WORKBOOK
IN SPANISH FIRST YEAR

By ROBERT J. NASSI

Former Teacher of Spanish
Los Angeles Valley Junior College
Los Angeles, California

Dedicated to serving

AMSCO

our nation's youth

When ordering this book, please specify

either

R 171 W

or

WORKBOOK IN SPANISH FIRST YEAR

AMSCO SCHOOL PUBLICATIONS, INC.

315 Hudson Street   New York, N. Y. 10013

WORKBOOK EDITION

ISBN 0-87720-503-5

Copyright, 1960, by

AMSCO SCHOOL PUBLICATIONS, INC.

Revised 1964

No part of this book may be reproduced in any
form without written permission from the publisher.

PRINTED IN THE UNITED STATES OF AMERICA

PREFACE

This *Workbook in Spanish First Year* offers the teacher and the student, not a textbook as such, but an equally valuable tool for mastering the fundamentals of Spanish. Certainly it is no substitute for a teacher; rather it frees the teacher to perform more creative work and give added practice in the aural-oral phases of the language. After the teacher has given appropriate motivation and explanation, he can then turn over the significant task of written drill to the workbook. In this workbook the teacher is secure, knowing that the job will be done thoroughly, logically and—most important—interestingly through a variety of exercises.

From the student's point of view, the workbook can be a pleasurable experience. Through conscientious use, he will reenforce what he has learned in class, be able to prepare successfully for examinations, review when the need occurs and—above all—find that his interest in the foreign language is not only sustained but increased. There is the added advantage of being able to write the answers directly in the book.

The material has been carefully divided into suitable topics: Verbs, Grammar, Idioms, Vocabulary, Civilization. Each lesson treats a specific point to be mastered and then offers an abundance of drill to insure that mastery. Medial review lessons and mastery exercises afford more comprehensive testing.

The work on vocabulary building, consisting of cognates, synonyms, antonyms and words frequently confused, is rarely found in an elementary text. The civilization section stresses the highlights of both Spain and Latin America. Artistic "cultural bits" have been interspersed throughout the book.

As culminating exercises, we have included several recent Citywide Examinations given in the schools of New York City.

The teacher as well as the student will find that this Workbook offers a significant supplement and enrichment to classroom instruction.

—R. J. N.

CONTENTS
Part I—Verbs

Lesson   *Page*

1. PRESENT TENSE OF REGULAR -AR VERBS.. 1
2. PRESENT TENSE OF REGULAR -ER AND -IR VERBS................................ 4
3. PRESENT TENSE OF STEM-CHANGING VERBS (E TO IE).......................... 7
4. PRESENT TENSE OF STEM-CHANGING VERBS (O TO UE)......................... 9
5. PRESENT TENSE OF STEM-CHANGING VERBS (E TO I)............................ 12
6. PRESENT TENSE OF IRREGULAR VERBS—PART I................................... 14
7. PRESENT TENSE OF IRREGULAR VERBS—PART II.................................. 16
   REVIEW OF VERB LESSONS 1-7.. 18
8. COMMANDS... 21
9. THE PRESENT PARTICIPLE (GERUND)... 23
10. REFLEXIVE VERBS... 25
11. PRETERITE TENSE OF REGULAR VERBS... 29
12. PRETERITE TENSE OF -IR STEM-CHANGING VERBS.............................. 32
13. PRETERITE TENSE OF IRREGULAR VERBS—PART I................................ 34
14. PRETERITE TENSE OF IRREGULAR VERBS—PART II.............................. 36
   REVIEW OF VERB LESSONS 8-14.. 38
15. IMPERFECT TENSE OF REGULAR AND IRREGULAR VERBS; USES OF THE IMPERFECT........ 40
16. PAST PARTICIPLE OF REGULAR VERBS; THE PERFECT TENSE.................. 44
17. IRREGULAR PAST PARTICIPLES... 47
18. FUTURE TENSE OF REGULAR VERBS.. 49
19. FUTURE TENSE OF IRREGULAR VERBS... 51
20. THE CONDITIONAL TENSE.. 53
   REVIEW OF VERB LESSONS 15-20.. 56
   MASTERY EXERCISES.. 59

Part II—Grammar

1. GENDER OF NOUNS; ARTICLES... 64
2. PLURAL OF NOUNS.. 66
3. THE CONTRACTIONS AL AND DEL; POSSESSION WITH DE........................ 67
4. AGREEMENT AND POSITION OF ADJECTIVES... 70
5. PERSONAL A.. 73
6. POSSESSIVE ADJECTIVES.. 74
   REVIEW OF GRAMMAR LESSONS 1-6.. 76
7. DEMONSTRATIVE ADJECTIVES.. 78
8. COMPARISON OF ADJECTIVES.. 80
9. SHORTENING OF ADJECTIVES.. 84
10. NUMBERS FROM 0 TO 99... 87
11. NUMBERS FROM 100 TO 1,000,000... 90
12. DAYS OF THE WEEK, MONTHS, SEASONS, DATES................................. 93
13. TIME EXPRESSIONS.. 96
14. USES OF ESTAR AND SER.. 99
   REVIEW OF GRAMMAR LESSONS 7-14.. 102
15. INTERROGATIVE WORDS.. 106
16. NEGATIVE WORDS.. 109
17. PREPOSITIONAL PRONOUNS... 111
18. DIRECT OBJECT PRONOUNS... 113
19. INDIRECT OBJECT PRONOUNS... 115
20. POSITION OF DIRECT AND INDIRECT OBJECT PRONOUNS...................... 118
   REVIEW OF GRAMMAR LESSONS 15-20.. 120
   MASTERY EXERCISES.. 122

Part III—Idioms

Lesson   *Page*

1. The Verb GUSTAR 125
2. Idioms with HACER 127
3. Idioms with TENER 129
4. Miscellaneous Verbal Idioms 131
5. Idioms with A, DE, EN and POR 134
6. Miscellaneous Idiomatic Expressions 137
    Mastery Exercises 140

Part IV—Vocabulary

1. Cognates 143
2. Indirect Cognates 145
3. Synonyms 151
4. Opposites 153
5. Words Frequently Confused 157
    Mastery Exercises 160

Part V—Hispanic Civilization

1. Spanish Influence in the United States 162
2. Our Spanish American Neighbors 166
3. Points of Interest in Spanish America 172
4. Famous Names in Spanish America 176
    Mastery Exercises on Spanish America 179
5. Spain, The Land 181
6. Spain, The People 187
7. Famous People of Spain 190
8. Spanish Life and Customs 193
    Mastery Exercises on Spain 196

    Examinations 198
    Spanish-English Vocabulary 208
    English-Spanish Vocabulary 214

ILLUSTRATIONS

	Page
CALDERÓN	6
BOLÍVAR	11
THE QUETZAL	13
A VILLAGE STREET IN SOUTHERN SPAIN	22
MIRANDA	24
THE MATADOR	31
IGUAZÚ FALLS	33
DÍAZ	37
MONTEZUMA II	43
THE CACAO TREE	48
GOYA	55
DON QUIJOTE AND SANCHO PANZA	58
MALLORCA	63
COLUMBUS	65
WEAVING CLOTH IN GUATEMALA	69
CHARLES V	75
FIESTA COSTUMES	79
THE PAN-AMERICAN UNION BUILDING	86
PIZARRO	89
THE JARABE TAPATÍO—MEXICAN HAT DANCE	92
EL PATIO DE LOS LEONES	95
CUZCO	98
TOMB OF COLUMBUS	101
FRANCO	105
ROSAS	112
UNAMUNO	117
MAKING TORTILLAS	124
RIVERA	133
BANANA GROWING IN HONDURAS	139
TAPPING RUBBER TREES	142
JUÁREZ	144
THE TAPIR	156
SPANISH MISSIONS	161

MAPS

CENTRAL AMERICA AND THE WEST INDIES	166
SOUTH AMERICA	167
PRODUCTS OF SOUTH AMERICA	169
MEXICO	172
SPAIN	181
PRODUCTS OF SPAIN	182
PROVINCES AND CITIES OF SPAIN	184

Part I—Verbs

Verb Lesson 1—PRESENT TENSE OF REGULAR -AR VERBS

hablar, to speak

SINGULAR			PLURAL		
yo	hablo	*I speak*	nosotros, -as	hablamos	*we speak*
tú	hablas	*you speak* (familiar)	vosotros, -as	habláis	*you speak* (familiar)
usted (Vd.) él ella	habla	*you speak* (polite) *he speaks* *she speaks*	ustedes (Vds.) ellos, -as	hablan	*you speak* (polite) *they speak*

Note

1. The present tense of regular **-ar** verbs is formed by dropping the ending **-ar** of the infinitive and adding **-o, -as, -a, -amos, -áis, -an.**

2. The present tense has several English translations.

    usted habla, you speak, you are speaking, you do speak
    él habla, he speaks, he is speaking, he does speak

3. Subject pronouns, except **usted (Vd.)** and **ustedes (Vds.),** are usually omitted in Spanish unless they are required for clearness, emphasis or in a compound subject.

Hablo inglés.	I speak English.
Hablan español.	They speak Spanish.

    But

Vd. habla bien.	You speak well.
Ella habla francés pero **él** habla alemán.	She speaks French but he speaks German.
Ella y yo hablamos portugués.	She and I speak Portuguese.

4. The feminine forms of **nosotros** and **vosotros** are **nosotras** and **vosotras.**

5. The **tú** and **vosotros** forms of the verb are used when addressing relatives, intimate friends or small children. In Spanish America, **Vds.** usually replaces the **vosotros** form.

6. When two verbs follow one another in a sentence, the second verb is generally in the infinitive.

Yo **deseo hablar.**	I wish to speak.

NEGATIVE FORM OF VERBS

A verb may be made negative by placing **no** before it.

María **no** habla español.	Mary does not speak Spanish.

INTERROGATIVE FORM OF VERBS

A verb may be made interrogative by placing the subject after the verb.

¿Habla Juan inglés?	Does John speak English?

COMMON -AR VERBS

bailar, to dance
cantar, to sing
comprar, to buy
contestar, to answer
desear, to wish
enseñar, to teach
entrar (en), to enter

escuchar, to listen (to)
estudiar, to study
explicar, to explain
hablar, to speak
invitar, to invite
mirar, to look at
necesitar, to need

preguntar, to ask
preparar, to prepare
tomar, to take
trabajar, to work
usar, to use
viajar, to travel
visitar, to visit

EXERCISES

A. Complete the English sentences.

1. Entran en la clase. _____ the class.

2. Preparamos la lección. _____ the lesson.

3. ¿Desea Vd. bailar? _____ ?

4. No estudio mucho. _____ much.

5. ¿Dónde trabajan Vds.? Where _____ ?

6. María canta bien. Mary _____ well.

7. Necesito el dinero. _____ the money.

8. Visitan a un amigo. _____ a friend.

9. ¿Por qué no invitas a Tomás? Why _____ Tom?

10. Toma el tren. _____ the train.

B. Write the correct form of the verb in the present tense.

1. Tú _____ bien. (bailar)

2. Yo _____ un lápiz. (desear)

3. Los alumnos _____ en la clase. (escuchar)

4. ¿Qué _____ el profesor? (preguntar)

5. ¿Cómo _____ Vds.? (contestar)

6. Nosotros _____ el español. (estudiar)

7. Ana y José _____ a la profesora. (mirar)

8. Carmen_____comprar un cuaderno. (desear)

9. Alicia y yo _____ tinta. (necesitar)

10. ¿Qué _____ los profesores? (enseñar)

C. Replace the blank with a correct subject pronoun.

1. _____ entra

2. _____ viajan

3. _____ explicamos

4. _____ trabajas

5. _____ preparo

D. Change each sentence to the negative.

1. Felipe habla inglés. _____

2. Compran la casa. _____

3. ¿Baila Vd. el tango? _____

[2]

4. Nosotros deseamos trabajar. _____

5. Rosa canta bien. _____

E. Change each statement to a question.

1. El profesor enseña la lección. _____

2. Vd. necesita papel. _____

3. Escuchan la música. _____

4. Juan estudia con un amigo. _____

5. Los alumnos entran en la escuela. _____

F. Translate into Spanish.

1. he asks _____

2. they listen _____

3. do you* use? _____

4. we sing _____

5. I do not work _____

6. she is explaining _____

7. Henry and I are studying _____

8. she doesn't answer _____

9. I wish to invite _____

10. you (tú) need _____

11. does Paul visit? _____

12. the children take _____

13. are you (Vds.) traveling? _____

14. who teaches? _____

15. I am looking at _____

G. Answer the following questions in complete Spanish sentences.

1. ¿Habla Vd. español? _____

2. ¿Estudia Vd. con un amigo? _____

3. ¿Qué enseña el profesor? _____

4. ¿Quién explica la lección? _____

5. ¿Baila Vd. bien? _____

6. ¿Cantan Vds. en la clase? _____

7. ¿Escucha Vd. el radio? _____

8. ¿Desea Vd. viajar a México? _____

9. ¿Qué necesita Vd. comprar? _____

10. ¿Preparan Vds. las lecciones en la escuela? _____

_____

*In all exercises in this book, *you* should be translated by **Vd.** unless otherwise indicated.

Verb Lesson 2—PRESENT TENSE OF REGULAR *-ER* AND *-IR* VERBS

com*er,* to eat

SINGULAR				PLURAL		
yo	com**o**	*I eat*	nosotros, -as	com**emos**	*we eat*
tú	com**es**	*you eat*	vosotros, -as	com**éis**	*you eat*
Vd.		*you eat*	Vds.		*you eat*
él	com**e**	*he eats*	ellos, -as	com**en**	*they eat*
ella		*she eats*			

viv*ir,* to live

SINGULAR				PLURAL		
yo	viv**o**	*I live*	nosotros, -as	viv**imos**	*we live*
tú	viv**es**	*you live*	vosotros, -as	viv**ís**	*you live*
Vd.		*you live*	Vds.		*you live*
él	viv**e**	*he lives*	ellos, -as	viv**en**	*they live*
ella		*she lives*			

Note

1. The present tense of regular **-er** verbs is formed by dropping the **-er** ending and adding -o, -es, -e, -emos, -éis, -en.
2. The present tense of regular **-ir** verbs is formed by dropping the **-ir** ending and adding -o, -es, -e, -imos, -ís, -en.
3. The endings for **-er** and **-ir** verbs are the same except for the **nosotros** and **vosotros** forms.

COMMON **-ER** VERBS

aprender, to learn
beber, to drink
comer, to eat

comprender, to understand
correr, to run
leer, to read

prometer, to promise
responder, to answer
vender, to sell

COMMON **-IR** VERBS

abrir, to open
decidir, to decide

escribir, to write
recibir, to receive

sufrir, to suffer
vivir, to live

EXERCISES

A. Add the correct ending of the present tense.

1. Los niños corr_____ en el parque.
2. Ellos viv_____ en San Francisco.
3. Un alumno le_____ la lección.
4. Nosotros aprend_____ el español.
5. ¿Recib_____ Vd. muchas cartas?
6. Nosotros escrib_____ en la pizarra.
7. Yo no comprend_____ la lección.
8. Alberto y yo decid_____ viajar.
9. ¿Promet_____ Vds. estudiar?
10. Dorotea y Perla sufr_____ mucho.
11. ¿Quién abr_____ la puerta?

12. ¿Qué vend_____ Vd.?

13. Nosotros no respond_____ en inglés.

14. ¿Com_____ (tú) en la cafetería hoy?

15. Yo vend_____ flores en el mercado.

B. Translate the sentences in Exercise A into English.

1. _____

2. _____

3. _____

4. _____

5. _____

6. _____

7. _____

8. _____

9. _____

10. _____

11. _____

12. _____

13. _____

14. _____

15. _____

C. Translate the English words into Spanish.

1. *I am learning* a hablar español. _____

2. *He promises* trabajar. _____

3. *¿Do you understand* Vds. la lección? _____

4. ¿Dónde *does he live?* _____

5. *We receive* el periódico todos los días. _____

6. Deciden *to sell* la casa. _____

7. *We eat* en el restaurante. _____

8. Tú siempre *run* a la clase. _____

9. *He does not drink* té. _____

10. ¿Por qué *don't you open* las ventanas? _____

D. Answer the following questions in complete Spanish sentences.

1. ¿Lee Vd. novelas? _____

2. ¿Aprenden Vds. mucho en la clase? _____
_____

3. ¿Comprende Vd. el español? _____

4. ¿Escriben Vds. la lección en la pizarra? _____

_____

5. ¿Bebe Vd. café? _____

6. ¿Come Vd. con mucho apetito? _____

7. ¿Quién recibe buenas notas (grades)? _____

8. ¿Promete Vd. estudiar? _____

9. ¿Qué venden en una tienda? _____

10. ¿En qué país viven Vds.? _____

    E. Complete the Spanish sentences.

1. Why is Peter running?

¿Por qué _____ Pedro?

2. Do you understand?

¿_____ Vds.?

3. The child does not answer.

El niño _____.

4. Paul decides to sell the bicycle.

Pablo _____ vender la bicicleta.

5. We read the exercises in class.

_____ los ejercicios en la clase.

6. We live in an apartment house.

_____ en una casa de apartamientos.

7. I promise to write to Jane.

_____ a Juana.

8. The boys are opening the packages.

Los muchachos _____ los paquetes.

9. They receive many gifts.

_____ muchos regalos.

10. What do you wish to eat?

¿Qué desea Vd. _____?

Pedro Calderón de la Barca (1600-1681) was the last of the great dramatists of Spain's Golden Age. His philosophical and religious dramas are unrivalled in the history of the Spanish theater. His best known work is "La Vida es Sueño." Calderón's plays are still performed today.

Verb Lesson 3—PRESENT TENSE OF STEM-CHANGING VERBS (*E TO IE*)

	pensar, to think	entender, to understand	preferir, to prefer
yo	*pienso*	*entiendo*	*prefiero*
tú	*piensas*	*entiendes*	*prefieres*
Vd., él, ella	*piensa*	*entiende*	*prefiere*
nosotros, -as	pensamos	entendemos	preferimos
vosotros, -as	pensáis	entendéis	preferís
Vds., ellos, -as	*piensan*	*entienden*	*prefieren*

Note

Many verbs with an **e** in the stem change the **e** to **ie** when that syllable is stressed. This change occurs in the last vowel of the stem in all forms of the present tense, except with **nosotros** and **vosotros**.

COMMON STEM-CHANGING VERBS (E TO IE)

cerrar, to close
comenzar, to begin
defender, to defend

empezar, to begin
entender, to understand
pensar, to think, to intend

perder, to lose
preferir, to prefer
sentir, to regret, to be sorry

EXERCISES

A. Write each verb in the present tense for the subject indicated.

1. yo

_____ (cerrar)

_____ (preferir)

_____ (entender)

_____ (pensar)

2. nosotros

_____ (defender)

_____ (sentir)

_____ (empezar)

_____ (entender)

3. ellos

_____ (perder)

_____ (comenzar)

_____ (preferir)

_____ (cerrar)

4. tú

_____ (empezar)

_____ (entender)

_____ (pensar)

_____ (preferir)

5. José

_____ (cerrar)

_____ (defender)

_____ (sentir)

_____ (perder)

B. Write the present tense of the italicized verbs for the subjects indicated.

1. yo *prefiero:* nosotros _____; Juan _____; Vds. _____

2. Tomás *pierde:* yo _____; los niños _____; nosotros _____

3. nosotros *entendemos:* ¿quién _____?; yo no _____; Pablo _____

4. Vd. *piensa:* Pepe y yo _____; ellos _____; yo _____

5. ellos *cierran:* yo _____; Ana _____; nosotros _____

C. Complete the Spanish sentences.

1. At what time does the picture begin? ¿A qué hora ----------------------------------- la película?
2. Do you understand Spanish? ¿-------------------------------------- el español?
3. They are very sorry. Lo -- mucho.
4. The child loses his pen. El niño ---------------------------------- su pluma.
5. We begin to work at nine. -------------------------------- a trabajar a las nueve.
6. What does Helen think of the house? ¿Qué ----------------------- Elena de la casa?
7. It is not necessary to close the door. No es necesario ------------------- la puerta.
8. I prefer this room. -- este cuarto.
9. Do you understand? ¿-- Vds.?
10. I always lose my books. Siempre ------------------------------- mis libros.

D. Answer the following questions in complete Spanish sentences.

1. ¿A qué hora comienza la clase de español? ---
----

2. ¿Prefiere Vd. viajar en avión? ---
----

3. ¿Entienden Vds. siempre al profesor? ---
----

4. ¿Quién cierra la puerta de la clase? --
5. ¿Cuándo empiezan las vacaciones de verano? ---
----

6. ¿Piensa Vd. trabajar hoy? ---
7. ¿A qué hora empieza Vd. a estudiar? --
----

8. ¿Prefieren Vds. hablar español? --
----

9. ¿Pierde Vd. muchas cosas? ---
10. ¿Desea Vd. defender a su patria? ---

E. Change the subject and verb in each sentence to the plural.

1. La clase empieza a las ocho. --------------------------------------
2. Yo no entiendo la lección. --------------------------------------
3. El soldado defiende el pueblo. --------------------------------------
4. Tú siempre pierdes la pelota. --------------------------------------
5. Yo lo siento mucho. --------------------------------------
6. ¿Qué piensa Vd. de este libro? --------------------------------------
7. Yo prefiero esta corbata. --------------------------------------
8. El alumno cierra las ventanas. --------------------------------------

[8]

	mostrar, to show	volver, to return	dormir, to sleep
yo	*muestro*	*vuelvo*	*duermo*
tú	*muestras*	*vuelves*	*duermes*
Vd., él, ella	*muestra*	*vuelve*	*duerme*
nosotros, -as	mostramos	volvemos	dormimos
vosotros, -as	mostráis	volvéis	dormís
Vds., ellos, -as	*muestran*	*vuelven*	*duermen*

Note

Many verbs with an **o** in the stem change the **o** to **ue** when that syllable is stressed. This change occurs in the last vowel of the stem in all forms of the present tense, except with **nosotros** and **vosotros**.

COMMON STEM-CHANGING VERBS (*O* TO **UE**)

almorzar, to lunch, to eat lunch
contar, to count, to relate
costar, to cost
dormir, to sleep

encontrar, to find, to meet
jugar (u to ue), to play
morir, to die
mostrar, to show

recordar, to remember
volar, to fly
volver, to return

EXERCISES

A. Write the present tense of each verb for the subjects indicated.

1. almorzar: yo _____; ¿_____ Vd.?; nosotros _____
2. dormir: tú _____; nosotros _____; ellos _____
3. volver: ¿_____ Vds.?; yo _____; nosotros _____
4. encontrar: Pedro _____; nosotros _____; los niños _____
5. volar: ¿quién _____?; ellos _____; nosotros _____
6. recordar: yo _____; José y yo _____; tú _____
7. contar: él _____; ellos _____; nosotros _____
8. mostrar: yo _____; ella _____; todos _____
9. morir: ¿quién _____?; ellos _____; nosotros _____
10. jugar: el niño _____; nosotros _____; yo _____

B. Write the infinitive form of each of the following verbs.

1. vuela _____
2. duerme _____
3. cuesta _____
4. recuerdan _____
5. almuerzo _____
6. cuento _____
7. muestras _____
8. encuentra _____
9. vuelve _____
10. juegan _____

[9]

C. Complete the English sentences.

1. Juan vuelve tarde a la casa.

    John _____ home late.

2. No recuerdo la dirección de su casa.

    _____ the address of his house.

3. Muchos aeroplanos vuelan por la ciudad todos los días.

    Many airplanes _____ over the city every day.

4. ¿Juega Vd. a la pelota?

    _____ ball?

5. El profesor cuenta la historia de su vida.

    The teacher _____ the story of his life.

6. ¿Cuánto cuestan los billetes?

    How much _____ the tickets _____?

7. Algunos niños duermen por la tarde.

    Some children _____ in the afternoon.

8. Almuerzo en casa.

    _____ at home.

9. María nos muestra fotografías de su familia.

    Mary _____ us pictures of her family.

10. ¿Dónde encuentro el camino más corto para ir a Tijuana?

    Where _____ the shortest road to go to Tijuana?

D. Translate the English words into Spanish.

1. Los alumnos *eat lunch* en la cafetería. _____

2. ¿*Do you remember* la fecha? _____

3. *It costs* cuatro dólares. _____

4. *They meet* a Pedro en la calle. _____

5. Los niños *play* en el parque. _____

6. ¿A qué hora *return* los alumnos? _____

7. *He shows* los regalos a sus amigos. _____

8. *We sleep* en este cuarto. _____

9. *They fly* en un avión de cuatro motores. _____

10. El hombre *counts* el dinero. _____

11. *We eat lunch* a las doce. _____

12. Ana *sleeps* en esta cama. _____

13. Las plantas *die* sin agua. _____

14. ¿Desea Vd. *to play* al béisbol mañana? _____

15. *We are returning* temprano. _____

E. Answer the following questions in complete Spanish sentences.

1. ¿Encuentra Vd. a sus amigos en la escuela? _____

_____

2. ¿Almuerzan Vds. en la cafetería? _____

_____

3. ¿Cuánto cuesta su cuaderno? _____

4. ¿Cuenta Vd. anécdotas? _____

5. ¿A qué hora vuelve Vd. a casa? _____

6. ¿Muestra Vd. sus notas (grades) a sus padres? _____

_____

7. ¿Juegan Vds. con sus compañeros en el patio de recreo (playground)? _____

_____

8. ¿Cuántas horas duerme Vd.? _____

9. ¿En qué estación vuelan los pájaros hacia el sur? _____

_____

0. ¿Recuerda Vd. los nombres de todos sus amigos? _____

_____

Simón Bolívar (1783-1830), known as "El Libertador" (The Liberator) was one of the great heroes in the war for South American independence. He liberated Colombia, Venezuela, Ecuador and northern Peru from Spanish rule, and founded a new country, Bolivia, which was named in his honor. He has been called the "George Washington of South America."

Bolívar was also a great statesman. His plan to establish an organization of American republics to strengthen the peace and security of the Americas was realized years later with the formation of the Pan-American Union, now known as the Organization of American States.

[11]

Verb Lesson 5—PRESENT TENSE OF STEM-CHANGING VERBS (*E* TO *I*)

servir, to serve

yo	*sirvo*	nosotros, -as	servimos
tú	*sirves*	vosotros, -as	servís
Vd., él, ella	*sirve*	Vds., ellos, -as	*sirven*

Note

Some **-ir** verbs with an **e** in the stem change the **e** to **i** when that syllable is stressed. This change occurs in the last vowel of the stem in all forms of the present tense, except with **nosotros** and **vosotros**.

COMMON STEM-CHANGING VERBS (E TO I)

pedir, to ask for, to order (food)   **repetir,** to repeat   **servir,** to serve

EXERCISES

A. Write the present tense of **pedir, servir** and **repetir** for the subjects indicated.

1. yo _____ _____ _____

2. Vds. _____ _____ _____

3. nosotros _____ _____ _____

4. tú _____ _____ _____

5. ¿quién _____? _____? _____?

B. Write the correct form of the verb in the present tense.

1. El hombre _____ una taza de café. (*pedir*)

2. Yo _____ las palabras del profesor. (*repetir*)

3. Nosotros no _____ mucho dinero. (*pedir*)

4. El mozo _____ la comida. (*servir*)

5. Los alumnos _____ la frase. (*repetir*)

C. Complete the sentences, rewriting the verbs for the subjects indicated.

1. Antonio repite la frase en voz alta.   Nosotros _____ la frase en voz alta.

2. Juana sirve los refrescos.   Juana y Dorotea _____ los refrescos.

3. ¿Qué pide Vd.?   ¿Qué _____ Vds.?

4. Yo sirvo el desayuno a las seis.   Nosotros _____ el desayuno a las seis.

5. Juan y yo pedimos café.   Yo _____ café

D. Translate the English words into Spanish.

1. *He repeats* el nombre muchas veces.   _____

2. ¿A qué hora *serve* Vds. el almuerzo?   _____

3. Tú siempre *order* té con limón.   _____

4. Lola me ayuda a *to serve* los refrescos.   _____

5. El criminal *asks for* perdón.   _____

[12]

E. Answer the following questions in complete Spanish sentences.

1. ¿A qué hora sirve su madre la comida? _____

_____

2. ¿Qué bebida (beverage) pide Vd. en el restaurante? _____

_____

3. ¿Repiten Vds. las frases en español? _____

_____

4. ¿Pide Vd. muchos favores a sus amigos? _____

_____

5. ¿Qué sirve Vd. a sus amigos cuando vienen a su casa? _____

_____

   The quetzal is a parrot-like bird found in the tropical jungles of Central America.
It has brilliant blue-green feathers and a tail approximately three feet long. The
Guatemalans chose the quetzal as their national emblem. Since this bird seldom
survives in captivity, it symbolizes for them the spirit of freedom. The quetzal
appears on Guatemala's flag, postage stamps and coins. In fact, the Guatemalan
unit of currency is called a "quetzal."

Verb Lesson 6—PRESENT TENSE OF IRREGULAR VERBS—PART I

The following verbs are irregular only in the first person singular.

> **caer,** to fall: *caigo,* caes, cae, caemos, caéis, caen
>
> **dar,** to give: *doy,* das, da, damos, dais, dan
>
> **hacer,** to do, to make: *hago,* haces, hace, hacemos, hacéis, hacen
>
> **poner,** to put: *pongo,* pones, pone, ponemos, ponéis, ponen
>
> **saber,** to know: *sé,* sabes, sabe, sabemos, sabéis, saben
>
> **salir,** to leave, to go out: *salgo,* sales, sale, salimos, salís, salen
>
> **traer,** to bring: *traigo,* traes, trae, traemos, traéis, traen
>
> **ver,** to see: *veo,* ves, ve, vemos, veis, ven

Note

The forms **dais** (from **dar**) and **veis** (from **ver**) do not have a written accent mark, since they consist of only one syllable.

EXERCISES

A. Write each verb in the present tense for the subject indicated.

1. yo

- ------------------------------ (poner)
- ------------------------------ (traer)
- ------------------------------ (salir)
- ------------------------------ (hacer)

2. nosotros

- ------------------------------ (dar)
- ------------------------------ (ver)
- ------------------------------ (salir)
- ------------------------------ (saber)

3. Pedro

- ------------------------------ (traer)
- ------------------------------ (hacer)
- ------------------------------ (ver)
- ------------------------------ (salir)

4. los niños

- ------------------------------ (caer)
- ------------------------------ (saber)
- ------------------------------ (dar)
- ------------------------------ (poner)

5. yo

- ------------------------------ (dar)
- ------------------------------ (caer)
- ------------------------------ (ver)
- ------------------------------ (saber)

B. Write the present tense of the italicized verbs for the subjects indicated.

1. yo *hago:* Vd. ----------------; nosotros ----------------; ellos ----------------

2. Elena *sabe:* yo ----------------; ¿---------------- Vds.?; tú ----------------

3. nosotros *damos:* Rosa y Ana ----------------; yo ----------------; ¿quién ----------------?

4. ellos *salen:* yo ----------------; nosotros ----------------; Alberto ----------------

5. tú *traes:* los alumnos ----------------; Vd. ----------------; yo ----------------

6. yo *pongo:* nosotros ----------------; ¿---------------- Vd.?; los niños ----------------

[14]

7. Vd. *ve:* ella y yo _____; mis amigos _____; yo _____

8. él *cae:* yo _____; el muchacho _____; nosotros _____

C. In the space at the left of each Spanish verb in Column I, write the letter of its meaning in Column II.

Column I	*Column II*
_____ **1.** da	*a.* he sees
_____ **2.** saben	*b.* they know
_____ **3.** ve	*c.* he puts
_____ **4.** doy	*d.* they leave
_____ **5.** traes	*e.* he gives
_____ **6.** salen	*f.* I do
_____ **7.** hago	*g.* they fall
_____ **8.** pone	*h.* I give
_____ **9.** caen	*i.* I know
_____ **10.** sé	*j.* you bring

D. Translate into Spanish.

1. I see _____

2. do you know? _____

3. we do not put _____

4. who makes? _____

5. I bring _____

6. they give _____

7. he falls _____

8. do you (*pl.*) see? _____

9. I am going out _____

10. we do _____

E. Answer the following questions in complete Spanish sentences.

1. ¿Dónde pone Vd. sus libros en casa? _____

_____

2. ¿Da Vd. regalos a sus amigos? _____

3. ¿Saben Vds. la dirección de la escuela? _____

_____

4. ¿Qué traen los alumnos a la escuela? _____

_____

5. ¿En qué día cae su cumpleaños? _____

6. ¿Ve Vd. a sus amigos todos los días? _____

_____

7. ¿Sabe Vd. una canción española? _____

8. ¿Hace Vd. su cama? _____

9. ¿A qué hora salen Vds. de la escuela? _____

_____

10. ¿Sale Vd. con sus amigos los sábados? _____

_____

Verb Lesson 7—PRESENT TENSE OF IRREGULAR VERBS—PART II

Other verbs irregular in the present tense are:

decir, to say, to tell: *digo, dices, dice,* decimos, decís, *dicen*

estar, to be: *estoy, estás, está,* estamos, estáis, *están*

ir, to go: *voy, vas, va, vamos, vais, van*

oír, to hear: *oigo, oyes, oye,* oímos, oís, *oyen*

poder, to be able, can: *puedo, puedes, puede,* podemos, podéis, *pueden*

querer, to want, to wish: *quiero, quieres, quiere,* queremos, queréis, *quieren*

ser, to be: *soy, eres, es, somos, sois, son*

tener, to have: *tengo, tienes, tiene,* tenemos, tenéis, *tienen*

venir, to come: *vengo, vienes, viene,* venimos, venís, *vienen*

EXERCISES

A. Write the plural form of the verb.

1. ¿puede Vd.?   ¿_____ Vds.?
2. yo voy   nosotros _____
3. el niño es   los niños _____
4. ¿oye Vd.?   ¿_____ Vds.?
5. tú tienes   vosotros _____
6. yo quiero   nosotros _____
7. la muchacha está las muchachas _____
8. Vd. viene   Vds. _____
9. yo digo   nosotros _____
10. yo tengo   nosotros _____

B. Write the English meaning and the infinitive form of each of the following verbs.

	English Meaning	*Infinitive*
1. tiene		
2. va		
3. estoy		
4. quieren		
5. vengo		
6. oyen		
7. es		
8. dice		
9. soy		
10. puede		

C. Underline the verb that best completes the meaning of the sentence.

1. Yo (doy, estoy, oigo) contento.

2. Yo no (vengo, tengo, digo) un automóvil.

3. ¿Quiere Vd. (venir, poder, oír) con nosotros?

4. (Oímos, Vamos, Decimos) la música.

5. Tú no (eres, vas, puedes) un amigo sincero.

6. Algunos alumnos (tienen, vienen, quieren) tarde a la escuela.

7. El hombre no (dice, está, puede) trabajar hoy.

8. El señor García (va, ve, oye) a la oficina.

9. Nosotros (somos, podemos, venimos) americanos.

10. Pablo (quiere, dice, oye) estudiar.

D. Translate the English words into Spanish.

1. El profesor *says* que Vd. es perezoso. _____

2. *¿Are you going* a la iglesia mañana? _____

3. *I can't* ver la pizarra. _____

4. *They have* dos hermanos. _____

5. ¿Cuándo *are coming* Vds. a nuestra casa? _____

6. *I want* comprar un sombrero. _____

7. Los alumnos *hear* la voz del profesor. _____

8. ¿Quieren Vds. *to go* al parque? _____

9. Jorge y su amigo *are* (estar) en el patio. _____

10. Tú siempre *come* tarde. _____

E. Answer the following questions in complete Spanish sentences.

1. ¿Es Vd. un alumno aplicado (una alumna aplicada)? _____
_____

2. ¿Qué quiere Vd. ser algún día? _____

3. ¿Van Vds. hoy a la biblioteca? _____
_____

4. ¿Quién está ausente hoy? _____

5. ¿Puede Vd. oír al profesor cuando habla? _____
_____

6. ¿Vienen Vds. a la escuela mañana? _____
_____

7. ¿Tiene Vd. una bicicleta? _____

8. ¿Qué dice el profesor cuando un alumno contesta bien en la clase? _____
_____

9. ¿Oye Vd. bien? _____

10. ¿Dónde está Vd. ahora? _____

REVIEW OF VERB LESSONS 1-7

A. Complete the English sentences.

1. ¿Qué piensan Vds. de Jorge? _____ of George?
2. Somos buenos amigos. _____ good friends.
3. Quiero comprar un periódico. _____ to buy a newspaper.
4. La clase empieza a las ocho. The class _____ at eight.
5. ¿Puede Vd. ayudar al muchacho? _____ help the boy?
6. Van al parque. _____ to the park.
7. No recuerdo su nombre. _____ your name.
8. ¿Qué dice Vd.? What _____?
9. Pierden el dinero. _____ the money.
10. ¿Oye Vd. la música? _____ the music?
11. Sé la respuesta. _____ the answer.
12. Juan nos muestra la carta. John _____ us the letter.
13. ¿Qué hago ahora? What _____ now?
14. Tomás lo siente mucho. Tom _____
15. Los alumnos traen lápices. The pupils _____ pencils.
16. ¿Ve Vd. el avión? _____ the airplane?
17. ¿Cuándo viene Vd. a mi casa? When _____ to my house?
18. Tienen un automóvil nuevo. _____ a new automobile.
19. No salgo de noche. _____ at night.
20. Pedro pide una taza de chocolate. Peter _____ a cup of chocolate.

B. Translate into Spanish.

1. we wish _____
2. he opens _____
3. they return _____
4. she is not able _____
5. I prefer _____
6. we go _____
7. the students do not understand _____
8. who sells? _____
9. Mary and Jane visit _____
10. do you begin? _____
11. I am (estar) _____
12. they see _____
13. I need _____
14. he sleeps _____

15. I bring   --

16. John and I receive   ------------------------------------

17. you are (ser)   --

18. he closes   --

19. they read   --

20. I play   ---

C. Write the English meaning and the infinitive form of each of the following verbs.

	English Meaning	*Infinitive*
1. encuentra		
2. doy		
3. oyen		
4. digo		
5. piden		
6. vengo		
7. pongo		
8. caigo		
9. voy		
10. entienden		
11. hago		
12. tiene		
13. puedo		
14. son		
15. sale		
16. quiero		
17. juega		
18. prometo		
19. ven		
20. muere		

D. Translate the English words into Spanish.

1. *I hear* un ruido (noise).   -----------------------------

2. Los niños *play* con sus compañeros.   ------------------

3. *He returns* a casa.   -------------------------------

4. *They serve* pasteles deliciosos.   ---------------------

5. ¿Quién *knows?*   ----------------------------------

6. *We give* los papeles al profesor.   --------------------

7. *I see* a Alicia todos los días.   -----------------------

8. *They are leaving* mañana.   -------------------------

[19]

9. *We can't* ir al cine. ------------------------------

10. ¿Qué color *do you prefer?* ------------------------------

11. Tomás *intends to travel* a Europa. ------------------------------

12. Lo *I am sorry* mucho. ------------------------------

13. *They order* una ensalada de frutas. ------------------------------

14. *¿Do you remember* el número? ------------------------------

15. ¿En qué día *falls* su cumpleaños? ------------------------------

16. Los niños *go* al circo. ------------------------------

17. El mozo *brings* una taza de café. ------------------------------

18. *I want* ser médico. ------------------------------

19. ¿Qué *are you* (Vds.) *doing* mañana? ------------------------------

20. La criada *puts* los platos en la mesa. ------------------------------

E. Answer the following questions in complete Spanish sentences.

1. ¿Dónde vive Vd.? ------------------------------

2. ¿Trabaja Vd. durante las vacaciones? ------------------------------
----

3. ¿Qué desea Vd. comprar? ------------------------------

4. ¿Escuchan los alumnos atentamente al profesor? ------------------------------
----

5. ¿Cómo son las clases? ------------------------------

6. ¿Qué periódico lee Vd.? ------------------------------

7. ¿Comen Vds. en la cafetería? ------------------------------

8. ¿Compra Vd. muchos discos de música popular? ------------------------------
----

9. ¿Son populares las orquestas latinoamericanas? ------------------------------
----

10. ¿Mira Vd. la televisión? ------------------------------

11. ¿A qué hora almuerza Vd.? ------------------------------

12. ¿Duerme Vd. en una cama cómoda? ------------------------------

13. ¿Qué hace Vd. hoy? ------------------------------

14. ¿Entiende Vd. el español? ------------------------------

15. ¿Tiene Vd. muchos amigos? ------------------------------

16. ¿Sabe Vd. la lección? ------------------------------

17. ¿Está Vd. ahora en la clase? ------------------------------

18. ¿Va Vd. al parque mañana? ------------------------------

19. ¿Es Vd. joven? ------------------------------

20. ¿Dice Vd. la verdad? ------------------------------

Verb Lesson 8—COMMANDS

Infinitive	Present Tense, First Singular	Command Form (Singular)	Command Form (Plural)	Translation
hablar	hablo	hable Vd.	hablen Vds.	speak
leer	leo	lea Vd.	lean Vds.	read
abrir	abro	abra Vd.	abran Vds.	open
cerrar	cierro	cierre Vd.	cierren Vds.	close
volver	vuelvo	vuelva Vd.	vuelvan Vds.	return
servir	sirvo	sirva Vd.	sirvan Vds.	serve
decir	digo	diga Vd.	digan Vds.	say, tell
hacer	hago	haga Vd.	hagan Vds.	do, make
ver	veo	vea Vd.	vean Vds.	see

Note

Commands of most verbs are formed as follows:

a. For -ar verbs, drop the final o of the yo form and add e for the **Vd.** form and **en** for the **Vds.** form.
b. For -er and -ir verbs, drop the final o and add **a** and **an**.

The following verbs form their commands irregularly:

Infinitive	Present Tense, First Singular	Commands	Translation
dar	*doy*	*dé* Vd., *den* Vds.	give
ir	*voy*	*vaya* Vd., *vayan* Vds.	go
ser	*soy*	*sea* Vd., *sean* Vds.	be

Note

Dé has an accent mark on the **e** to differentiate it from **de** (*of*). The plural **den** has no accent.

EXERCISES

A. Underline the verb that correctly translates the English command.

1. listen   (escucha, escuche) Vd.
2. read   (lean, leen) Vds.
3. leave   (sale, salga) Vd.
4. work   (trabajen, trabajan) Vds.
5. bring   (trae, traiga) Vd.
6. give   (den, dan) Vds.
7. see   (ve, vea) Vd.
8. study   (estudian, estudien) Vds.
9. tell   (dice, diga) Vd.
10. do   (haga, hace) Vd.

B. Write the first person singular of the present tense, the command forms, and the English translation of the command forms.

	Present Tense	Commands		Translation
EXAMPLE: tomar	tomo	tome Vd.	tomen Vds.	take
1. mirar	----	----	----	----
2. comer	----	----	----	----
3. escribir	----	----	----	----

4. pensar $\quad$ ----------------- $\quad$ ----------------- $\quad$ ----------------- $\quad$ -----------------

5. dormir $\quad$ ----------------- $\quad$ ----------------- $\quad$ ----------------- $\quad$ -----------------

6. pedir $\quad$ ----------------- $\quad$ ----------------- $\quad$ ----------------- $\quad$ -----------------

7. tener $\quad$ ----------------- $\quad$ ----------------- $\quad$ ----------------- $\quad$ -----------------

8. poner $\quad$ ----------------- $\quad$ ----------------- $\quad$ ----------------- $\quad$ -----------------

9. ir $\quad$ ----------------- $\quad$ ----------------- $\quad$ ----------------- $\quad$ -----------------

10. ser $\quad$ ----------------- $\quad$ ----------------- $\quad$ ----------------- $\quad$ -----------------

C. Add the correct ending to form the command.

1. entr _____ Vds.
2. cuent _____ Vd.
3. recib _____ Vd.
4. veng _____ Vds.
5. respond _____ Vds.

6. oig _____ Vd.
7. muestr _____ Vd.
8. repit _____ Vds.
9. caig _____ Vd.
10. defiend _____ Vds.

D. Complete the Spanish sentences.

1. Learn the lesson. ----------------------------------- Vds. la lección.
2. Put the glass on the table. ----------------------------------- Vd. el vaso sobre la mesa.
3. Go to the store. ----------------------------------- Vd. a la tienda.
4. Be sincere. ----------------------------------- Vds. sinceros.
5. Read the lesson in Spanish. ----------------------------------- Vds. la lección en español.
6. Invite Jane. ----------------------------------- Vd. a Juana.
7. Give this letter to your sister. ----------------------------------- Vd. esta carta a su hermana.
8. Order a chicken salad. ----------------------------------- Vd. una ensalada de pollo.
9. Come to my house tomorrow. ----------------------------------- Vds. a mi casa mañana.
10. Sleep in that bed. ----------------------------------- Vd. en esa cama.

Most villages in southern Spain have narrow, winding streets covered with cobblestones. Nearly every home has a balcony, grilled windows and a flower-filled patio, or inner courtyard. From time to time, vendors with small donkeys pass along the streets and call out their wares.

Verb Lesson 9—THE PRESENT PARTICIPLE (GERUND)

PRESENT PARTICIPLES (GERUNDS) OF REGULAR VERBS

hablar, to speak	hablando, speaking
comer, to eat	comiendo, eating
vivir, to live	viviendo, living

Note

1. To form the present participle of regular -ar verbs, drop the -ar ending and add -ando.
2. To form the present participle of regular -er or -ir verbs, drop the -er or -ir ending and add -iendo.

PRESENT PARTICIPLES OF -IR STEM-CHANGING VERBS

dormir, to sleep	durmiendo, sleeping
sentir, to regret	sintiendo, regretting
servir, to serve	sirviendo, serving

Note

The stem vowel o becomes u and the stem vowel e becomes i in the present participle.

PRESENT PARTICIPLES ENDING IN -YENDO

caer, to fall	cayendo, falling
creer, to believe	creyendo, believing
ir, to go	yendo, going
leer, to read	leyendo, reading
oír, to hear	oyendo, hearing
traer, to bring	trayendo, bringing

IRREGULAR PRESENT PARTICIPLES

decir, to say, to tell	diciendo, saying, telling
poder, to be able	pudiendo, being able
venir, to come	viniendo, coming

USE OF ESTAR WITH THE PRESENT PARTICIPLE

The verb estar is used with the present participle to form the present progressive tense.

Juan está estudiando.	John is studying.
Los alumnos están leyendo.	The pupils are reading.

EXERCISES

A. Write the present participle of the following verbs.

1. volver	----------------------		6. cerrar	----------------------
2. decir	----------------------		7. volar	----------------------
3. visitar	----------------------		8. aprender	----------------------
4. venir	----------------------		9. caer	----------------------
5. repetir	----------------------		10. dormir	----------------------

B. Add the correct ending to form the present participle.

1. com_____   4. est_____   7. abr_____

2. entr_____   5. tra_____   8. pens_____

3. viv_____   6. vend_____   9. mir_____

C. In the space at the left of each present participle in Column I, write the letter of its meaning in Column II.

Column I	Column II
_____ 1. dando	a. hearing
_____ 2. pudiendo	b. being
_____ 3. oyendo	c. losing
_____ 4. pidiendo	d. giving
_____ 5. siendo	e. coming
_____ 6. creyendo	f. seeing
_____ 7. perdiendo	g. going
_____ 8. viniendo	h. asking for
_____ 9. yendo	i. believing
_____ 10. viendo	j. being able

D. Write the following in Spanish, using the present progressive tense (estar + present participle).

1. They are dancing. _____

2. Charles is running. _____

3. We are working. _____

4. The students are reading. _____

5. I am studying. _____

6. Who is speaking? _____

7. The children are sleeping. _____

8. The maid is serving. _____

9. I am listening. _____

10. The boys are playing. _____

Francisco Miranda (1750-1816), a native of Caracas, Venezuela, led the first important movement to liberate South America from the autocratic rule of Spain. Captured by Spanish troops, he was placed in a prison dungeon, where he died. But his struggle was not in vain. The revolutionary cause was continued by one of Miranda's most able lieutenants, Simón Bolívar.

Verb Lesson 10—REFLEXIVE VERBS

lavarse, to wash oneself

PRESENT TENSE

I wash myself, you wash yourself, etc.

yo *me lavo*	nosotros, -as *nos lavamos*
tú *te lavas*	vosotros, -as *os laváis*
Vd., él, ella *se lava*	Vds., ellos, -as *se lavan*

PRESENT PARTICIPLE (GERUND)

washing myself, washing yourself, etc.

lavándome, lavándote, lavándose, etc.

COMMANDS

lávese Vd., *wash yourself*	no se lave Vd., *don't wash yourself*
lávense Vds., *wash yourselves*	no se laven Vds., *don't wash yourselves*

Note

1. Reflexive verbs in the infinitive are identified by the attached pronoun **me, te, se, nos** or **os.**
2. A reflexive pronoun must always be used with a reflexive verb.

POSITION OF REFLEXIVE PRONOUNS

Reflexive pronouns, like other object pronouns, are generally placed *before* the verb. However, they follow and are attached to the verb when used with:

a. an affirmative command
b. an infinitive
c. a present participle

NORMAL POSITION:

Los niños *se* lavan.	The children wash themselves.

EXCEPTIONS:

. Affirmative Command.

Láve*se* Vd.	Wash yourself.
But	
No *se* lave Vd.	Don't wash yourself.

. Infinitive.

Voy a lavar*me.*	I am going to wash myself.

. Present Participle.

Están lavándo*se.*	They are washing themselves.

Note

1. Reflexive pronouns are attached to the affirmative command, but are placed *before* the *negative* command.

2. When a reflexive pronoun is attached to an affirmative command or present participle, a written accent mark is generally required on the vowel that is stressed.

[25]

COMMON REFLEXIVE VERBS

acostarse (ue), to go to bed
bañarse, to take a bath
desayúnarse, to eat breakfast
despertarse (ie), to wake up
divertirse (ie), to enjoy oneself,
   to have a good time
irse, to go away

lavarse, to wash (oneself),
   to get washed
levantarse, to get up
llamarse, to be named
pasearse, to take a walk
peinarse, to comb one's hair
ponerse, to put on

quedarse, to remain
quitarse, to take off
sentarse (ie), to sit down
sentirse (ie), to feel
vestirse (i), to dress (oneself),
   to get dressed

Note

1. Many verbs are reflexive in Spanish but not in English.

nos quedamos	we remain
se siente	he feels

2. Some reflexive verbs are also stem-changing verbs. The stem change is indicated after the infinitive by **(ue), (ie)** or **(i),** as seen above.

me ac*ue*sto	I go to bed
se div*ie*rte	he enjoys himself
se v*i*sten	they get dressed

EXERCISES

A. Replace the blank with the correct reflexive pronoun, and translate each sentence into English. Supply an accent mark where required.

1. Los muchachos _____ levantan temprano.

_____

2. Nosotros _____ acostamos tarde.

_____

3. Yo _____ desayuno a las siete.

_____

4. Alberto _____ siente malo.

_____

5. Vds. no están divirtiendo _____.

_____

6. Voy a bañar _____.

_____

7. ¿Por qué no _____ sientas en el sofá?

_____

8. No _____ vayan Vds.

_____

9. Necesitamos vestir _____.

_____

10. María está peinando _____.

_____

B. Write each verb in the present tense for the subject indicated.

1. yo

----------------------------- (levantarse)

----------------------------- (llamarse)

----------------------------- (bañarse)

2. él

----------------------------- (desayunarse)

----------------------------- (divertirse)

----------------------------- (quedarse)

3. los niños

----------------------------- (sentarse)

----------------------------- (vestirse)

----------------------------- (despertarse)

4. nosotros

----------------------------- (acostarse)

----------------------------- (irse)

----------------------------- (pasearse)

5. tú

----------------------------- (ponerse)

----------------------------- (quitarse)

----------------------------- (sentirse)

C. Write the affirmative and negative command with **Vd.** for each of the following verbs.

	Affirmative	*Negative*
EXAMPLE: lavarse	lávese Vd.	no se lave Vd.
1. levantarse		
2. sentarse		
3. acostarse		
4. desayunarse		
5. vestirse		
6. despertarse		
7. peinarse		
8. quedarse		
9. pasearse		
10. bañarse		

D. Write the present participle of the verb in parentheses.

1. Tú no estás ----------------------------------. (lavarse)

2. Estoy ----------------------------. (peinarse)

3. Estamos ----------------------------. (desayunarse)

4. Están ----------------------. (divertirse)

5. María está ----------------------. (bañarse)

6. Pedro está ----------------------. (vestirse)

7. José y Alicia están ----------------------------. (pasearse)

E. Complete the Spanish sentences.

1. My friend's name is Jane. Mi amiga ---------------------- Juana.

2. We get up early. -- temprano.

3. I do not wish to eat breakfast. No deseo _____.

4. Do you feel ill? ¿_____ Vd. enfermo?

5. Put on your hat. _____ Vd. el sombrero.

6. Do not take off your coat. _____ el abrigo.

7. The children enjoy themselves. Los niños _____.

8. Why are you going away? ¿Por qué _____ Vd.?

9. We remain at home. _____ en casa.

10. The pupils sit down. Los alumnos _____.

11. Wake up! ¡_____ Vds.!

12. I am dressing myself. Estoy _____.

F. Answer the following questions in complete Spanish sentences.

1. ¿Cómo se llama Vd.? _____

2. ¿A qué hora se levanta Vd.? _____

3. ¿Se viste Vd. inmediatamente? _____

4. ¿Se baña Vd. todos los días? _____

5. ¿Se desayuna su familia en casa o en un restaurante? _____

_____

6. ¿Se siente Vd. bien? _____

7. ¿Se pone Vd. un abrigo cuando hace frío? _____

_____

8. ¿Se divierten Vds. en la clase de español? _____

9. ¿Se sientan Vds. cuando entra el profesor? _____

_____

10. ¿Va Vd. a pasearse hoy con su amigo? _____

11. ¿Se acuesta Vd. tarde o temprano? _____

12. ¿Se queda Vd. en casa los sábados? _____

G. Translate into Spanish.

1. They wake up. _____

2. He takes a bath. _____

3. She gets dressed. _____

4. I comb my hair. _____

5. We eat breakfast. _____

6. I put on my (el) coat. _____

7. They take a walk. _____

8. We don't wish to stay at home. _____

9. My father doesn't feel well. _____

10. Go to bed early. _____

Verb Lesson 11—PRETERITE TENSE OF REGULAR VERBS

	hablar, to speak	**comer,** to eat	**vivir,** to live
	I spoke, *did speak,* *etc.*	*I ate,* *did eat,* *etc.*	*I lived,* *did live,* *etc.*
yo	habl*é*	com*í*	viv*í*
tú	habl*aste*	com*iste*	viv*iste*
Vd., él, ella	habl*ó*	com*ió*	viv*ió*
nosotros, -as	habl*amos*	com*imos*	viv*imos*
vosotros, -as	habl*asteis*	com*isteis*	viv*isteis*
Vds., ellos, -as	habl*aron*	com*ieron*	viv*ieron*

Note

1. The preterite tense of regular verbs is formed by dropping the ending of the infinitive and adding:

> for **-ar** verbs, **-é, -aste, -ó, -amos, -asteis, -aron.**
> for **-er** and **-ir** verbs, **-í, -iste, -ió, -imos, -isteis, -ieron.**

2. The first person plural (**nosotros** form) of regular **-ar** and **-ir** verbs is the same in the present and preterite tenses.

> **tomamos,** we take, we took
> **vivimos,** we live, we lived

EXERCISES

A. Write each verb in the preterite for the subjects indicated.

1. hablar: yo _____; ¿quién _____?; ellos _____

2. escribir: el profesor _____; Vds. _____; yo _____

3. vender: nosotros _____; yo _____; José _____

4. comprar: Vd. _____; tú _____; nosotros _____

5. recibir: Juan y yo _____; él _____; tú _____

6. prometer: ellos _____; Vd. _____; yo _____

7. estudiar: el alumno _____; yo _____; Ana y María _____

8. salir: los muchachos _____; él _____; nosotros _____

9. ver: ¿quién _____?; nosotros _____; ellos _____

10. quedarse: nadie _____; los niños _____; yo _____

B. Complete the English sentences.

1. Hablé a Juan por teléfono.   _____ to John on the phone.

2. ¿Qué compraron Vds.?   What _____?

3. Vendieron la casa.   _____ the house.

4. Corrió a casa.   _____ home.

5. Recibí una carta de Alicia.   _____ a letter from Alice.

6. No comimos mucho.   _____ much.

7. Trabajó anoche.   _____ last night.

[29]

8. ¿Por qué abriste la caja?   Why _____ the box?

9. Visitamos a Pablo ayer.   _____ Paul yesterday.

10. ¿Estudiaste la lección?   _____ the lesson?

C. Write the correct form of the verb in the preterite.

1. El profesor _____ en la clase. (entrar)

2. ¿Quién _____ las ventanas? (abrir)

3. Yo _____ a nadar el verano pasado. (aprender)

4. Los alumnos _____ a las tres. (salir)

5. Nosotros no _____ la casa. (comprar)

6. ¿_____ Vds. a Ernesto ayer? (ver)

7. Yo _____ a mis amigos. (invitar)

8. Mi hermano y yo _____ muchos regalos. (recibir)

9. Los niños _____ temprano. (levantarse)

10. El hombre _____ un vaso de vino. (beber)

D. Translate the English words into Spanish.

1. *I helped* a mi padre ayer.   _____

2. *We took* el tren a las dos.   _____

3. *He did not understand* todas las palabras.   _____

4. *They decided* comprar un automóvil.   _____

5. Muy bien, *answered* el señor.   _____

6. ¿*Did you listen to* el radio anoche?   _____

7. *We promised* pagar el dinero.   _____

8. La profesora *sang* una canción española.   _____

9. Anoche *I saw* a su hermano.   _____

10. *They traveled* por Europa el año pasado.   _____

E. Answer the following questions in complete Spanish sentences.

1. ¿Trabajó Vd. el verano pasado? _____

_____

2. ¿Qué comió Vd. anoche? _____

3. ¿Se lavó Vd. las manos esta mañana? _____

_____

4. ¿Dónde vivió su familia el año pasado? _____

_____

5. ¿A qué hora entraron Vds. en la clase de español? _____

_____

6. ¿Qué lección aprendieron Vds. hoy? _____

7. ¿Escuchó Vd. al profesor con atención? _____

_____

8. ¿Escribió Vd. las frases en la pizarra? _____

_____

9. ¿Comprendieron los alumnos la lección? _____

_____

10. ¿Cuándo salieron Vds. de la escuela? _____

_____

F. Translate into Spanish.

1. they promised _____   6. I looked at _____
2. we wrote _____   7. we sold _____
3. I did not open _____   8. who ate? _____
4. he decided _____   9. did they buy? _____
5. they danced _____   10. we needed _____

The matador is the bullfighter assigned to kill the bull. He first makes a series of passes with his cape. If the passes are executed with skill and daring, the spectators show their approval by shouting "olé" (bravo). To kill the bull, the matador must thrust a sword between the bull's shoulder blades. If he kills the bull with a single thrust, he is wildly acclaimed with flowers, hats and other articles thrown into the ring.

Verb Lesson 12—PRETERITE TENSE OF -IR STEM-CHANGING VERBS

	servir, to serve	**dormir,** to sleep
	I served,	*I slept,*
	did serve, etc.	*did sleep, etc.*
yo	serví	dormí
tú	serviste	dormiste
Vd., él, ella	*sirvió*	*durmió*
nosotros, -as	servimos	dormimos
vosotros, -as	servisteis	dormisteis
Vds., ellos, -as	*sirvieron*	*durmieron*

Note

1. Stem-changing verbs ending in **-ir** change the stem vowel **e** to **i** and **o** to **u** in the third person singular and plural of the preterite tense.

2. Stem-changing verbs ending in **-ar** or **-er** do *not* change the stem vowel in the preterite tense.

pensar, to think: pensé, pensaste, pensó, etc.
volver, to return: volví, volviste, volvió, etc.

EXERCISES

A. Write each verb in the preterite tense for the subject indicated.

1. Vd.

------------------------------ (dormir)

------------------------------ (pedir)

------------------------------ (sentirse)

2. nosotros

------------------------------ (servir)

------------------------------ (vestirse)

------------------------------ (preferir)

3. él

------------------------------ (sentir)

------------------------------ (volver)

------------------------------ (morir)

4. yo

------------------------------ (pedir)

------------------------------ (dormir)

------------------------------ (repetir)

5. ellos

------------------------------ (morir)

------------------------------ (divertirse)

------------------------------ (cerrar)

B. Change the verbs in italics from the present to the preterite, using the same subject.

1. La criada *sirve* la comida. ------------------------------

2. Los niños *duermen*. ------------------------------

3. *Encuentran* a su amigo. ------------------------------

4. *Pide* un plato de sopa. ------------------------------

5. *Prefieren* este cuarto. ------------------------------

6. ¿Por qué no *cierras* la puerta? ------------------------------

7. Lo *siento* mucho. ------------------------------

8. Los soldados *mueren*. ------------------------------

9. *Volvemos* a casa. ----------------------------------

10. *Se divierte* mucho. ----------------------------------

C. Translate the English words into Spanish.

1. *He slept* en una cama cómoda. ----------------------------------

2. *They served* muchos refrescos. ----------------------------------

3. *I ordered* huevos fritos. ----------------------------------

4. El niño *got dressed*. ----------------------------------

5. Lo *we regretted* mucho. ----------------------------------

6. Los alumnos *repeated* las palabras. ----------------------------------

7. *He died* en la guerra. ----------------------------------

8. *We slept* bien. ----------------------------------

9. *¿Did you (pl.) enjoy yourselves* ayer? ----------------------------------

10. *They asked for* el menú. ----------------------------------

D. Answer the following questions in complete Spanish sentences.

1. ¿Cuántas horas durmió Vd. anoche? ----------------------------------

2. ¿A qué hora se vistió Vd.? ----------------------------------

3. ¿Quién sirvió el desayuno esta mañana? ----------------------------------

----

4. ¿Pidió Vd. huevos con jamón? ----------------------------------

5. ¿Se divirtieron Vds. hoy? ----------------------------------

Iguazú Falls, located at the boundary of Brazil and Argentina, ranks among the world's greatest waterfalls. At certain points, huge volumes of water drop in roaring torrents from a height of 230 feet—70 feet higher than the largest waterfall at Niagara!

Verb Lesson 13—PRETERITE TENSE OF IRREGULAR VERBS—PART I

The verbs listed below are irregular in the preterite tense. They have the following endings, with no accent marks: **-e, -iste, -o, -imos, -isteis, -ieron (-eron** if **j** precedes).

andar, to walk: *anduve, anduviste, anduvo, anduvimos, anduvisteis, anduvieron*

decir, to say, to tell: *dije, dijiste, dijo, dijimos, dijisteis, dijeron*

estar, to be: *estuve, estuviste, estuvo, estuvimos, estuvisteis, estuvieron*

hacer, to do, to make: *hice, hiciste, hizo, hicimos, hicisteis, hicieron*

poder, to be able, can: *pude, pudiste, pudo, pudimos, pudisteis, pudieron*

poner, to put: *puse, pusiste, puso, pusimos, pusisteis, pusieron*

querer, to want, to wish: *quise, quisiste, quiso, quisimos, quisisteis, quisieron*

saber, to know: *supe, supiste, supo, supimos, supisteis, supieron*

tener, to have: *tuve, tuviste, tuvo, tuvimos, tuvisteis, tuvieron*

traer, to bring: *traje, trajiste, trajo, trajimos, trajisteis, trajeron*

venir, to come: *vine, viniste, vino, vinimos, vinisteis, vinieron*

EXERCISES

A. Write each verb in the preterite tense for the subjects indicated.

1. estar: ella _____; nosotros _____; yo _____; ellos _____

2. poder: yo _____; Vds. _____; Rosa _____; nosotros _____

3. poner: ¿quién _____?; yo _____; él y yo _____; los niños _____

4. andar: ¿_____ Vd.?; nosotros _____; yo _____; ellos _____

5. tener: yo _____; los alumnos _____; ¿quién _____?; nosotros _____

6. saber: Vd. _____; Ana y yo _____; yo _____; tú _____

7. querer: ellos _____; mi amigo _____; yo _____; nosotros _____

8. decir: Pablo _____; nosotros _____; los profesores _____; yo _____

9. venir: yo _____; Alberto y yo _____; nadie _____; ellos _____

10. hacer: tú _____; él _____; Vds. _____; yo _____

B. Complete the English sentences.

1. No pudimos venir. _____ to come.

2. No vino tarde. _____ late.

3. ¿Dónde puse las llaves? Where _____ the keys?

4. Quisieron ver la película. _____ to see the movie.

5. ¿Qué dijeron Vds.? What _____?

6. Tuve un examen ayer. _____ an examination yesterday.

7. ¿Quién trajo los dulces? Who _____ the candy?

8. Vine a tiempo. _____ on time.

9. Estuve en México el año pasado. _____ in Mexico last year.

10. ¿Por qué lo pusiste allí? Why _____ it there?

[34]

C. Translate the English words into Spanish.

1. *He put* el sombrero en la silla. _____

2. ¿Quién *said* eso? _____

3. Nosotros *did* el ejercicio. _____

4. *He had* que trabajar el sábado. _____

5. Algunos niños *couldn't* entrar. _____

6. ¿Por qué *didn't they come* a la fiesta? _____

7. *We walked* por la plaza con nuestros amigos. _____

8. ¿*Did you* (*pl.*) *bring* los discos? _____

9. Nadie *wanted* ir al centro. _____

10. Yo lo *did* anoche. _____

D. Write the verb in parentheses in the present and preterite tenses.

	Present	Preterite
1. Yo (decir) la verdad.	_____	_____
2. Las muchachas (poner) flores en la mesa.	_____	_____
3. Nosotros (venir) temprano.	_____	_____
4. Yo no (querer) ir al cine.	_____	_____
5. ¿Dónde (estar) Ricardo?	_____	_____
6. Mis padres (tener) que trabajar.	_____	_____
7. ¿Cómo lo (saber) Vds.?	_____	_____
8. Nosotros no (hacer) nada.	_____	_____
9. José no (poder) jugar.	_____	_____
10. Yo (traer) un regalo.	_____	_____

E. Answer the following questions in complete Spanish sentences.

1. ¿Pudo Vd. estudiar anoche? _____

2. ¿Dónde puso Vd. sus libros? _____

3. ¿A qué hora vino Vd. a casa? _____

4. ¿Qué hizo Vd. en casa ayer? _____

5. ¿Dónde estuvo Vd. a las dos de la tarde? _____
_____

6. ¿Quiso Vd. ir a la escue'a hoy? _____

7. ¿Tuvieron Vds. que escribir la lección en la pizarra? _____
_____

8. ¿Qué trajo Vd. ayer a la escuela? _____

9. ¿Qué dijo el profesor a los alumnos? _____
_____

10. ¿Anduvo Vd. por el parque el domingo? _____

Verb Lesson 14—PRETERITE TENSE OF IRREGULAR VERBS—PART II

The following irregular preterites have an accented **i** except in the third person (singular and plural) where **i** changes to **y**.

> **caer,** to fall: caí, caíste, *cayó,* caímos, caísteis, *cayeron*
>
> **creer,** to believe: creí, creíste, *creyó,* creímos, creísteis, *creyeron*
>
> **leer,** to read: leí, leíste, *leyó,* leímos, leísteis, *leyeron*
>
> **oír,** to hear: oí, oíste, *oyó,* oímos, oísteis, *oyeron*

In the preterite, **dar** has the endings of regular **-er, -ir** verbs; **ser** and **ir** have identical forms in the preterite.

> **dar,** to give: *di, diste, dió, dimos, disteis, dieron*
>
> **ser,** to be; **ir,** to go: *fui, fuiste, fué, fuimos, fuisteis, fueron*

EXERCISES

A. Write each verb in the preterite tense for the subject indicated.

1. yo

_____ (caer)

_____ (dar)

_____ (ser)

2. Vds.

_____ (dar)

_____ (leer)

_____ (ir)

3. Alberto

_____ (oír)

_____ (ir)

_____ (dar)

4. nosotros

_____ (creer)

_____ (dar)

_____ (ser)

5. tú

_____ (oír)

_____ (ser)

_____ (dar)

B. Complete the English sentences.

1. Ana no lo creyó.

Ann _____ it.

2. No leí el periódico.

_____ the newspaper.

3. No fué a la oficina hoy.

_____ to the office today.

4. Oyeron un sonido.

_____ a sound.

5. Mis amigos no fueron invitados.

My friends _____ not invited.

6. Dió el libro al profesor.

_____ the book to the teacher.

7. ¿Dónde cayó?

Where _____?

8. Fuí al teatro.

_____ to the theater.

9. Los alumnos leyeron el cuento.

The pupils _____ the story.

10. ¿Cuánto dieron Vds.?

How much _____?

C. Translate the English words into Spanish.

1. *It was* necesario vender el automóvil. _____
2. *We gave* el cheque al propietario. _____
3. Carlos y yo *went* a la playa. _____
4. El profesor *read* la lección. _____
5. Los platos *fell* al suelo. _____
6. Lo *I gave* a mi hermano. _____
7. *We did not read* el artículo. _____
8. Ellos no me *believed*. _____
9. *I went* al mercado. _____
10. *I heard* una explosión. _____

D. Change the verb in italics from the present to the preterite.

1. *Caemos* enfermos. _____
2. *Van* a casa. _____
3. *Lee* la carta. _____
4. ¿Cuánto dinero *da* Vd.? _____
5. *Oye* un ruido. _____
6. *Voy* a la escuela. _____
7. Le *creen*. _____
8. *Es* importante. _____
9. *Leo* la novela. _____
10. *Dan* el premio a Teresa. _____

E. Answer the following questions in complete Spanish sentences.

1. ¿Leyó Vd. la lección de hoy? _____
2. ¿Dió el profesor un examen esta semana? _____
   _____
3. ¿Fueron Vds. al salón de actos (auditorium) la semana pasada? _____
   _____
4. ¿A qué hora fué Vd. a casa? _____
5. ¿Qué dió Vd. a su amigo(-a) para su cumpleaños? _____
   _____

General Porfirio Díaz (1830-1915) was dictator of Mexico for over thirty years. During his time in power, Mexico enjoyed some degree of economic prosperity. Very little, however, was done to improve the conditions of the masses. As a result, the people revolted in 1910, forcing Díaz to flee the country.

[37]

REVIEW OF VERB LESSONS 8-14

A. Write the first person singular of the present tense, the command with **Vd.**, and the present participle of each of the following verbs.

	Present Tense	Command	Present Participle
EXAMPLE: entrar	entro	entre Vd.	entrando
1. tomar			
2. correr			
3. venir			
4. ir			
5. poner			
6. dar			
7. traer			
8. decir			
9. cerrar			
10. dormir			
11. lavarse			
12. volver			
13. sentarse			
14. hacer			
15. salir			

B. Write the correct form of the verb in the preterite.

1. Yo no (poder) visitar a Inés.
2. ¿A qué hora (volver) Vds. a casa?
3. Yo (salir) de casa a las ocho.
4. Nosotros (comer) en un restaurante.
5. Yo (comprar) pan y leche.
6. Pedro (vender) su bicicleta.
7. El hombre (pedir) la cuenta.
8. Los niños no (dormir) bien.
9. ¿(Encontrar) Vds. a sus amigos?
10. ¿Quién (oír) las noticias?
11. Juana y yo (ir) al cine.
12. Pedro (venir) temprano.
13. El muchacho no (contestar).
14. Mis hermanos (tener) que trabajar.
15. ¿Cuánto dinero (dar) Vd. a Tomás?

C. Underline the correct Spanish verb.

1. He got dressed.   Se (viste, vistió, vestí).
2. I did not want to work.   No (quise, quiso, quiero) trabajar.
3. He died in peace.   (Muere, Murió, Muera) en paz.
4. He did not give the book to me.   No me (dé, da, dió) el libro.
5. What did you say?   ¿Qué (dijo, dice, diga) Vd.?
6. Read the lesson.   (Lean, Leyeron, Leen) Vds. la lección.
7. He closed the door.   (Cierra, Cerré, Cerró) la puerta.
8. Mary takes a bath.   María se (bañó, bañé, baña).
9. Do not remain at home.   No se (queda, quedó, quede) Vd. en casa.
10. The letter carrier brought a letter.   El cartero (traje, trae, trajo) una carta.
11. He went to the movies.   (Fuí, Fué, Va) al cine.
12. At what time did they come?   ¿A qué hora (vengan, vienen, vinieron)?
13. Where did they put the suitcases?   ¿Dónde (ponen, pusieron, pongan) las maletas?
14. They served us refreshments.   Nos (sirvieron, servimos, sirven) refrescos.
15. What fell?   ¿Qué (cayó, caiga, cae)?

D. Answer the following questions in complete Spanish sentences.

1. ¿A dónde fué Vd. ayer? _____
2. ¿Hizo Vd. una cita (date) con su amigo(-a)? _____
   _____
3. ¿Leyó Vd. el periódico hoy? _____
4. ¿Cuándo vió Vd. a sus amigos? _____
5. ¿Se divirtieron Vds.? _____
6. ¿A qué hora se acuesta Vd.? _____
7. ¿Se levanta Vd. temprano los sábados? _____
   _____
8. ¿Quién estuvo en su casa ayer? _____
9. ¿Anduvo Vd. por la calle anoche? _____
   _____
10. ¿Preparó Vd. la lección para mañana? _____
    _____
11. ¿A qué hora comió Vd.? _____
12. ¿Qué está Vd. haciendo ahora? _____
13. ¿Cuántas horas durmió Vd. anoche? _____
14. ¿Cuándo vino Vd. a casa? _____
15. ¿Se quedó Vd. en casa? _____

Verb Lesson 15—IMPERFECT TENSE OF REGULAR AND IRREGULAR VERBS; USES OF THE IMPERFECT

IMPERFECT TENSE OF REGULAR VERBS

	hablar, to speak	**comer,** to eat	**vivir,** to live
	I was speaking, used to speak, spoke, etc.	*I was eating, used to eat, ate, etc.*	*I was living, used to live, lived, etc.*
yo	habl*aba*	com*ía*	viv*ía*
tú	habl*abas*	com*ías*	viv*ías*
Vd., él, ella	habl*aba*	com*ía*	viv*ía*
nosotros, -as	habl*ábamos*	com*íamos*	viv*íamos*
vosotros, -as	habl*abais*	com*íais*	viv*íais*
Vds., ellos, -as	habl*aban*	com*ían*	viv*ían*

Note

The imperfect tense of regular verbs is formed by dropping the ending of the infinitive and adding:

for -**ar** verbs, -aba, -abas, -aba, -ábamos, -abais, -aban.

for -**er** and -**ir** verbs, -ía, -ías, -ía, -íamos, -íais, -ían.

IMPERFECT TENSE OF IRREGULAR VERBS

The following are the only verbs irregular in the imperfect tense.

ir, to go: *iba, ibas, iba, íbamos, ibais, iban*

ser, to be: *era, eras, era, éramos, erais, eran*

ver, to see: *veía, veías, veía, veíamos, veíais, veían*

USES OF THE IMPERFECT

The imperfect is used:

1. To express a continuous action in the past.

   La muchacha **cantaba** mientras **bailábamos**.

   The girl sang (= was singing) while we danced (= were dancing).

2. To express a repeated or customary action in the past.

   Pedro me **invitaba** a menudo a su casa.

   Peter often invited (= used to invite) me to his home.

   Yo siempre **trabajaba** durante las vacaciones.

   I always worked (= used to work) during the vacation.

3. To describe persons or things in the past.

   Juana **era** alta y bonita.

   Jane was tall and pretty.

   La ciudad **estaba** en ruinas.

   The city was in ruins.

4. To describe what was going on in the past (*imperfect*) when something else happened (*preterite*).

   Yo **escribía** una carta cuando él **llegó**.

   I was writing a letter when he arrived.

EXERCISES

A. Write each verb in the imperfect tense for the subject indicated.

1. Juan

_____ (beber)

_____ (recibir)

_____ (amar)

2. los niños

_____ (invitar)

_____ (tener)

_____ (abrir)

3. yo

_____ (venir)

_____ (trabajar)

_____ (prometer)

4. tú

_____ (pensar)

_____ (creer)

_____ (decir)

5. nosotros

_____ (salir)

_____ (llegar)

_____ (saber)

B. Write the correct form of the verb in the imperfect tense.

1. Nosotros _____ buenos amigos. (ser)

2. Nosotros _____ al cine los sábados. (ir)

3. Su hermana _____ muy hermosa. (ser)

4. Yo _____ a su casa con frecuencia. (ir)

5. Los señores González _____ ricos. (ser)

6. Mi amigo y yo los _____ a menudo. (ver)

7. Ellos _____ a vender la casa. (ir)

8. Yo _____ a mi amigo todos los días. (ver)

9. ¿_____ Vd. a visitar a Ana? (ir)

10. Algunas veces Pablo la _____ en el mercado. (ver)

C. Complete the English sentences.

1. Los muchachos corrían por el parque.

The boys _____ through the park.

2. Yo vivía en Colorado.

_____ in Colorado.

3. Juan nos visitaba frecuentemente.

John _____ us frequently.

4. Comíamos en aquel restaurante.

_____ in that restaurant.

5. Todas las muchachas cantaban.

All the girls _____

6. Le admirábamos mucho.

_____ him a great deal.

7. ¿Qué decías a Pedro?

What _____ Peter?

8. Los niños iban a la escuela.

The children _____ to school.

9. La lección era difícil.

The lesson _____ difficult.

10. Le veíamos a menudo.

We _____ him often.

D. Translate the English words into Spanish.

1. *I was reading* una novela.
2. *We were* alumnos de la misma escuela.
3. ¿Por qué *were you crying?*
4. *It was* imposible convencerle.
5. *He was going* a comprar un automóvil.
6. *We used to come* aquí en el verano.
7. *I used to see* a Enrique con frecuencia.
8. ¿A dónde *were you (pl.) going?*
9. *They were listening* atentamente.
10. *He used to be* mi profesor de español.
11. *They used to see* a Carlos todos los días.
12. Vds. *used to live* en Cuba, ¿verdad?
13. ¿*Were you* su amigo?
14. *I was not able* estudiar.
15. *I was* muy pobre.
16. Carlos y María *were dancing.*
17. *We were going* a pasar una semana en el campo.
18. ¿Quién *used to say* eso?
19. *We were working* todo el día.
20. El profesor *was writing* en la pizarra.

E. Complete the Spanish sentences.

1. It was raining when we left.

   ------------------- cuando ----------------------.

2. I used to buy shoes in that store.

   ------------------------------- zapatos en esa tienda.

3. What were you doing during the day?

   ¿Qué ------------------- Vds. durante el día?

4. She used to earn a great deal of money.

   --------------------------------- mucho dinero.

5. We used to receive many letters from him.

   --- muchas cartas de él.

6. They were selling fruits and vegetables.

   ------------------------------- frutas y legumbres.

7. Paul used to study much.

   Pablo -------------------------- mucho.

8. The birds were singing in the trees.

   Los pájaros ------------------------ en los árboles.

[42]

9. I was carrying the suitcases.

   _____ las maletas.

10. Anthony and I were looking at the airplanes.

    Antonio y yo _____ los aviones.

11. I always played with my friends in the afternoon.

    Siempre _____ con mis amigos por la tarde.

12. It was one o'clock when they arrived.

    _____ la una cuando _____.

13. We often went to the country in the summer.

    A menudo _____ al campo en el verano.

14. He was blond and had blue eyes.

    _____ rubio y _____ los ojos azules.

15. The mother read while the children slept.

    La madre _____ mientras los niños _____.

16. We were eating when he called.

    _____ cuando _____.

17. When I was young, I believed in ghosts.

    Cuando _____ joven, _____ en los fantasmas.

18. What were you doing while I was downtown?

    ¿Qué _____ Vds. mientras yo _____ en el centro?

19. Who was calling me?

    ¿Quién me _____?

20. They were very tired.

    _____ muy cansados.

Montezuma II (1480?-1520) was emperor of the Aztecs when Cortés arrived in Mexico (1519). Because Montezuma was imprisoned by Cortés, the Aztecs rose in revolt. Montezuma pleaded with his people not to attack the palace, but the Aztecs, believing that he had turned traitor, stoned him to death.

Verb Lesson 16—PAST PARTICIPLE OF REGULAR VERBS; THE PERFECT TENSE

PAST PARTICIPLES OF REGULAR VERBS

habl*ar,* to speak hspace habl*ado,* spoken
com*er,* to eat com*ido,* eaten
viv*ir,* to live viv*ido,* lived

Note

The past participle of regular verbs is formed by dropping the infinitive ending (**-ar, -er, -ir**) and adding **-ado** for **-ar** verbs and **-ido** for **-er** or **-ir** verbs.

PERFECT TENSE

	hablar, to speak	**comer,** to eat	**vivir,** to live
	I have spoken, etc.	*I have eaten, etc.*	*I have lived, etc.*
yo	*he* habl*ado*	*he* com*ido*	*he* viv*ido*
tú	*has* habl*ado*	*has* com*ido*	*has* viv*ido*
Vd., él, ella	*ha* habl*ado*	*ha* com*ido*	*ha* viv*ido*
nosotros, -as	*hemos* habl*ado*	*hemos* com*ido*	*hemos* viv*ido*
vosotros, -as	*habéis* habl*ado*	*habéis* com*ido*	*habéis* viv*ido*
Vds., ellos, -as	*han* habl*ado*	*han* com*ido*	*han* viv*ido*

Note

1. The perfect tense is made up of two verb forms, the present tense of the verb **haber** (*to have*) and the past participle.
2. To make a verb in the perfect tense negative, place **no** before the verb **haber**. To form a question, place the subject after the past participle.

Pablo **no ha** trabajado.   Paul has not worked.
¿Han **comido los niños?**   Have the children eaten?

EXERCISES

A. Write the past participle and its English meaning for each of the following verbs.

	Past Participle	*English Meaning*
EXAMPLE: invitar	invitado	invited
1. entrar	------	------
2. prometer	------	------
3. prohibir	------	------
4. tomar	------	------
5. salir	------	------
6. dar	------	------
7. ir	------	------
8. ser	------	------
9. cerrar	------	------
10. responder	------	------

[44]

B. Write the correct form of **haber.**

1. Mi familia y yo _____ viajado por Europa.

2. ¿_____ comido Vds.?

3. Nosotros _____ recibido el cheque.

4. ¿Quién _____ visitado a España?

5. Yo _____ pagado la cuenta.

6. Sus padres _____ vivido en México.

7. Tú no _____ estudiado la lección.

8. Mi tío _____ vendido la casa.

9. Lola no _____ bebido la leche.

0. ¿_____ comprado Vd. los billetes?

C. Change the verbs in parentheses to the perfect tense, and then translate each sentence into English.

1. Los alumnos no _____ sus lecciones. (preparar)

_____

2. Yo _____ su carta. (contestar)

_____

3. El mozo _____ la comida. (servir)

_____

4. ¿Me _____ Vds.? (comprender)

_____

5. Nosotros no _____ el tiempo. (tener)

_____

6. Tú no _____ (estudiar)

_____

7. Los habitantes _____ mucho. (sufrir)

_____

8. Nosotros _____ dos asientos. (reservar)

_____

9. Carmen _____ una falda. (comprar)

_____

10. Yo no _____ visitar el club. (poder)

_____

D. Complete the Spanish sentences.

. We have bought a television set.

_____ un aparato de televisión.

. I have not received a telegram.

_____ un telegrama.

[45]

3. My mother has gone to the market.

Mi madre _____ al mercado.

4. What have they decided to do?

¿Qué _____ hacer?

5. Has the train arrived yet?

¿_____ el tren todavía?

6. We have learned much.

_____ mucho.

7. Have you given the gift to your cousin?

¿_____ el regalo a su primo?

8. He has not eaten the bread.

_____ el pan.

9. I have invited all my friends.

_____ a todos mis amigos.

10. Some television programs have been interesting.

Algunos programas de televisión _____ interesantes.

E. Answer the following questions in complete Spanish sentences.

1. ¿Qué han aprendido Vds. hoy en la clase de español? _____

_____

2. ¿Ha recibido Vd. buenas notas este semestre? _____

_____

3. ¿Han celebrado Vds. el Día Panamericano este año? _____

_____

4. ¿Qué ha comido Vd. hoy? _____

5. ¿Ha visitado Vd. a México? _____

Verb Lesson 17—IRREGULAR PAST PARTICIPLES

PAST PARTICIPLES ENDING IN -ÍDO

caer, to fall	**caído,** fallen
creer, to believe	**creído,** believed
leer, to read	**leído,** read
oír, to hear	**oído,** heard
traer, to bring	**traído,** brought

PAST PARTICIPLES ENDING IN -TO

abrir, to open	**abierto,** opened
escribir, to write	**escrito,** written
morir, to die	**muerto,** died
poner, to put	**puesto,** put
ver, to see	**visto,** seen
volver, to return	**vuelto,** returned

PAST PARTICIPLES ENDING IN -CHO

decir, to say, to tell	**dicho,** said, told
hacer, to do, to make	**hecho,** done, made

EXERCISES

A. Write the infinitive form of the following past participles.

1. hecho _____
2. escrito _____
3. vuelto _____
4. puesto _____
5. visto _____
6. dicho _____
7. traído _____
8. muerto _____
9. abierto _____
10. oído _____

B. Translate into English.

1. hemos vuelto _____
2. han caído _____
3. he escrito _____
4. has visto _____
5. ha puesto _____
6. han muerto _____
7. ¿ha abierto Vd.? _____
8. he hecho _____
9. han creído _____
10. hemos dicho _____

C. Translate the English words into Spanish.

1. *I have not read* el periódico. _____
2. *We have told* la verdad. _____
3. ¿*Have you seen* esta película? _____
4. ¿Quién *has heard* su orquesta? _____
5. Sus abuelos *have died.* _____
6. Tú *have not written* la carta. _____
7. José y su hermano *have returned* de la playa. _____
8. *I have done* mi trabajo. _____

[47]

9. ¿Dónde *has Mary put* la revista? --

10. *We have opened* los paquetes. --

D. Answer the following questions in complete Spanish sentences.

1. ¿Quién ha escrito la lección en la pizarra? --------------------------------

----

2. ¿Ha traído Vd. su libro de español a la escuela? --------------------------

----

3. ¿Han leído Vds. un cuento interesante? ------------------------------------

----

4. ¿Ha hecho su familia un viaje a México? ----------------------------------

----

5. ¿Ha visto Vd. jamás (ever) una corrida de toros? --------------------------

----

The cacao tree is found in the tropical forests of Latin America. Curiously, the pods grow directly from the tree's trunk and limbs. Within each pod are the many beans from which chocolate and cocoa are made. Cacao is an important crop in Ecuador, Brazil, Venezuela and the Dominican Republic.

	hablar, to speak	**comer,** to eat	**vivir,** to live
	I shall (will) speak, etc.	*I shall (will) eat, etc.*	*I shall (will) live, etc.*
yo	hablar*é*	comer*é*	vivir*é*
tú	hablar*ás*	comer*ás*	vivir*ás*
Vd., él, ella	hablar*á*	comer*á*	vivir*á*
nosotros, -as	hablar*emos*	comer*emos*	vivir*emos*
vosotros, -as	hablar*éis*	comer*éis*	vivir*éis*
Vds., ellos, -as	hablar*án*	comer*án*	vivir*án*

Note

The future tense of regular verbs is formed by adding **-é, -ás, -á, -emos, -éis, -án** to the infinitive form of the verb.

EXERCISES

A. Add the correct ending of the future tense and translate each sentence into English.

1. Pablo pasar_____ sus vacaciones en el campo.

_____

2. ¿A qué hora comer_____ los niños?

_____

3. Yo abrir_____ los paquetes. _____

4. Vds. ver_____ muchas cosas interesantes.

_____

5. Nosotros ir_____ a la playa. _____

6. José me dar _____ el dinero. _____

7. Tú ser_____ muy feliz. _____

8. ¿Cuándo volver_____ Vd.? _____

9. La fiesta comenzar_____ a las nueve.

_____

10. Luisa y yo ayudar _____ a Rosa. _____

B. Underline the Spanish verb in parentheses that correctly translates the English verb.

1. I shall give (darán, dará, daré)

2. we shall win (ganamos, ganaremos, ganábamos)

3. she will sing (cantará, canta, cantaré)

4. they will dance (bailan, bailarán, bailarás)

5. Paul will bring Pablo (traerá, trae, traeré)

6. I shall celebrate (celebré, celebra, celebraré)

7. will you promise? ¿(promete, prometerá, prometeré) Vd.?

8. we shall drink (bebimos, beberemos, beberán)

[49]

9. he will believe   (creerá, cree, creyó)

10. will you serve?   ¿(servirás, servirán, servirá) Vds.?

C. Change the verbs in italics from the present to the future tense, keeping the same subject.

1. *Reciben* muchos regalos.   ----------------------------------

2. *Leo* esta novela.   ----------------------------------

3. Mi hermana *compra* un automóvil.   ----------------------------------

4. ¿Con quién *vive* Vd.?   ----------------------------------

5. *Invitamos* a nuestros amigos.   ----------------------------------

6. Los alumnos *van* a la escuela.   ----------------------------------

7. Pedro *cierra* las ventanas.   ----------------------------------

8. *Aprendemos* a hablar español.   ----------------------------------

9. José *es* médico.   ----------------------------------

10. *Vuelven* esta noche.   ----------------------------------

D. Translate the English words into Spanish.

1. *I shall speak* a Pedro mañana.   ----------------------------------

2. Vds. *will lose* el dinero.   ----------------------------------

3. La criada *will prepare* la comida.   ----------------------------------

4. Los niños *will play* en el parque.   ----------------------------------

5. *We shall visit* al señor Pereda.   ----------------------------------

6. *¿Will you write* a su primo Carlos?   ----------------------------------

7. *I shall be* allí dos semanas.   ----------------------------------

8. ¿Cuánto *will it cost?*   ----------------------------------

9. *We will arrive* a las diez.   ----------------------------------

10. *¿Will I need* un pasaporte?   ----------------------------------

E. Answer the following questions in complete Spanish sentences.

1. ¿Cuándo terminarán las clases este semestre? ----------------------------------
   ----

2. ¿Estarán Vds. contentos? ----------------------------------

3. ¿Recibirá Vd. buenas notas? ----------------------------------

4. ¿Estudiará Vd. el español el año próximo? ----------------------------------
   ----

5. ¿En qué año se graduará Vd.? ----------------------------------

6. ¿Asistirá Vd. a la universidad? ----------------------------------

7. ¿Qué será Vd. algún día? ----------------------------------

8. ¿Irá su familia al campo este año? ----------------------------------

9. ¿Viajarán Vds. en avión? ----------------------------------

10. ¿Trabajará Vd. durante el verano? ----------------------------------

Verb Lesson 19—FUTURE TENSE OF IRREGULAR VERBS

The following verbs drop the **e** of the infinitive ending before adding the endings of the future tense.

poder, to be able: *podré, podrás, podrá, podremos, podréis, podrán*

querer, to want, to wish: *querré, querrás, querrá, querremos, querréis, querrán*

saber, to know: *sabré, sabrás, sabrá, sabremos, sabréis, sabrán*

The following verbs replace the **e** or **i** of the infinitive ending with a **d** before adding the endings of the future tense.

poner, to put: *pondré, pondrás, pondrá, pondremos, pondréis, pondrán*

salir, to leave, to go out: *saldré, saldrás, saldrá, saldremos, saldréis, saldrán*

tener, to have: *tendré, tendrás, tendrá, tendremos, tendréis, tendrán*

venir, to come: *vendré, vendrás, vendrá, vendremos, vendréis, vendrán*

Other verbs irregular in the future are:

decir, to say, to tell: *diré, dirás, dirá, diremos, diréis, dirán*

hacer, to do, to make: *haré, harás, hará, haremos, haréis, harán*

EXERCISES

A. Write the verbs in parentheses in the correct form of the future tense.

1. Yo no _____ nada. (decir)

2. Ana y yo _____ a las ocho. (venir)

3. ¿Cuándo _____ Vds.? (salir)

4. Tú _____ que estudiar más. (tener)

5. ¿Lo _____ Vd. mañana? (hacer)

6. José _____ ver la revista. (querer)

7. Los niños _____ ir al circo. (querer)

8. ¿Quién _____ ayudar a Luis? (poder)

9. Yo _____ los paquetes en el automóvil. (poner)

10. Yo _____ la respuesta mañana. (saber)

B. Underline the verb in parentheses that correctly completes the Spanish sentence.

1. I shall not be able to work tomorrow.   No (podré, pondré) trabajar mañana.

2. We shall want to see the monuments. (Queremos, Querremos) ver los monumentos.

3. They will come with their friends.   (Vendrán, Venderán) con sus amigos.

4. Peter will know his address.   Pedro (sabrá, saldrá) su dirección.

5. What will they say to their parents?   ¿Qué (dirán, darán) a sus padres?

6. You will have many opportunities.   Vd. (tenga, tendrá) muchas oportunidades.

7. I shall make the meal.   (Haré, Hace) la comida.

8. We shall put the radio in the kitchen.   (Ponemos, Pondremos) el radio en la cocina.

9. They will know how to solve the problem.   (Subirán, Sabrán) resolver el problema.

10. I shall leave tomorrow.   (Saldré, Sale) mañana.

[51]

C. Translate the English words into Spanish.

1. ¿Qué *shall we do* ahora? -------------------
2. *You will have* que pagar el precio. -------------------
3. *They will not know* que soy su hermano. -------------------
4. *I shall tell* la verdad. -------------------
5. *I shall come* temprano. -------------------
6. ¿Cuándo *will you leave* para San Francisco? -------------------
7. *They will not be able* visitar a sus primos. -------------------
8. *I shall have* que comprar dos cuadernos. -------------------
9. ¿Dónde *shall we put* las flores? -------------------
10. ¿*Will he want* viajar en avión? -------------------

D. Change the verb from the present to the future tense, keeping the same subject.

1. Carlos tiene ------------------- 6. yo sé -------------------
2. ¿pueden Vds.? ------------------- 7. mis amigos vienen -------------------
3. yo hago ------------------- 8. tú dices -------------------
4. nosotros decimos ------------------- 9. yo pongo -------------------
5. ¿quién quiere? ------------------- 10. ellos salen -------------------

E. Answer the following questions in complete Spanish sentences.

1. ¿Tendrán Vds. que ir a la escuela mañana? -------------------
----
2. ¿A qué hora saldrá Vd. de casa? -------------------
3. ¿Vendrá Vd. a la escuela tarde o temprano? -------------------
----
4. ¿Qué dirán Vds. al profesor al entrar (on entering) en la clase? -------------------
----
5. ¿Qué harán Vds. en la clase de español? -------------------
----
6. ¿Sabrá Vd. la lección mañana? -------------------
7. ¿Querrá Vd. estudiar el español el año próximo? -------------------
----
8. ¿Podrá Vd. jugar con sus compañeros después de la clase? -------------------
----
9. ¿Pondrá Vd. sus libros en el ropero (locker)? -------------------
----
10. ¿A qué hora saldrán Vds. de la escuela? -------------------
----

Verb Lesson 20—THE CONDITIONAL TENSE

REGULAR VERBS

	hablar, to speak	**comer,** to eat	**vivir,** to live
	I would speak, etc.	*I would eat, etc.*	*I would live, etc.*
yo	hablar*ía*	comer*ía*	vivir*ía*
tú	hablar*ías*	comer*ías*	vivir*ías*
Vd., él, ella	hablar*ía*	comer*ía*	vivir*ía*
nosotros, -as	hablar*íamos*	comer*íamos*	vivir*íamos*
vosotros, -as	hablar*íais*	comer*íais*	vivir*íais*
Vds., ellos, -as	hablar*ían*	comer*ían*	vivir*ían*

Note

The conditional tense of regular verbs is formed by adding **-ía, -ías, -ía, -íamos, -íais, -ían** to the infinitive form of the verb.

IRREGULAR VERBS

Verbs irregular in the future have the same irregular stems in the conditional.

poder, to be able: *podría, podrías, podría, podríamos, podríais, podrían*
querer, to want, to wish: *querría, querrías, querría, querríamos, querríais, querrían*
saber, to know: *sabría, sabrías, sabría, sabríamos, sabríais, sabrían*

poner, to put: *pondría, pondrías, pondría, pondríamos, pondríais, pondrían*
salir, to leave, to go out: *saldría, saldrías, saldría, saldríamos, saldríais, saldrían*
tener, to have: *tendría, tendrías, tendría, tendríamos, tendríais, tendrían*
venir, to come: *vendría, vendrías, vendría, vendríamos, vendríais, vendrían*

decir, to say, to tell: *diría, dirías, diría, diríamos, diríais, dirían*
hacer, to do, to make: *haría, harías, haría, haríamos, haríais, harían*

EXERCISES

A. Write each verb in the conditional tense for the subject indicated.

1. Vd.

---------------------------- (hablar)

---------------------------- (comer)

---------------------------- (vivir)

---------------------------- (poner)

2. nosotros

---------------------------- (ir)

---------------------------- (ser)

---------------------------- (dar)

---------------------------- (tener)

[53]

3. Pancho

----------------------------- (saber)

----------------------------- (salir)

----------------------------- (ver)

----------------------------- (hacer)

4. Vds.

----------------------------- (querer)

----------------------------- (pasar)

----------------------------- (traer)

----------------------------- (poder)

5. yo

----------------------------- (venir)

----------------------------- (decir)

----------------------------- (leer)

----------------------------- (estar)

B. Write each verb in the correct form of the future, conditional and imperfect.

	Future	*Conditional*	*Imperfect*
EXAMPLE: José (vivir)	vivirá	viviría	vivía
1. yo (escribir)			
2. nosotros (vender)			
3. los niños (tomar)			
4. Isabel (tener)			
5. Vds. (decir)			
6. tú (poder)			
7. Vd. (salir)			
8. yo (saber)			
9. nadie (poner)			
10. Pablo y yo (hacer)			

C. Answer the following questions in complete Spanish sentences.

1. ¿Qué haría Vd. con un millón de dólares? ------------------------------

----

2. ¿En qué mes preferiría Vd. ir al campo? ------------------------------

----

3. ¿Irían Vds. a la escuela en día de fiesta? ------------------------------

----

4. ¿Cuánto costaría un ramo (bouquet) de rosas? ------------------------------

----

5. ¿Sería posible estar contento sin mucho dinero? ------------------------------

----

6. ¿Trabajaría Vd. en una fábrica de aeroplanos? ------------------------------

----

7. ¿Podría Vd. vivir sin comer? ------------------------------

8. ¿Querrían Vds. ver una película española? _____

_____

9. ¿Qué regalo daría Vd. a un niño para su cumpleaños? _____

_____

0. ¿Tendrían Vds. que estudiar para recibir buenas notas? _____

_____

D. Complete the Spanish sentences.

1. My friends would not leave without me.

Mis amigos no _____ sin mí.

2. I would not invite Charles.

Yo no _____ a Carlos.

3. It would be very difficult.

_____ muy difícil.

4. We would not have the time to visit him.

No _____ el tiempo para visitarle.

5. Would you be able to find the road?

¿_____ Vds. encontrar el camino?

6. Where would you go?

¿A dónde _____ Vd.?

7. Mary would know why he did it.

María _____ por qué lo hizo.

8. At what time would we arrive?

¿A qué hora _____?

9. Henry said that he would not need the money.

Enrique dijo que no _____ el dinero.

0. I would do it immediately.

Yo lo _____ inmediatamente.

Francisco Goya (1746-1828) was one of the great masters of Spanish painting. He had a fiery temperament, and was brutally realistic in his art. In his paintings and etchings, he exposed the horrors of war, the stupidity of the Spanish rulers and the corrupt society of 18th and 19th century Spain. Among his better-known works are "Los Fusilamientos del Dos de Mayo," "La Familia de Carlos IV" and "Los Caprichos."

REVIEW OF VERB LESSONS 15-20

A. Underline the Spanish verb in parentheses that correctly translates the English verb.

1. I was leaving   (salía, saldré, saldría)

2. they were studying   (estudiaron, estudiarán, estudiaban)

3. I used to be   (era, seré, sería)

4. we would go   (íbamos, iríamos, iremos)

5. I shall prepare   (preparé, prepararé, preparaba)

6. they will be able   (podrán, pudieron, pueden)

7. I would do   (hacía, haría, haré)

8. will you tell?   ¿(diré, dirá, diría) Vd.?

9. he has written   (he escrito, había escrito, ha escrito)

10. they will know   (sabían, supieron, sabrán)

11. he was reading   (leía, leería, leerá)

12. they would come   (vendrían, venían, vinieron)

13. we shall have   (tenemos, teníamos, tendremos)

14. I have put   (ha puesto, he puesto, has puesto)

15. they have taken   (has tomado, han tomado, habéis tomado)

B. Underline the correct verb form.

1. Juan (venía, vino) a verme todos los días.

2. Mientras yo (leía, leí), mi hermano (escuchaba, escuchó) la radio.

3. Carmen (estudiaba, estudió) cuando yo (entraba, entré).

4. ¿Quién ha (abría, abierto) la ventana?

5. Pedro lo (hará, haga) mañana.

6. Josefina y yo (éramos, somos) amigas cuando asistíamos a la escuela.

7. Dijo que (vendría, vino) la semana próxima.

8. Si hace frío, no (salía, saldré).

9. Pablo era moreno y (tenía, tendría) los ojos negros.

10. No (hemos, tenemos) visto esa película.

C. Write the English translation and the infinitive form of the following verbs.

      Translation   *Infinitive*

1. eran ------------------------ ------------------------

2. querrá ------------------------ ------------------------

3. he hecho ------------------------ ------------------------

4. han vuelto ------------------------ ------------------------

5. pondré ------------------------ ------------------------

6. saldremos ------------------------ ------------------------

7. yo daría ------------------------ ------------------------

8. él oía _____ _____

9. iban _____ _____

.0. estábamos _____ _____

.1. he dicho _____ _____

.2. podrían _____ _____

.3. diré _____ _____

.4. haríamos _____ _____

.5. sabrán _____ _____

D. Answer the following questions in complete Spanish sentences.

1. ¿Ha ido Vd. hoy a la escuela? _____

2. ¿Qué hacía el profesor cuando Vds. entraron en la clase? _____

_____

3. ¿Han estudiado Vds. la lección de hoy? _____

_____

4. ¿Escuchaban Vds. al profesor mientras él explicaba la lección? _____

_____

5. ¿Han aprendido Vds. una canción española? _____

_____

6. ¿Desearían Vds. cantar la canción? _____

_____

7. ¿A qué hora saldrán Vds. de la clase? _____

8. ¿Se quedará Vd. en casa mañana? _____

9. ¿Tendrá Vd. que trabajar este verano? _____

_____

0. ¿Qué preferiría Vd. hacer durante las vacaciones? _____

_____

E. Translate the English words into Spanish.

1. *I was eating* cuando llegó. _____

2. *He used to work* aquí. _____

3. *They have not received* mi carta. _____

4. *¿Have you bought* la blusa? _____

5. *We have opened* las ventanas de la cocina. _____

6. *I shall arrive* a las nueve. _____

7. *He will see* los monumentos. _____

8. *We will come* mañana. _____

9. *¿Would you believe* eso? _____

0. *They would not be able* vivir allí. _____

11. Dorotea y Vicente *were dancing*. --

12. *It was* un edificio moderno. --

13. *I have written* una carta a Elisa. --

14. *We used to go* al campo todos los veranos. --

15. *They will help* a los estudiantes. --

16. *I would put* este cuadro en la sala. --

17. ¿Cuánto tiempo *will you have?* --

18. *I was* enfermo todo el día. --

19. *It would be* imposible hacerlo. --

20. *We were visiting* a nuestros abuelos. --

Cervantes' novel "Don Quijote de la Mancha," the most famous work in Spanish literature, has two main characters: Don Quijote and Sancho Panza.

Don Quijote is a kindly man who loses his mind reading tales of chivalry. He imagines himself a knight and sets out in search of adventure. Accompanying him is his short, chubby squire, Sancho Panza. Their experiences furnish many amusing incidents.

Cervantes' original purpose in writing this novel was to poke fun at the books of chivalry popular at the time. But as he proceeded, the work deepened into a vast panorama of Spanish society. In Don Quijote's devotion to the ideals of bravery, justice, loyalty, generosity and self-sacrifice, we find a hero who personifies all that is noble in mankind, but who, at the same time, is an impractical dreamer. Sancho Panza, on the contrary, typifies the simple-minded, practical and realistic person who is more concerned with his own comforts than with ideals. The philosophy of life symbolized by these two opposite types has made this novel one of the world's great masterpieces.

MASTERY EXERCISES

A. Underline the correct translation of the Spanish sentence.

1. ¿Qué dió Vd. a Tomás?

   a. What did you say to Thomas?
   b. What did you give to Thomas?
   c. What did you do to Thomas?

2. Hablará a Ana.

   a. He spoke to Ann.
   b. He will speak to Ann.
   c. I shall speak to Ann.

3. Los niños iban al circo.

   a. The children were at the circus.
   b. The children were going to the circus.
   c. The children will go to the circus.

4. Oigo un ruido.

   a. I hear a noise.
   b. He heard a noise.
   c. I heard a noise.

5. Ve la casa.

   a. He sees the house.
   b. I saw the house.
   c. He goes home.

6. Ha prometido venir.

   a. He had promised to come.
   b. I have promised to come.
   c. He has promised to come.

7. Fué al hospital.

   a. He went to the hospital.
   b. I went to the hospital.
   c. I was at the hospital.

8. Comimos en la cocina.

   a. We eat in the kitchen.
   b. We ate in the kitchen.
   c. We were eating in the kitchen.

9. Pide el reloj.

   a. He asks for the watch.
   b. He loses the watch.
   c. He put on the watch.

10. Recibíamos muchas cartas.

   a. We should receive many letters.
   b. We used to receive many letters.
   c. We will receive many letters.

11. Vine a tiempo.

   a. He comes on time.
   b. He came on time.
   c. I came on time.

12. Saldremos temprano.

   a. We leave early.
   b. We shall leave early.
   c. We left early.

13. No escuchaban la música.

   a. They were not listening to the music.
   b. They are not listening to the music.
   c. They would not listen to the music.

14. Digo la verdad.

   a. He told the truth.
   b. I tell the truth.
   c. Tell the truth.

15. Trajo el libro.

   a. He brought the book.
   b. I brought the book.
   c. I bring the book.

16. ¿Cuándo llegaron?

   a. When will they arrive?
   b. When did they arrive?
   c. When are they arriving?

17. Vuelven a la oficina.

   a. They were returning to the office.
   b. They returned to the office.
   c. They return to the office.

18. Era tarde.

   a. It was late.
   b. I went late.
   c. It will be late.

19. Visitó la escuela.

   a. He visited the school.
   b. I visited the school.
   c. I visit the school.

20. ¿Qué dirán?

   a. What will they say?
   b. What were they saying?
   c. What will they do?

B. Draw a line through the verb that is *incorrect* for the subject indicated.

1. José (quiero, quiso, querrá, ha querido) vender el reloj.

2. Yo no (sé, supo, sabré, he sabido) nada.

3. Ellos (vienen, vinieron, vendrán, ha venido) de México.

4. Nosotros (tenemos, tuvimos, tendrían, hemos tenido) que estudiar.

5. Ella me (digo, dijo, dirá, ha dicho) la verdad.

6. Yo (puedo, pudo, podré, he podido) hacerlo fácilmente.

7. ¿Qué (haces, hizo, hará, ha hecho) Vd.?

8. María y yo (vamos, fuimos, iremos, he ido) al teatro.

9. El profesor (lee, leyó, leeré, ha leído) un cuento.

10. Los muchachos (salía, salieron, saldrán, han salido) de la clase.

11. Yo (compro, compré, compraré, ha comprado) el sombrero.

12. La criada (cierre, cerró, cerrará, ha cerrado) la puerta.

13. Nosotros (creemos, creímos, creyeron, hemos creído) el cuento.

14. Ellos (abren, abrieron, abriré, han abierto) las puertas.

15. Vd. (duermo, durmió, dormirá, ha dormido) ocho horas.

C. Write the correct form of the verb in the tense indicated.

Present:

1. yo (hacer) _____

2. ellos (encontrar) _____

3. él (bañarse) _____

4. Vd. (preferir) _____

5. yo (ser) _____

Preterite:

6. nosotros (ver) _____

7. yo (poner) _____

8. él (vivir) _____

9. Vds. (querer) _____

10. ella (sentarse) _____

Imperfect:

11. yo (estar) _____

12. Vds. (comer) _____

13. Rosa (salir) _____

14. nosotros (ir) _____

15. Vd. (ser) _____

Future:

16. nosotros (tener) _____

17. yo (quedarse) _____

18. los niños (recibir) _____

19. tú (ver) _____

20. nadie (saber) _____

Conditional:

21. ella (estar) _____

22. yo (venir) _____

23. nosotros (desayunarse) _____

24. ellos (decir) _____

25. Pablo y yo (ir) _____

Perfect:

26. yo (escribir) _____

27. ellos (viajar) _____

28. nosotros (ver) _____

29. Vds. (creer) _____

30. el muchacho (prometer) _____

Present Progressive: (**estar** + present participle)

31. Alberto (leer) _____

32. los alumnos (estudiar) _____

33. nosotros (comer) _____

34. la madre (servir) _____

35. yo (escribir) _____

Command:

36. (abrir) Vd. _____

37. (volver) Vds. _____

38. (tomar) Vd. _____

39. (levantarse) Vd. _____

40. (traer) Vds. _____

Infinitive:

41. oye _____

42. vaya _____

43. anduvo _____

44. muerto _____

45. cayeron _____

D. Write the correct form of the verb in parentheses.

1. Mi hermano (venir) ayer. --------------------------------
2. Yo (tener) el dinero mañana. --------------------------------
3. (Darme) Vd. los libros, por favor. --------------------------------
4. Ahora Pepe y yo (ser) buenos amigos. --------------------------------
5. Está (escribir) una carta. --------------------------------
6. Cuando estaba en México, yo (hablar) español todos los días. --------------------------------
7. Nosotros no hemos (poder) hallarlo. --------------------------------
8. Me dijo que (ir) al centro mañana. --------------------------------
9. Ella siempre (ponerse) los guantes antes de salir. --------------------------------
10. Anoche yo (acostarse) muy tarde. --------------------------------

E. Translate the English words into Spanish.

1. Ayer *I visited* a mi primo. --------------------------------
2. *He enjoys himself* mucho. --------------------------------
3. *We went* al teatro. --------------------------------
4. El viaje *was* interesante. --------------------------------
5. *I used to live* en esta casa. --------------------------------
6. *¿Have you read* el periódico? --------------------------------
7. *We shall come* a verlos mañana. --------------------------------
8. Dijo que nos *they would give* el dinero. --------------------------------
9. Los niños están *playing* en el patio. --------------------------------
10. *Come* Vds. mañana, por favor. --------------------------------
11. *They returned* a casa. --------------------------------
12. *I shall not be able* asistir a la fiesta. --------------------------------
13. ¿Dónde *have they put* mi sombrero? --------------------------------
14. ¿Cuánto *does it cost?* --------------------------------
15. Miguel *has lost* su reloj. --------------------------------
16. *Close* Vd. la puerta. --------------------------------
17. Carlos está *working*. --------------------------------
18. *I want to go* al cine. --------------------------------
19. Jorge *had* que trabajar ayer. --------------------------------
20. ¿A qué hora *do you go to bed?* --------------------------------
21. *He received* una carta de Pablo. --------------------------------
22. *They entered* en la casa. --------------------------------
23. ¿*Do you understand* el inglés? --------------------------------
24. *I don't know* el número de la casa. --------------------------------
25. *She prefers* este cuarto. --------------------------------
26. La criada *served* la comida. --------------------------------

7. *They came* temprano. --

8. *We gave* el paquete a Rosa. --

9. *He said* que estaba enfermo. --

0. *It was* imposible hacerlo ayer. --

1. *We have invited* a nuestros vecinos. --

2. ¿Qué *did you buy?* --

3. *I have decided* estudiar para médico. --

4. *They were listening to* la música. --

5. *I believe* que está en su cuarto. --

6. Margarita y José *will be* muy felices. --

7. Mi hermano *has not returned* todavía. --

8. Yo *would go* en avión.

9. Los niños están *sleeping.* --

0. ¿Qué *will you do?* --

1. ¿A qué hora *does it begin?*

2. Sus padres *died* el año pasado. --

3. *Look at* aquel monumento.

4. *I do not remember* la fecha de su cumpleaños. --

5. *I sold* mi bicicleta a Enrique. --

6. Nuestro amigo nos *will help.* --

7. *We used to see* a Tomás todos los días. --

8. *I brought* los discos. --

9. *We couldn't* dormir anoche. --

0. Todos *have gone out* a pasearse. --

Mallorca is the largest of the Balearic Islands, located in the Mediterranean Sea off the eastern coast of Spain. Its picturesque setting, luxuriant vegetation and delightful climate attract tourists from all parts of the world. Mallorca has been called the "Pearl of the Mediterranean."

Part II—Grammar

Grammar Lesson 1—GENDER OF NOUNS; ARTICLES

GENDER OF NOUNS

All nouns in Spanish are either masculine or feminine. Nouns ending in **-o**, or referring to male beings, are generally masculine. Nouns ending in **-a, -d, -ión**, or referring to female beings, are generally feminine.

MASCULINE	FEMININE
el libro, the book	**la tinta**, the ink
el padre, the father	**la ciudad**, the city
	la lección, the lesson
	la madre, the mother

The gender of other nouns must be learned individually.

MASCULINE	FEMININE
el lápiz, the pencil	**la flor**, the flower
el papei, the paper	**la sal**, the salt

The articles used before masculine singular nouns are **el** (*the*) and **un** (*a, an*). The articles used before feminine singular nouns are **la** (*the*) and **una** (*a, an*).

MASCULINE	FEMININE
el hombre, the man	**la mujer**, the woman
un cuadro, a picture	**una silla**, a chair

EXERCISES

A. Write the correct form of the article (**el** or **la**) before each of the following nouns.

1. _____ muchacho
2. _____ papel
3. _____ alumna
4. _____ señor
5. _____ estación
6. _____ sociedad
7. _____ mesa
8. _____ hombr
9. _____ mujer

B. Write the correct form of the article (**un** or **una**) before each of the following nouns.

1. La banana es _____ fruta.
2. ¿Usa usted _____ lápiz?
3. Es _____ pluma.
4. Pedro es _____ amigo sincero.
5. España es _____ nación.
6. Es _____ clase interesante.
7. Hay rosas y violetas en _____ jardín.
8. Harvard es _____ universidad.
9. La rosa es _____ flor.
10. Es _____ lección difícil.

[64]

C. Write the Spanish article for the English.

1. Felipe es un amigo de *the* familia.   -----------

2. San Francisco es *a* ciudad importante.   -----------

3. Alberto es *a* alumno inteligente.   -----------

4. ¿Dónde está *the* escuela?   -----------

5. Ana vive en *a* casa grande.   -----------

6. Hay muchas plantas en *the* parque.   -----------

7. ¿Quién es *the* profesor de español?   -----------

8. Tomás recibe *an* invitación a la fiesta.   -----------

9. *The* burro es un animal.   -----------

10. La señora Adams es *the* madre de Pablo.   -----------

D. Translate into Spanish.

1. the class	-----------------	6. a door	-----------------
2. the lesson	-----------------	7. a window	-----------------
3. the pencil	-----------------	8. a boy	-----------------
4. the pen	-----------------	9. a girl	-----------------
5. the notebook	-----------------	10. an animal	-----------------

When Columbus made his triumphal entry into Spain on his return from the New World, he was given a royal reception by Ferdinand and Isabella. Columbus not only described the riches of the newly discovered regions, but exhibited as proof gold trinkets, tropical birds, rare plants and even native Indians he had brought along with him. Ferdinand and Isabella bestowed on Columbus many honors and privileges, naming him "Admiral of the Ocean Sea."

Grammar Lesson 2—PLURAL OF NOUNS

Nouns ending in a vowel form the plural by adding -s.

SINGULAR	PLURAL
el libro, the book	**los libros,** the books
la pluma, the pen	**las plumas,** the pens

Nouns ending in a consonant form the plural by adding -es.

el profesor, the teacher	**los profesores,** the teachers
la ciudad, the city	**las ciudades,** the cities

Nouns ending in -z change z to c before adding -es.

el lápiz, the pencil	**los lápices,** the pencils
la actriz, the actress	**las actrices,** the actresses

Nouns ending in -n or -s with an accent mark in the last syllable drop the accent mark in the plural.

la lección, the lesson	**las lecciones,** the lessons
el inglés, the Englishman	**los ingleses,** the Englishmen

Note

The articles **el** and **la** become **los** and **las** when used with plural nouns.

EXERCISES

A. Write in the plural.

1. el niño _____   6. el lápiz _____
2. la república _____   7. la flor _____
3. la montaña _____   8. el francés _____
4. el amigo _____   9. el plan _____
5. el color _____   10. el jardín _____

B. Write the correct form of the article (**el, la, los** or **las**) before each of the following nouns.

1. _____ novelas   4. _____ actores   7. _____ mujeres
2. _____ opinión   5. _____ automóviles   8. _____ verdad
3. _____ continente   6. _____ chocolate   9. _____ vacaciones

C. Translate the English words into Spanish.

1. *The students* estudian en mi escuela. _____
2. *The teachers* son populares. _____
3. El señor Smith es *the principal* de la escuela. _____
4. *The seats* están reservados. _____
5. *The windows* son grandes. _____
6. En *the walls* hay cuadros. _____
7. En una pared hay dos *flags*. _____
8. ¿Quién tiene *the pencils?* _____
9. Los muchachos preparan *the lessons*. _____
10. El profesor escribe en *the blackboard* con tiza. _____

THE CONTRACTIONS *AL* AND *DEL*

The preposition **a** (*to*) combines with **el** (*the*) to form **al** (*to the*).

María va **al** mercado.	Mary goes to the market.
El profesor habla **al** alumno.	The teacher speaks to the student.

The preposition **de** (*of, from*) combines with **el** (*the*) to form **del** (*of the, from the*).

Jorge es el presidente **del** club.	George is the president of the club.
Ana recibe dinero **del** banco.	Ann receives money from the bank.

The prepositions **a** and **de** never combine with **la, los,** or **las.**

Rosa va **a la** tienda.	Rose goes to the store.
El profesor habla **a los** alumnos.	The teacher speaks to the pupils.
¿Recibe usted cartas **de las** niñas?	Do you receive letters from the girls?

POSSESSION WITH *DE*

Possession in Spanish is expressed by **de** or **de** + the article before the possessor. There is no apostrophe *s* in Spanish.

el libro **de** Alberto	Albert's book (the book of Albert)
la casa **del** hombre	the man's house (the house of the man)
el reloj **de la** muchacha	the girl's watch (the watch of the girl)
los pupitres **de los** alumnos	the pupils' desks (the desks of the pupils)

EXERCISES

A. Complete each sentence with **al, a la, a los,** or **a las.**

1. La madre lee un cuento _____ niño.

2. Carmen escribe una carta _____ muchacho.

3. Alicia va _____ escuela.

4. El hombre habla _____ señoritas.

5. Pedro da los papeles _____ profesor.

6. El muchacho va _____ cine.

7. El alumno pasa _____ pizarra.

8. El profesor explica la lección _____ alumnos.

9. El director habla _____ clase.

10. La niña vende flores _____ señores.

B. Complete each sentence with **de, del, de la, de los,** or **de las.**

1. ¿Quién es el padre _____ niño?

2. El señor Adams es el profesor _____ clase.

3. El color _____ sombrero es negro.

4. La mujer recibe un paquete _____ tienda.

5. Dorotea es una _____ alumnas.

6. Muchos _____ habitantes son indios.

7. Denver es la capital _____ estado de Colorado.

8. Alicia es la hermana _____ María.

9. ¿Dónde está el cuarto _____ niño?

10. Pablo es el amigo _____ Enrique.

C. Complete the Spanish sentences.

1. The president of the nation is an important person.

El presidente _____ nación es una persona importante.

2. My family is going to the country in August.

Mi familia va _____ campo en agosto.

3. The color of the dress is red.

El color _____ vestido es rojo.

4. Guatemala is one of the republics of Central America.

Guatemala es una _____ repúblicas de Centro América.

5. The doctor goes to the office.

El doctor va _____ oficina.

6. Henry goes to the circus.

Enrique va _____ circo.

7. February is the second month of the year.

Febrero es el segundo mes _____ año.

8. The teacher gives books to the students.

El profesor da libros _____ estudiantes.

9. The mother receives flowers from the children.

La madre recibe flores _____ niños.

10. The boys speak to the girls.

Los muchachos hablan _____ muchachas.

D. Translate the English words into Spanish.

1. Pedro es *the president of the class.* _____

2. Los alumnos dan un regalo *to the teacher.* _____

3. ¿Quién es *the principal of the school?* _____

4. Muchos *of the students* son inteligentes. _____

5. El hombre va *to the hotel.* _____

6. La muchacha recibe flores *from the boy.* _____

7. Recuerdos (Regards) *to the family.* _____

8. Es *the capital of the nation.* _____

9. El profesor habla *to the students.* _____

10. El señor Pérez es el autor *of the book.* _____

E. Rearrange the Spanish words in parentheses to translate the English expression.

1. my neighbor's dog (mi de vecino perro el)

2. the king's palace (palacio rey el del)

3. the nation's capital (la nación la de capital)

4. Carmen's husband (de esposo el Carmen)

5. the child's maid (la del criada niño)

6. the girl's parents (padres los la de muchacha)

7. Helen's sister (de hermana Elena la)

8. the children's toys (los niñas las de juguetes)

9. the boys' room (cuarto muchachos el de los)

10. today's lesson (lección de la hoy)

F. Translate into Spanish.

1. the boy's mother _____

2. Peter's friends _____

3. the girl's house _____

4. Jane's father _____

5. the teacher's book _____

6. Henry's wife _____

7. the students' cafeteria _____

8. the man's daughter _____

9. Mary's son _____

10. the women's club _____

The Indians of Guatemala are skilled in the art of weaving cloth, a craft passed down to them by their ancestors. Woven by hand, the cloth is famous for its rich variety of colors, designs and patterns.

FEMININE OF ADJECTIVES

Adjectives ending in **-o** change **-o** to **-a** when describing a feminine singular noun.

El libro es **negro**.	The book is black.
La pluma es **negra**.	The pen is black.

Adjectives not ending in **-o** remain the same when describing a feminine singular noun.

El edificio es **grande**.	The building is large.
La casa es **grande**.	The house is large.
El ejercicio es **difícil**.	The exercise is difficult.
La lección es **difícil**.	The lesson is difficult.

Adjectives of nationality which end in a consonant add an **-a** when describing a feminine singular noun.

El muchacho es **español**.	The boy is Spanish.
La muchacha es **española**.	The girl is Spanish.

PLURAL OF ADJECTIVES

Adjectives must be made plural when describing plural nouns. The plural of adjectives, like the plural of nouns, is formed by adding **-s** if the adjective ends in a vowel, or **-es** if the adjective ends in a consonant.

SINGULAR	PLURAL
El libro es **negro**.	Los libros son **negros**.
La pluma es **negra**.	Las plumas son **negras**.
El muchacho es **español**.	Los muchachos son **españoles**.
La muchacha es **española**.	Las muchachas son **españolas**.
El edificio es **grande**.	Los edificios son **grandes**.
La lección es **difícil**.	Las lecciones son **difíciles**.

Note

1. Adjectives ending in **-o** and adjectives of nationality have four forms.

   negro, negra, negros, negras
   español, española, españoles, españolas

2. Adjectives not ending in **-o** have two forms, one for the singular and one for the plural.

   grande (*m. and f. sing.*), **grandes** (*m. and f. pl.*)
   difícil (*m. and f. sing.*), **difíciles** (*m. and f. pl.*)

3. Adjectives of nationality with an accent mark in the last syllable drop the accent mark in the feminine singular and in both plural forms.

   inglés, inglesa, ingleses, inglesas, English
   francés, francesa, franceses, francesas, French
   alemán, alemana, alemanes, alemanas, German

POSITION OF ADJECTIVES

Descriptive adjectives generally follow the nouns they modify.

un libro **rojo**	a red book
una escuela **grande**	a large school
un muchacho **español**	a Spanish boy

Adjectives expressing number or quantity generally come before the nouns they modify.

algunos alumnos   some pupils
mucho dinero   much money
cada año   each year

EXERCISES

A. Complete each sentence by underlining the correct form of the adjective in parentheses.

1. La camisa es (rojo, roja, rojos, rojas).

2. Los libros son (interesante, interesantes).

3. Juana es (español, española, españoles, españolas).

4. La pluma es (azul, azules).

5. Las señoritas son (francés, francesa, franceses, francesas).

6. El niño es (bueno, buena, buenos, buenas).

7. Las lecciones son (fácil, fáciles).

8. La corbata es (verde, verdes).

9. Los papeles son (blanco, blanca, blancos, blancas).

10. Los niños son (inglés, inglesa, ingleses, inglesas).

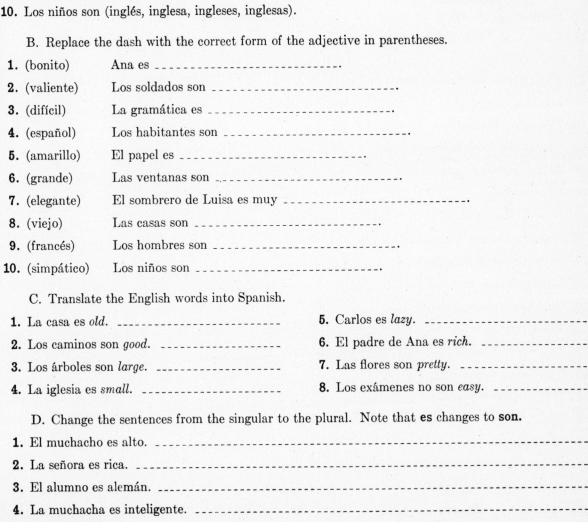

B. Replace the dash with the correct form of the adjective in parentheses.

1. (bonito)   Ana es _____.

2. (valiente)   Los soldados son _____.

3. (difícil)   La gramática es _____.

4. (español)   Los habitantes son _____.

5. (amarillo)   El papel es _____.

6. (grande)   Las ventanas son _____.

7. (elegante)   El sombrero de Luisa es muy _____.

8. (viejo)   Las casas son _____.

9. (francés)   Los hombres son _____.

10. (simpático)   Los niños son _____.

C. Translate the English words into Spanish.

1. La casa es *old*. _____

2. Los caminos son *good*. _____

3. Los árboles son *large*. _____

4. La iglesia es *small*. _____

5. Carlos es *lazy*. _____

6. El padre de Ana es *rich*. _____

7. Las flores son *pretty*. _____

8. Los exámenes no son *easy*. _____

D. Change the sentences from the singular to the plural. Note that **es** changes to **son.**

1. El muchacho es alto. _____

2. La señora es rica. _____

3. El alumno es alemán. _____

4. La muchacha es inteligente. _____

5. La flor es azul. _____

6. El libro es interesante. ---

7. La actriz es famosa. ---

8. El ejercicio es fácil. --

9. El jardín es bonito. ---

10. La nación es pequeña. ---

E. Place the correct form of the adjective in the proper position.

1. (alto)   Son ----------------------- hombres -----------------------.

2. (mucho)   Hay ----------------------- alumnos ----------------------- en la clase.

3. (inglés)   Es un ----------------------- actor -----------------------.

4. (alguno)   Deseo comprar ----------------------- libros -----------------------.

5. (pequeño)   ¿Vive Vd. en una ----------------------- casa -----------------------?

6. (popular)   Es una ----------------------- canción -----------------------.

7. (todo)   El director habla a ----------------------- los alumnos -----------------------.

8. (azul)   La ----------------------- blusa ----------------------- es bonita.

9. (bonito)   Juana es una ----------------------- muchacha -----------------------.

10. (fácil)   Los profesores dan ----------------------- exámenes -----------------------.

F. Translate the English words into Spanish.

1. Ana es *a tall girl*. --

2. ¿Tiene Vd. *blue ink?* --

3. Hay *an American flag* en la clase. --

4. *All the teachers* no son simpáticos. --

5. Es *a large city*. --

6. Necesita dos *small tables*. --

7. *Many classes* son interesantes. --

8. La rosa es mi *favorite flower*. --

9. El señor Gómez es *a rich man*. --

10. *Some students* son aplicados. --

11. Tiene *a red tie*. --

12. Es *a national hero*. --

13. Son *famous monuments*. --

14. Vive en *a modern hotel*. --

15. México y Chile son *important countries*. --

16. Inés tiene *blue eyes*. --

17. ¿Tiene Vd. *some comfortable chairs?* --

18. *All the stores* son grandes. --

19. *Each room* es diferente. --

20. Hay *many large restaurants*. --

Grammar Lesson 5—PERSONAL *A*

In Spanish, the preposition **a** is required when the direct object of a verb is one or more definite persons. The preposition **a,** when used this way, is known as the personal **a,** and is not translated into English.

Ana visita **a Pedro.**	Ann visits Peter.
El niño ve **al hombre.**	The child sees the man.
Pablo invita **a sus amigos.**	Paul invites his friends.
But	
Ana visita la escuela.	Ann visits the school.
El niño ve la pelota.	The child sees the ball.

Note

The personal **a** is not used after the verb **tener** (*to have*).

Tiene una hermana bonita.	He has a pretty sister.
Tengo muchos amigos.	I have many friends.

EXERCISES

A. Replace the blank space by **a** if it is needed.

1. No comprendo _____ la profesora.
2. Leemos _____ los ejercicios.
3. Juan invita _____ Carlos a la fiesta.
4. No veo _____ los niños.
5. Tomás abre _____ la puerta.

6. Visito _____ mi amigo todos los días.
7. ¿Tiene Vd. _____ un amigo sincero?
8. El profesor enseña _____ la lección.
9. Admiramos _____ María.
10. No tengo _____ hermanos.

B. Complete the Spanish sentences.

1. Charles helps the teacher.   Carlos ayuda _____.
2. They invite many friends.   Invitan _____.
3. He has three sisters.   Tiene _____.
4. Alice does not eat fruits.   Alicia no come _____.
5. Do you see the children?   ¿Ve Vd. _____?
6. They have an automobile.   Tienen _____.
7. Lucy loves Alfred.   Lucía ama _____.
8. The students visit the library.   Los estudiantes visitan _____.
9. I wish to see the rooms.   Deseo ver _____.
10. The principal calls the boy.   El director llama _____.

C. Answer the following questions in complete Spanish sentences.

1. ¿A quién (Whom) visita Vd. durante las vacaciones? _____
2. ¿A quién ve Vd. todos los días? _____
3. ¿Cuántas clases tiene Vd.? _____
4. ¿Qué explica el profesor? _____
5. ¿Comprende Vd. al profesor cuando habla español? _____

	SINGULAR	PLURAL
my	*mi* amigo (-a)	*mis* amigos (-as)
your (*fam. sing.*)	*tu* amigo (-a)	*tus* amigos (-as)
your, his, her, its, their	*su* amigo (-a)	*sus* amigos (-as)
our	{ *nuestro* amigo { *nuestra* amiga	*nuestros* amigos *nuestras* amigas
your (*fam. pl.*)	{ *vuestro* amigo { *vuestra* amiga	*vuestros* amigos *vuestras* amigas

Note

1. Possessive adjectives agree in form with what is possessed, not with the possessor.

<blockquote>
nuestra madre   our mother
sus libros   her books
</blockquote>

2. **Su** and **sus** may mean *your, his, her, its, their.*
3. **Nuestro** and **vuestro** have four forms; the other possessive adjectives have two forms.

EXERCISES

A. Underline the correct form of the adjective in parentheses.

1. Cada nación tiene *its* bandera. (su, sus)

2. ¿Dónde está *my* reloj? (mi, mis)

3. ¿Vives cerca de *your* amigos? (tu, tus)

4. *My* vecinos son simpáticos. (Mi, Mis)

5. *His* hermana es bonita. (Su, Sus)

6. ¿Tiene Vd. *your* libros? (su, sus)

7. *Their* casa es grande. (Su, Sus)

8. Miguel y Tomás son *her* hermanos. (su, sus)

9. *Our* clases son interesantes. (Nuestro, Nuestra, Nuestros, Nuestras)

10. Hay siete personas en *our* familia. (nuestro, nuestra, nuestros, nuestras)

B. Translate into Spanish.

1. my automobile   ------------------------------------

2. our school   ------------------------------------

3. his parents   ------------------------------------

4. your seats   ------------------------------------

5. my teachers   ------------------------------------

6. their maid   ------------------------------------

7. our town   ------------------------------------

8. her dog   ------------------------------------

9. your hat _____

10. their rooms _____

C. Change to the plural.

1. El alumno estudia su lección. _____

2. Mi amigo es alto. _____

3. Nuestra profesora es buena. _____

4. La muchacha invita a su amiga. _____

5. El niño abre su paquete. _____

6. ¿Dónde está tu lápiz? _____

7. Su padre es rico. _____

8. Nuestro primo vive en San Francisco. _____
_____

9. Mi clase es interesante. _____

10. ¿Quién es su actor favorito? _____

D. Answer the following questions in complete Spanish sentences.

1. ¿Estudia Vd. con sus amigos? _____

2. ¿Cuántas personas hay en su familia? _____
_____

3. ¿Trabaja Vd. con mi hermano? _____

4. ¿Desea Vd. ver mis regalos? _____

5. ¿Es popular nuestro presidente? _____

Charles V (1500-1558), grandson of Ferdinand and Isabella, was the most powerful monarch in Europe from 1516 to 1556. His empire, including possessions throughout Europe and America, was so vast that it was said, "En su imperio nunca se ponía el sol." (The sun never set on his empire.) In 1556, he abdicated the throne in favor of his son, Philip II, and retired to a monastery.

REVIEW OF GRAMMAR LESSONS 1-6

A. Write the correct form of the article (el, la, los, las) before each of the following nouns.

1. _____ sombrero   4. _____ lección   7. _____ padre
2. _____ frutas   5. _____ jardín   8. _____ flores
3. _____ libros   6. _____ ciudades   9. _____ hombres

B. Translate into Spanish.

1. a new bicycle _____
2. a comfortable seat _____
3. an interesting book _____
4. a modern building _____
5. a tall man _____
6. a pretty girl _____
7. a Spanish university _____
8. each student _____
9. black ink _____
10. much money _____
11. my notebook _____
12. her friends _____
13. their house _____
14. our neighbors _____
15. his teachers _____
16. your brother _____
17. our school _____
18. her house _____
19. my class _____
20. your books _____

C. Replace the dash with al, a la, a los, a las, de, del, de la, de los, or de las.

1. El padre _____ Ana trabaja aquí.
2. Los alumnos van _____ parque.
3. Pedro es el presidente _____ club.
4. La mujer va _____ mercado para comprar frutas.
5. La señorita Domínguez es la profesora _____ clase.
6. Las flores _____ jardín son bonitas.
7. La hermana _____ Juan es alta.
8. El profesor habla _____ alumnos.
9. ¿Desea Vd. ir _____ cine?
10. La señora Pérez es la madre _____ niños.

D. Complete the following sentences.

1. Visitan _____ sus amigos.

2. ¿Quién tiene mi pluma y _____ libros?

3. Inés desea visitar _____ hermano de José.

4. ¿Tiene Vd. mis billetes? Sí, tengo _____ billetes.

5. Carlos invita _____ los niños.

6. La rosa es _____ flor.

7. Algunos alumnos no comprenden _____ profesor.

8. Boston es _____ ciudad importante.

9. _____ es roja, blanca y azul.

10. José tiene _____ automóvil.

E. Complete the Spanish sentences.

1. Who is the child's father?
   ¿Quién es _____?

2. His parents are English.
   _____ padres son _____.

3. Their family is very rich.
   _____ familia es muy _____.

4. They live in a red house.
   Viven en _____.

5. All the rooms are large.
   _____ son _____.

6. Peter and I prepare our lessons.
   Pedro y yo preparamos _____.

7. Some exercises are difficult.
   _____ son _____.

8. The intelligent students receive good grades.
   _____ reciben buenas notas.

9. We admire your sister Charlotte.
   Admiramos _____ Carlota.

10. There are many interesting stories in the book.
   Hay _____ en el libro.

Grammar Lesson 7—DEMONSTRATIVE ADJECTIVES

Demonstrative adjectives, like other adjectives, must agree with their nouns in gender and number

	MASCULINE	FEMININE
this	*este* libro	*esta* casa
these	*estos* libros	*estas* casas
that (near you)	*ese* libro	*esa* casa
those (near you)	*esos* libros	*esas* casas
that (at a distance)	*aquel* libro	*aquella* casa
those (at a distance)	*aquellos* libros	*aquellas* casas

EXERCISES

A. Underline the correct form of the adjective in parentheses.

1. Hay muchas tiendas en (esta, ese, aquellas) calle.

2. ¿Ve Vd. (esta, esas, aquel) avión?

3. ¿Quién es (este, esa, aquellas) mujer?

4. (Estos, Esas, Aquel) asientos están reservados.

5. El señor Galindo vive en (este, esa, aquellos) hotel.

6. ¿De quién es (estos, ese, aquella) sombrero?

7. (Esta, Esos, Aquellas) montañas son altas.

8. (Estas, Esos, Aquel) monumentos son famosos.

9. ¿Cuál es la capital de (este, esas, aquella) nación?

10. (Estas, Esos, Aquellos) revistas son interesantes.

B. Translate the English words into Spanish.

1. Yo tomo *that* tren todos los días. ----------------------

2. *This* pueblo es interesante. ----------------------

3. *Those* corbatas son más baratas. ----------------------

4. *These* lecciones son muy largas. ----------------------

5. Un artista famoso pintó *those* cuadros. ----------------------

6. ¿Cuánto cuesta *that* blusa? ----------------------

7. *This* niña es muy buena. ----------------------

8. *That* ciudad es antigua. ----------------------

9. ¿Sabe Vd. el nombre de *those* árboles? ----------------------

10. *These* cuartos son pequeños. ----------------------

C. Translate into Spanish.

1. those countries (far away) --

2. this town --

3. those buildings (near you) --

4. that park (near you) _____

5. those trees (at a distance) _____

6. these flowers _____

7. this morning _____

8. that bird (at a distance) _____

9. this restaurant _____

10. that store (near you) _____

D. Change to the plural.

1. Ese hombre es mexicano. _____

2. Esta alumna es inteligente. _____

3. Aquel muchacho es mi vecino. _____

4. El profesor explica este ejercicio. _____

5. El niño canta esa canción. _____

6. Aquella casa es muy bonita. _____

7. Este señor es español. _____

8. Esa mujer trabaja aquí. _____

9. Aquel mozo tiene su maleta. _____

10. ¿Quién vive en ese apartamiento? _____

During fiesta time, the traditional costumes of Spain may be seen. Crowning the woman's costume is a mantilla, a headdress made of black or white lace draped gracefully over the head. A large ornamental comb (peineta) holds up the mantilla. Covering the woman's shoulders is a brilliantly embroidered silk shawl, called a mantón. The man's dashing costume usually consists of a high-crowned hat with a broad brim, a short jacket, long tight trousers and a sash (faja) worn around the waist.

Grammar Lesson 8—COMPARISON OF ADJECTIVES

	COMPARATIVE	SUPERLATIVE
rico, -a rich	**más** rico, -a richer	**el más** rico, **la más rica** (the) richest
caros, -as expensive	**más** caros, -as more expensive	**los más** caros, **las más** caras (the) most expensive
interesante interesting	**menos** interesante less interesting	**el (la) menos** interesante (the) least interesting

Note

1. The comparative of an adjective is formed by placing **más** or **menos** before the adjective.
2. The superlative of an adjective is formed by placing the definite article (**el, la, los, las**) before the comparative form.
3. A noun modified by the superlative form of the adjective follows the definite article and precedes **más** or **menos**.

el hombre **más rico**	the richest man
las lecciones **menos importantes**	the least important lessons

4. A possessive adjective may replace the definite article in the superlative.

su hermana *más rica*	his richest sister

5. After a superlative, *in* is translated by **de.**

Alicia es la niña más alta *de* la clase.	Alice is the tallest girl in the class.

TRANSLATION OF *THAN*

Than is generally translated by **que.**

Pedro es más fuerte **que** Ricardo.	Peter is stronger than Richard.

Than is translated by **de** before a number, except when the sentence is negative.

Tengo más **de** cinco dólares.	I have more than five dollars.
Roberto gasta menos **de** ocho dólares.	Robert spends less than eight dollars.
But	
No tengo **más que** cinco dólares.	I do not have more than five dollars. (I have only five dollars.)

IRREGULAR COMPARISON OF ADJECTIVES

	COMPARATIVE	SUPERLATIVE
bueno, -a good	**mejor** better	**el (la) mejor** (the) best
malo, -a bad	**peor** worse	**el (la) peor** (the) worst
grande large, great	**mayor** older. greater	**el (la) mayor** (the) oldest, greatest
pequeño, -a small	**menor** younger, lesser	**el (la) menor** (the) youngest, least

Note

1. When **grande** and **pequeño** refer to size, they are compared regularly: **más grande** (*larger*), **más grande** (*largest*), **más pequeño** (*smaller*) and **el más pequeño** (*smallest*).

Este cuarto es *más grande* que ese cuarto.   This room is larger than that room.
Es *el* cuarto *más pequeño* de la casa.   It is the smallest room in the house.

2. **Mejor** and **peor** generally precede the noun they modify.

el *mejor* periódico   the best newspaper
la *peor* revista   the worst magazine

3. **Mayor** and **menor** generally follow the noun they modify when they refer to age.

el hermano *mayor*   the oldest brother
la hija *menor*   the youngest daughter

EXERCISES

A. Rewrite each sentence, changing the adjective to the comparative and superlative forms.

EXAMPLE: José es alto.
José es más alto.
José es el más alto.

1. Arturo es fuerte.

---

2. Elena es bonita.

---

3. José y Arturo son aplicados.

---

4. Estas casas son pequeñas.

---

5. Este restaurante es bueno.

---

6. Esta persona es mala.

---

7. El Hotel Prado es grande.

---

8. Estos trajes son caros.

---

9. Esta película es buena.

_____

_____

10. Estas faldas son baratas.

_____

_____

B. Replace the dash with the correct form of *than*.

1. Carlos es mayor _____ Antonio.

2. Pepe es más bajo _____ Alfredo.

3. Cuesta menos _____ diez centavos.

4. Su casa es más moderna _____ la casa de Juana.

5. Mi hermana gana más _____ cuatro dólares.

6. Esta lección es menos difícil _____ la otra.

7. Jorge trabaja menos _____ cinco horas.

8. No tengo más _____ tres billetes.

9. Este camino es mejor _____ el otro.

10. Esta corbata vale más _____ dos dólares.

C. Complete the Spanish sentences.

1. Jane is prettier than Frances.

Juana es _____ Francisca.

2. This apartment is more expensive than your apartment.

Este apartamiento es_____su apartamiento de Vd.

3. These exercises are less important than the others.

Estos ejercicios son _____ los otros.

4. Los Angeles is the largest city in California.

Los Angeles es _____ California.

5. There are fewer than forty seats in the classroom.

Hay _____ cuarenta asientos en la clase.

6. These stories are the least interesting in the book.

Estos cuentos son _____ libro.

7. Paul is my oldest brother.

Pablo es mi _____.

8. He spends more than eighty cents a day.

Gasta _____ ochenta centavos al día.

9. Our team is better than your team.

Nuestro equipo _____ su equipo.

10. My sister is younger than Charlotte.

Mi hermana es _____ Carlota.

[82]

1. Spring is the best season of the year.

La primavera es _____ estación del año.

2. This movie is worse than the other.

Esta película es _____ la otra.

3. She has only two dresses.

No tiene _____ dos vestidos.

4. Rio de Janeiro has one of the most beautiful ports in the world.

Río de Janeiro tiene uno de _____ mundo.

5. Henry is the most intelligent boy in the class.

Enrique es _____ la clase.

D. Answer the following questions in complete Spanish sentences.

1. ¿Es Vd. el (la) mayor de su familia? _____

_____

2. ¿Quién es su mejor amigo(-a)? _____

3. ¿Es su amigo más alto o más bajo que Vd.? _____

4. ¿Es Vd. menor que él? _____

5. ¿Quién es el alumno (la alumna) más perezoso(-a) de la clase? _____

_____

6. ¿Cuál es el estado más pequeño de los Estados Unidos? _____

_____

7. ¿Gana Vd. más de diez dólares cada semana? _____

_____

8. ¿Es más rápido viajar por tren o por automóvil? _____

_____

9. ¿Cuál es el edificio más alto de Nueva York? _____

_____

10. ¿Cuál es el mes más corto del año? _____

_____

Grammar Lesson 9—SHORTENING OF ADJECTIVES

ADJECTIVES WHICH DROP THE FINAL -O

The following adjectives drop the final -o before a masculine singular noun.

Adjective	Shortened Form Before a Masculine Singular Noun
uno, a, an, one	**un** centavo, a (one) cent
primero, first	el **primer** piso, the first floor
tercero, third	el **tercer** mes, the third month
bueno, good	un **buen** muchacho, a good boy
malo, bad	un **mal** año, a bad year
alguno, some	**algún** dinero, some money
ninguno, no	**ningún** dinero, no money

Note

1. The complete forms are used when the above adjectives follow a masculine singular noun, when they modify a feminine or plural noun.

un muchacho **bueno**	a good boy
una **mala** muchacha	a bad girl
algunos libros	some books

2. The shortened form of **alguno** and **ninguno** requires an accent mark on the **u** (**algún, ningún**

ADJECTIVES WHICH DROP THE LAST TWO LETTERS

Santo becomes **San** before the name of a masculine saint, unless the name begins with **To-** or **D**

San Fernando	Saint Ferdinand
San Francisco	Saint Francis
But	
Santo Tomás	Saint Thomas
Santo Domingo	Saint Dominic
Santa María	Saint Mary

Grande becomes **gran** before a singular noun and means *great*. When **grande** follows the noun, means *large* or *big*.

un **gran** hombre	a great man
una **gran** mujer	a great woman
But	
una casa **grande**	a large house

Ciento becomes **cien** before a plural noun, and before the numbers **mil** (*thousand*) or **millones** (*m lions*).

cien asientos	one hundred seats
cien mesas	one hundred tables
cien mil	one hundred thousand
cien millones	one hundred million
But	
ciento treinta asientos	one hundred thirty seats

EXERCISES

A. Underline the correct form of the adjective in parentheses.

1. ¿Necesita Vd. (algún, alguno, alguna) cosa?
2. El hombre es (malo, mala, mal).
3. ¿Cuál es el (primero, primera, primer) día de la semana?
4. Los alumnos estudian el (tercero, tercera, tercer) capítulo del libro.
5. El Brasil es una (grande, gran) nación.
6. Mi amigo vive en (San, Santo, Santa) Bárbara.
7. Es un (bueno, buena, buen) camino.
8. (Ningún, Ninguno, Ninguna) periódico es imparcial.
9. Vive en una casa (gran, grande).
10. Es una ciudad de (ciento, cien) mil habitantes.

B. Write the correct form of the adjective in parentheses.

1. (malo) Hoy hace _____ tiempo.
2. (Bueno) _____ días, señor Pereda.
3. (primero) Su asiento está en la _____ fila.
4. (tercero) Viven en el _____ piso.
5. (ciento) El aparato de televisión cuesta _____ ochenta dólares.
6. (Santo) ¿Dónde está _____ Domingo?
7. (grande) Es una _____ actriz.
8. (Alguno) _____ lecciones son difíciles.
9. (Ninguno) _____ hombre es perfecto.
10. (uno) Voy a comprar _____ docena de naranjas.

C. Write the Spanish for the English words.

1. Es una *good* idea. _____
2. ¿Hay *some* remedio? _____
3. Hoy es el *first* de agosto. _____
4. No hay una *great* diferencia entre los dos países. _____
5. *Saint* Juan es la capital de Puerto Rico. _____
6. Es una *bad* persona. _____
7. *No* tienda está abierta. _____
8. Celebran una fiesta el día de *Saint* Tomás. _____
9. El número de su teléfono es cinco, cero, cuatro, *one*. _____
10. Tengo *one hundred* dólares en el banco. _____

D. Translate into Spanish.

1. some day _____
2. a great president _____

3. a good voice   _____

4. a bad trip   _____

5. no nation   _____

6. the first year   _____

7. the third row   _____

8. Saint Peter   _____

9. one hundred students   _____

10. a good friend   _____

11. some cities   _____

12. a big dog   _____

13. one million   _____

14. one hundred million   _____

15. the third Saturday   _____

The Pan-American Union building in Washington, D. C., is the permanent headquarters of the Organization of American States. This magnificent marble structure, donated by Andrew Carnegie in 1910, has sometimes been called the "House of the Americas."

Flags of the twenty-one American Republics and busts of their heroes are displayed in the central hall. One of the attractions of this building is its tropical patio in which are found brilliantly colored birds and exotic plants from the American nations.

0-10

0	cero	6	seis
1	uno (un), una	7	siete
2	dos	8	ocho
3	tres	9	nueve
4	cuatro	10	diez
5	cinco		

11-19

11	once	16	diez y seis
12	doce	17	diez y siete
13	trece	18	diez y ocho
14	catorce	19	diez y nueve
15	quince		

20-99

20	veinte	30	treinta
21	veinte y uno	31	treinta y uno, etc.
22	veinte y dos	40	cuarenta
23	veinte y tres	50	cincuenta
24	veinte y cuatro	60	sesenta
25	veinte y cinco	70	setenta
26	veinte y seis	80	ochenta
27	veinte y siete	90	noventa
28	veinte y ocho	99	noventa y nueve
29	veinte y nueve		

Note

1. Compound numbers from 16-99 are connected by **y**.
2. Numbers 16-19 and 21-29 may be written as one word. When this is done, **y** becomes **i**.

   dieciséis, diecisiete, dieciocho, diecinueve
   veintiuno, veintidós, veintitrés, veinticuatro, veinticinco, veintiséis, veintisiete, veintiocho, veintinueve

3. **Uno** and combinations of **uno** (**veinte y uno, treinta y uno,** etc.) become **un** before a masculine noun and **una** before a feminine noun.

un libro	one book
una mesa	one table
veinte y **un** asientos	twenty-one seats
treinta y **una** sillas	thirty-one chairs

EXERCISES

A. **¿Sí o No?** If the statement is true, write **sí**; if it is false, write **no**.

. Hay seis días en una semana.   ----------

. Hay veinte días en un mes.   ----------

. Hay doce meses en un año.   ----------

. Hay veinte y cuatro horas en un día.   ----------

. Hay treinta días en el mes de mayo.   ----------

. Hay ochenta asientos en la clase de español.   ----------

7. Hay noventa y cinco páginas en este libro. ---------

8. Hay setenta minutos en una hora. ---------

9. Veinte y cinco dólares y quince dólares son cincuenta dólares. ---------

10. Cuarenta centavos y veinte centavos son ochenta centavos. ---------

B. Write the Spanish words for the following numbers.

4	----------------------------------	35	----------------------------------
7	----------------------------------	41	----------------------------------
9	----------------------------------	54	----------------------------------
11	----------------------------------	69	----------------------------------
13	----------------------------------	76	----------------------------------
16	----------------------------------	83	----------------------------------
18	----------------------------------	97	----------------------------------
22	----------------------------------	99	----------------------------------

C. Replace the dash with **uno, un,** or **una.**

1. Tomás vive en la calle Main número noventa y ----------.

2. Necesito ---------- dólar.

3. Las frutas cuestan cincuenta y ---------- centavos.

4. Hay cuarenta y ---------- lecciones en el libro.

5. Once y diez son veinte y ----------.

D. Answer the following questions in complete Spanish sentences.

1. ¿Cuántos alumnos hay en la clase de español? ------------

2. ¿Cuántos son muchachos? ¿Cuántas son muchachas? ------------

3. ¿Cuál es el número de su teléfono? ------------

4. ¿Cuántos estados hay en los Estados Unidos? ------------

5. ¿Cuántos días tiene el mes de diciembre? ------------

6. ¿Cuántas manzanas hay en una docena? ------------

7. ¿Cuántas banderas americanas hay en la clase? ------------

8. ¿Cuántos relojes hay en la clase? ------------

9. ¿Cuántas letras hay en el alfabeto? ------------

[88]

10. ¿Qué lección estudia Vd. en este libro? _____

_____

E. Translate into Spanish.

1. sixty days _____

2. thirty-eight seats _____

3. twenty-one dollars _____

4. seventy-five cents _____

5. six months _____

6. forty-one pages _____

7. fifty students _____

8. thirteen years _____

9. one week _____

10. ninety pounds _____

When Pizarro arrived in Peru (1532), he invited the Inca Emperor Atahualpa to visit him. Atahualpa accepted the invitation and, accompanied by his courtiers, went to meet Pizarro. At a given moment, Pizarro signaled for an attack. Spanish soldiers, hidden in nearby buildings, opened fire on the Incas. They seized Atahualpa and massacred several thousands of his men. To obtain his release, Atahualpa offered to fill with gold and silver the room in which he was confined. The precious metals were brought in as promised, but Pizarro did not keep his part of the bargain. Fearful of releasing Atahualpa, Pizarro ordered the Inca chief strangled to death in the public square.

Grammar Lesson 11—NUMBERS FROM 100 TO 1,000,000

100-900

100	ciento, cien	600	seiscientos, -as
200	doscientos, -as	700	*setecientos, -as*
300	trescientos, -as	800	ochocientos, -as
400	cuatrocientos, -as	900	*novecientos, -as*
500	*quinientos, -as*		

1,000-1,000,000

1,000	mil	100,000	cien mil
2,000	dos mil	1,000,000	un millón (de)
2,500	dos mil quinientos		

Note

1. **Ciento** becomes **cien** before a masculine or feminine noun, and before the numbers **mil** or **millones.**

cien libros	one hundred books
cien casas	one hundred homes
cien mil habitantes	one hundred thousand inhabitants
cien millones	one hundred million
But	
ciento veinte libros	one hundred twenty books

2. The numbers **doscientos, trescientos,** etc., become **doscientas, trescientas,** etc., before a feminine noun.

doscientas libras	two hundred pounds
novecientas páginas	nine hundred pages

3. Hundreds beyond a thousand, such as 1,100, 1,200, etc., must be expressed in Spanish by thousands and hundreds and not by hundreds, as in English.

mil doscientos	twelve hundred (one thousand two hundred)
mil novecientos cincuenta	nineteen hundred fifty (one thousand nine hundred fifty)
dos mil quinientos	twenty-five hundred (two thousand five hundred)

4. The English word *a* or *one* is not translated before **ciento** and **mil,** but must be translated before **millón. Millón** (*pl.*, millones) requires **de** when a noun follows.

ciento diez alumnos	a (one) hundred ten pupils
mil pesos	a (one) thousand pesos
But	
un millón de pesos	a (one) million pesos
dos millones de habitantes	two million inhabitants

EXERCISES

A. Write the number for the Spanish.

1. cuatro mil doscientos	----------	6. treinta y dos mil ochocientos	----------
2. quince mil ciento once	----------	7. cien mil	----------
3. novecientos noventa y nueve	----------	8. setenta mil seiscientos	----------
4. mil ciento	----------	9. doce mil cuatrocientos	----------
5. quinientos catorce	----------	10. setecientos cuarenta	----------

B. Replace the dash with **ciento** or **cien.**

1. Tengo _____ veinte dólares en el banco.

2. Hay _____ páginas en ese libro.

3. Este reloj vale _____ dólares.

4. Hay asientos para _____ personas.

5. Es un país de _____ millones de habitantes.

6. Mi amiga pesa (weighs) _____ diez libras.

7. Hay _____ tarjetas en cada paquete.

8. Vivo en la calle _____ cuarenta y nueve.

9. Hay _____ profesores en nuestra escuela.

10. Setenta y treinta son _____.

C. Complete the following sentences, writing the answers in Spanish words.

1. Ciento diez y ciento quince son _____

2. Doscientos y trescientos son _____

3. Cuatrocientos y quinientos son _____

4. Seiscientos y doscientos son _____

5. Setecientos y trescientos son _____

6. Novecientos y ochocientos son _____

7. Dos mil y ocho mil son _____

8. Ochocientos mil y doscientos mil son _____

9. Cien mil y cien mil son _____

10. Un millón y un millón son _____

D. Write the Spanish words for the following numbers.

245 _____

359 _____

478 _____

514 _____

692 _____

781 _____

866 _____

933 _____

1,500 _____

1,958 _____

2,400 _____

5,000 _____

E. Answer the following questions in complete Spanish sentences.

1. ¿Cuántos días hay en un año? _____

_____

2. ¿Cuántos años hay en un siglo? _____

3. ¿Cuántos centavos hay en un dólar? _____

4. ¿Cuántas páginas hay en este libro? _____

_____

5. ¿Cuántas libras pesa Vd.? (**pesar,** to weigh) _____

_____

F. Translate into Spanish.

1. one hundred dollars   _____

2. a million soldiers   _____

3. ten thousand inhabitants   _____

4. three hundred pounds   _____

5. five hundred rooms   _____

6. seventeen hundred students   _____

7. one hundred ninety homes   _____

8. nine hundred chairs   _____

9. a hundred children   _____

10. three million pesos   _____

The jarabe tapatío, commonly called the Mexican Hat Dance, is considered the national folk dance of Mexico. It is a lively dance with a variety of steps, and is performed by a man and woman dressed in native costumes. The highlight of the dance is the finale in which the man throws his hat at the feet of his partner. She dances gaily around the brim, picks up the hat and dons it. The couple then dance away together.

Grammar Lesson 12—DAYS OF THE WEEK, MONTHS, SEASONS, DATES

DAYS OF THE WEEK

lunes, Monday	**viernes,** Friday
martes, Tuesday	**sábado,** Saturday
miércoles, Wednesday	**domingo,** Sunday
jueves, Thursday	

Note

On before a day of the week is expressed by **el** in the singular and by **los** in the plural.

el lunes, on Monday	*los* lunes,* on Mondays
el viernes, on Friday	*los* viernes,* on Fridays
el sábado, on Saturday	*los* sábados, on Saturdays
el domingo, on Sunday	*los* domingos, on Sundays

* Note that days ending in **-s** in the singular remain the same in the plural.

MONTHS

enero, January	**mayo,** May	**septiembre,** September
febrero, February	**junio,** June	**octubre,** October
marzo, March	**julio,** July	**noviembre,** November
abril, April	**agosto,** August	**diciembre,** December

SEASONS

la primavera, spring	**el otoño,** autumn, fall
el verano, summer	**el invierno,** winter

Note

The name of a season is generally preceded by **el** or **la.**

La primavera es mi estación favorita.	Spring is my favorite season.
Hace frío en *el* invierno.	It is cold in winter.

DATES

¿Cuál es la fecha?	What is the date?
Es el primero de enero.	It is January 1.
Es el dos de febrero.	It is February 2.
Es el tres (cuatro, etc.) **de mayo.**	It is May 3 (4, etc.).
mil ochocientos doce	1812
el quince de abril de mil novecientos cincuenta y uno	April 15, 1951

Note

1. In giving the date in Spanish, *first* is expressed by **primero;** *second, third, fourth,* etc., are expressed by **dos, tres, cuatro,** etc.

2. The year is expressed in Spanish by thousands and hundreds and not by hundreds alone, as in English.

3. The month and the year are connected by the preposition **de.**

[93]

EXERCISES

A. Complete the following sentences.

1. Hoy es jueves; mañana es _____.
2. Mi familia va a la iglesia los _____.
3. Hay treinta días en el mes de _____.
4. Hay treinta y un días en el mes de _____.
5. El mes de _____ tiene veinte y ocho o veinte y nueve días.
6. Los alumnos no van a la escuela durante los meses de _____ y _____.
7. _____ es una estación del año.
8. El cumpleaños de Washington se celebra _____.
9. Nací (I was born) en el año _____.
10. Hoy es el treinta y uno de marzo; mañana es _____.

B. Translate the English words into Spanish.

1. ¿Va Vd. al cine *on Saturday?* _____.
2. Estudio con mi amigo *on Wednesdays.* _____.
3. Hace calor en *summer.* _____.
4. *Autumn* es mi estación favorita. _____.
5. *¿What is the date* de hoy? _____.
6. Hoy es *August 1.* _____.
7. Hay una fiesta en su casa *March 25.* _____.
8. La fiesta nacional de los Estados Unidos se celebra *July 4.* _____.
9. Murió (He died) en el año *1947.* _____.
10. Colón descubrió a América *October 12, 1492.* _____
_____.

C. Write the Spanish for the following dates.

1. September 9 _____
2. November 30 _____
3. June 21 _____
4. October 1 _____
5. January 18 _____
6. March 27 _____
7. May 31 _____
8. August 16 _____
9. September 3 _____
10. July 11 _____

D. Write the Spanish for the following dates.

1. March 15, 1958 _____

2. February 2, 1588 _____

3. April 17, 1942 _____

4. May 25, 1848 _____

5. July 14, 1789 _____

6. January 30, 1660 _____

7. July 18, 1936 _____

8. December 13, 1929 _____

9. June 22, 1453 _____

10. March 25, 1953 _____

E. Answer the following questions in complete Spanish sentences.

1. ¿Qué día de la semana es hoy? _____

2. ¿Qué día visita Vd. a sus amigos? _____

_____

3. ¿Trabaja su padre los sábados? _____

4. ¿Cuántas estaciones hay en un año? _____

5. ¿Cuál es su estación favorita? _____

_____

6. ¿Cuántos días hay en los meses de enero y marzo? _____

_____

7. ¿Cuál es la fecha de hoy? _____

_____

8. ¿Cuándo es su cumpleaños? _____

_____

9. ¿Cuándo se celebra el Año Nuevo? _____

_____

10. ¿En qué año nació (was born) su padre? _____

_____

El Patio de los Leones (Courtyard of the Lions) is one of the many exquisitely wrought patios found in the Alhambra. The Alhambra, in Granada, Spain, is the outstanding example of the Moorish genius in architecture. In his "Tales of the Alhambra," Washington Irving describes the magnificence of this 13th century palace and fortress.

Grammar Lesson 13—TIME EXPRESSIONS

In time expressions, *it is* is expressed by **es la** with *one o'clock* and by **son las** with *two o'clock*, *three o'clock*, etc.

Es la una.	It is one o'clock.
Son las dos (tres, etc.).	It is two (three, etc.) o'clock.
¿Qué hora es?	What time is it?

Time *after* or *past* the hour is expressed by **y**; time *before* the hour is expressed by **menos.**

Es la una **y** diez.	It is ten (minutes) after (past) one.
Son las dos **menos** veinte.	It is twenty (minutes) to (of) two.

Half past is expressed by **y media**; *a quarter* is expressed by **cuarto.**

Son las seis **y media.**	It is half past six.
Son las nueve menos **cuarto.**	It is a quarter to nine.
Son las diez y **cuarto.**	It is a quarter after ten.

OTHER TIME EXPRESSIONS

¿a qué hora?	at what time?
a la una	at one o'clock
a las dos (tres, etc.)	at two (three, etc.) o'clock
de la mañana	in the morning, A.M.
de la tarde	in the afternoon, P.M.
de la noche	in the evening, P.M.
Es mediodía.	It is noon.
Es medianoche.	It is midnight.
Es tarde.	It is late.
Es temprano.	It is early.
a tiempo	on time

EXERCISES

A. Complete the Spanish sentences by underlining the correct words in parentheses.

1. It is eleven o'clock.   (Es, Son) las once.

2. It is half past one.   Es la una (y cuarto, y media).

3. At what time does the train arrive?   ¿(A qué hora, Qué hora es) llega el tren?

4. It arrives at 4:00 P.M.   Llega a las cuatro (de la tarde, de la noche).

5. It is ten after five.   Son las (diez y cinco, cinco y diez).

6. It is twenty to eight.   Son las ocho (y veinte, menos veinte).

7. It is a quarter past one.   (Es, Son) la una y cuarto.

8. The train leaves at 6:00 A.M.   El tren sale (a las seis de la mañana, son las seis de la mañana).

9. He arrives on time.   Llega a (hora, tiempo).

10. It is noon.   Es (mediodía, medianoche).

B. Write in Spanish the time indicated on each clock.

EXAMPLE: Son las dos.

1.   2.   3.   4.   5.

6.   7.   8.   9.   10.

1. _____

2. _____

3. _____

4. _____

5. _____

6. _____

7. _____

8. _____

9. _____

10. _____

C. Write the Spanish for the following time expressions.

1. It is seven o'clock. _____

2. It is a quarter past ten. _____

3. What time is it? _____

4. At what time? _____

5. at five o'clock _____

6. at one o'clock _____

7. at 11:00 P.M. _____

8. at half past four _____

9. It is five minutes to one. _____

[97]

10. It is early. _____

11. He arrives late. _____

12. It is midnight. _____

13. The train leaves on time. _____

14. at 8:25 A.M. _____

15. It is not late. _____

D. Answer the following questions in complete Spanish sentences.

1. ¿Qué hora es? _____

2. ¿A qué hora llega Vd. a la escuela? _____

3. ¿Llega Vd. temprano? _____

4. ¿Quién llega tarde? _____

5. ¿A qué hora comienza (begins) la clase de español? _____

_____

6. ¿A qué hora termina la clase de español? _____

_____

7. ¿Llega el profesor a tiempo? _____

8. ¿A qué hora va Vd. a casa? _____

9. ¿A qué hora estudia Vd.? _____

10. ¿A qué hora come Vd.? _____

Cuzco, the former capital of the Inca Empire, is today a picturesque city in Peru located more than 11,000 feet above sea level and surrounded by majestic mountains. Gigantic ruins of palaces, fortresses and other structures built by the Incas are found here. These massive ruins were used by the conquering Spaniards as foundations for their colonial dwellings and churches, many of which can be seen today.

Grammar Lesson 14—USES OF *ESTAR* AND *SER*

Estar (*to be*) is used to express:

1. *Location or position.*

El libro está en la mesa.	The book is on the table.
¿Dónde están los niños?	Where are the children?
San Francisco está en California.	San Francisco is in California.

2. *Health.*

¿Cómo está Vd.?	How are you?
Estoy bien, gracias.	I am fine, thanks.
María está enferma.	Mary is sick.

3. *Change from a previous state or condition.*

La sopa está caliente.	The soup is hot.
Estoy cansado.	I am tired.
Estamos ocupados.	We are busy.
Dolores está triste.	Dolores is sad.

Ser (*to be*) is used to express:

1. *Characteristics or essential qualities.*

El cuarto es pequeño.	The room is small.
María es alta.	Mary is tall.
El señor Salas es rico.	Mr. Salas is rich.
Mi hermana es joven.	My sister is young.

2. *Origin, possession and material, with* **de.**

Es un producto de México.	It is a product of Mexico.
Son amigos de Carmen.	They are Carmen's friends.
Es una casa de madera.	It is a wooden house.

3. *Occupations and nationalities.*

Mi hermano es médico.	My brother is a doctor.
Pedro es español.	Peter is Spanish.

4. *Time and dates.*

Es la una.	It is one o'clock.
Es el tres de marzo.	It is March 3.

Note

1. Adjectives used with **estar** or **ser** must agree with the subject in number and gender.

Ana no está *ocupada*.	Ann is not busy.
Sus padres son *viejos*.	His parents are old.

2. In questions, the predicate adjective generally follows the verb.

¿Es difícil la lección?	Is the lesson difficult?
¿Son altos sus hermanos?	Are your brothers tall?

EXERCISES

A. Underline the form of **estar** or **ser** which correctly completes the sentence.

1. Su casa (es, está) grande.
2. (Soy, Estoy) muy cansado.
3. Juana no (es, está) en casa.
4. (Son, Están) las cuatro.
5. ¿Quién (es, está) ausente hoy?
6. El señor Vargas (es, está) viejo.
7. (Somos, Estamos) ocupados.
8. El profesor no (es, está) en la clase.
9. José (es, está) enfermo.
10. El agua (es, está) caliente.
11. El libro (es, está) rojo.

12. ¿Dónde (es, está) Antonio?
13. (Somos, Estamos) norteamericanos.
14. (Son, Están) pobres.
15. María no (es, está) contenta.
16. Este edificio (es, está) nuevo.
17. Su hermano (es, está) médico.
18. Hoy (es, está) el cinco de abril.
19. Pablo y Andrés (son, están) hermanos de Felipe.
20. La muchacha (es, está) triste.

B. Rewrite the following sentences, using the subjects indicated.

1. El cuarto es pequeño.   Los cuartos ------------------------------.
2. Su padre es alto.   Su madre --------------------.
3. El libro está en mi cuarto.   Los libros -----------------------------------.
4. Ana es bonita.   Ana y Dolores ----------------------------.
5. Yo estoy enfermo.   Nosotros -----------------------------.
6. El alumno está presente.   Los alumnos ------------------------- -----------.
7. El café está frío.   La comida --------------------------.
8. Vd. está triste.   Vds. -----------------------------.
9. ¿Es rico el señor Ortega?   ¿ -------------------- la señora Ortega?
10. Nosotros somos mexicanos.   Yo --------------------------------.

C. Complete the Spanish sentences.

1. Is the book interesting?   ¿Es ---?
2. His friend is young.   Su amigo --------------------.
3. The coffee is hot.   El café ---------------------------.
4. Where is the teacher?   ¿Dónde ------------------------?
5. We are tired.   Nosotros -----------------------------.
6. Your friends are here.   Sus amigos ----------------------.
7. Are the rooms large?   ¿Son ----------------------- -----------------?
8. Who are you?   ¿Quién --------------?
9. Jane is ill.   Juana ----------------------.
10. The girls are busy.   Las muchachas ------------------------.

D. Answer the following questions in complete Spanish sentences.

1. ¿Es Vd. alto(-a)? --

2. ¿Dónde están sus amigos? --

3. ¿Es grande su escuela? ---

4. ¿Son Vds. buenos alumnos? ---

5. ¿Quién está ausente hoy? ---

6. ¿Están Vds. en la clase ahora? -------------------------------------

----

7. ¿Quién es un alumno (una alumna) inteligente? ----------------------

----

8. ¿Cómo está Vd.? --

9. ¿Está Vd. triste? ---

10. ¿Está Vd. contento(-a)? ¿Por qué? -------------------------------

----

In the Cathedral of Seville, there is an impressive tomb containing the remains of Columbus. The four bronze figures carrying the coffin on their shoulders represent the regions of Castile, León, Aragón and Navarra. The remains of Columbus were first buried in the Cathedral of Santo Domingo. They were removed to Havana, Cuba, in 1795, when Santo Domingo became a French possession. After Cuba gained her independence in 1898, the remains of Columbus were brought back to Spain and placed in the Cathedral of Seville.

REVIEW OF GRAMMAR LESSONS 7-14

A. Complete the following sentences.

1. Nieva (It snows) mucho en _____ _____.

2. ¿Quién es el alumno más aplicado _____ la clase?

3. Hay _____ meses en un año.

4. Hay _____ días en el mes de octubre.

5. Pedro es más fuerte _____ su amigo.

6. _____ es el primer mes del año.

7. No vamos a la escuela _____ sábados.

8. Hoy es martes; mañana es _____.

9. La Navidad (Christmas) se celebra _____

_____.

10. Inés desea invitar _____ hermano de José.

11. Un buen reloj cuesta más _____ veinte dólares.

12. ¿Prefiere Vd. esta corbata o _____ corbata?

13. Setenta y treinta son _____.

14. Cuesta un millón _____ dólares.

15. Nací (I was born) en el año _____

B. Write the Spanish for the words in parentheses.

1. (taller than)   Dorotea es _____ su hermana.

2. (the most important city in) Madrid es _____ España.

3. (better than)   Este hotel es _____ el otro.

4. (this)   Deseo comprar _____ reloj.

5. (these)   _____ frutas son deliciosas.

6. (that)   Carlos trabaja en _____ oficina.

7. (those)   ¿Cuánto cuestan _____ cuadros?

8. (good)   El señor Gallegos es un _____ hombre.

9. (third)   Hoy es el _____ de marzo.

10. (great)   Washington es un _____ héroe nacional.

11. (the oldest daughter) Juana es _____.

12. (less expensive than) Este vestido es _____ ese vestido.

13. (that)   ¿Puede Vd. ver _____ avión?

14. (third)   El señor Vargas vive en el _____ piso.

15. (Saint)   Mi hermano vive en _____ Luis.

C. Complete each sentence with the present tense of **estar** or **ser**.

1. ¿Quién _____ el presidente de los Estados Unidos?

2. ¿Dónde _____ la Casa Blanca?

3. ¿_____ Vds. ocupados?

4. La señorita Domínguez _____ bonita.

5. Nosotros _____ cansados.

6. ¿_____ Vd. enfermo?

7. Yo _____ americano.

8. Este sombrero _____ de México.

9. Los niños _____ en el patio.

10. Pedro y yo _____ hermanos.

11. Mi madre _____ en el mercado.

12. El señor Pereda _____ viejo.

13. Yo _____ bien.

14. Su padre _____ profesor.

15. Carlos _____ ausente hoy.

D. Write the Spanish for the following numbers.

9 _____

14 _____

26 _____

35 _____

47 _____

58 _____

61 _____

70 _____

82 _____

93 _____

150 _____

290 _____

360 _____

480 _____

575 _____

630 _____

720 _____

840 _____

910 _____

1,000 _____

E. Translate into Spanish.

1. on Thursday _____

2. on Fridays _____

3. on time _____

[103]

4. twenty-one cents

5. one pound

6. one hundred years

7. ten million inhabitants

8. two hundred pages

9. eighteen hundred dollars

10. three thousand students

F. Write the Spanish for the following dates.

1. February 11, 1952

2. June 20, 1960

3. August 31, 1958

4. November 2, 1947

5. March 1, 1934

6. January 3, 1956

7. July 27, 1925

8. April 14, 1898

9. December 11, 1783

10. October 4, 1555

G. Write the Spanish for the following time expressions.

1. What time is it?

2. It is a quarter to one.

3. It is half past eight.

4. It is five to nine.

5. It is ten after eleven.

6. at one o'clock

7. at two o'clock

8. at 10:00 A.M.

9. at 7:00 P.M.

10. at three o'clock in the afternoon

H. Write the opposites of the words in italics.

1. Agosto es un *buen* mes para viajar.

2. Es *mediodía*.

3. Es *temprano*.

4. *Algún* soldado viene.

5. Hoy es el *último* (last) día de las vacaciones.

6. ¿Va Vd. al campo en *el verano?*

7. Son las ocho de *la noche*.

8. La señora Galindo es *mayor* que su hermana. _____

9. Este camino es *mejor* que el otro. _____

10. Cuesta *más* de ocho pesos. _____

I. Answer the following questions in complete Spanish sentences.

1. ¿Dónde está Vd. ahora? _____

2. ¿Cuándo ve Vd. a sus amigos? _____

_____

3. ¿Cuál es su estación favorita? _____

_____

4. ¿Cuánto dinero recibe Vd. cada semana? _____

_____

5. ¿Cuántas libras pesa Vd.? _____

6. ¿Qué día es hoy? _____

7. ¿Cuál es la fecha? _____

8. ¿Cuándo celebra Vd. su cumpleaños? _____

_____

9. ¿Qué hora es? _____

10. ¿A qué hora va Vd. a la escuela? _____

_____

11. ¿Es Vd. el alumno (la alumna) más inteligente de la clase de español? _____

_____

12. ¿Qué escuela tiene el mejor equipo de fútbol? _____

_____

13. ¿Hay más de mil estudiantes en su escuela? _____

_____

14. ¿Cuál es el primer mes del año? _____

15. ¿Cuál es el tercer día de la semana? _____

_____

General Francisco Franco is the present ruler of Spain. He led the Nationalist forces against the Republican government during the Spanish Civil War (1936-1939). This bitter struggle attracted men from other nations who came to help one side or the other. After the overthrow of the Republic in 1939, Franco became dictator of Spain.

Grammar Lesson 15—INTERROGATIVE WORDS

¿qué?, what?, which?

¿Qué compra Vd.?	What are you buying?
¿Qué libro desea Vd.?	What (Which) book do you wish?

¿quién (*pl.* **quiénes**)?, who?

¿Quién es el alumno?	Who is the pupil?
¿Quiénes son los alumnos?	Who are the pupils?

¿a quién?, whom?

¿A quién admira Vd.?	Whom do you admire?

¿de quién?, whose?

¿De quién es el libro?	Whose book is it?
	(Of whom is the book?)

¿cuál (*pl.* **cuáles**)?, which?, which one(s)?, what?

¿Cuál de los libros necesita Vd.?	Which (one) of the books do you need?
¿Cuáles necesita Vd.?	Which (ones) do you need?
¿Cuál es la capital de Cuba?	What is the capital of Cuba?
¿Cuáles son las capitales de Bolivia y Chile?	What are the capitals of Bolivia and Chile?

¿cuándo?, when?

¿Cuándo trabaja Vd.?	When do you work?

¿cuánto, -a?, how much?

¿Cuánto dinero paga Vd.?	How much money do you pay?

¿cuántos, -as?, how many?

¿Cuántas muchachas hay?	How many girls are there?

¿cómo?, how?

¿Cómo está Vd.?	How are you?

¿dónde?, wnere?

¿Dónde está Ana?	Where is Ann?

¿por qué?, why?

¿Por qué no estudia Vd.?	Why don't you study?

Note

1. All interrogative words have a written accent mark. The accent mark is omitted when these words do not introduce a question.

¿Cuándo prepara Juan las lecciones? *But*	When does John prepare the lessons?
Prepara las lecciones *cuando* está en casa.	He prepares the lessons when he is at home.

2. The interrogative word *which* is translated by **qué** before a noun and by **cuál** before a verb or phrase introduced by **de**.

¿*Qué* corbata prefiere Vd.?   Which tie do you prefer?
¿*Cuál* (or ¿*Cuál* de estas corbatas)   Which (or Which of these ties) do you prefer?
prefiere Vd.?

3. The interrogative word *what*, followed by the verb *to be* and a noun, is translated by **cuál** instead of **qué**, except when asking for the definition of a word.

¿*Cuál* es su dirección?   What is your address?
¿*Cuáles* son las ciudades importantes de   What are the important cities of Mexico?
México?

But

¿*Qué* es un gaucho?   What is a Gaucho?

4. The interrogative word *where* is translated by **a dónde** (also written **adónde**) before a verb of motion.

¿*A dónde* va Vd.?   Where are you going?

EXERCISES

A. Complete the English sentences.

1. ¿Dónde vive Enrique?   _____ does Henry live?
2. ¿Cómo prepara Vd. este plato?   _____ do you prepare this dish?
3. ¿A quién llama Vd.?   _____ are you calling?
4. ¿Cuándo llega el tren?   _____ does the train arrive?
5. ¿Quién habla?   _____ is speaking?
6. ¿Por qué llora Vd.?   _____ are you crying?
7. ¿Qué lee Vd.?   _____ are you reading?
8. ¿De quién es esta pluma?   _____ pen is this?
9. ¿Cuántos alumnos hay en la clase?   _____ pupils are there in the class?
10. ¿Cuál desea Vd.?   _____ do you want?

B. Underline the Spanish words that correctly translate the English.

1. (Dónde, A dónde)   ¿*Where* van Vds.?
2. (Qué, Cuál)   ¿*What* es esto?
3. (Cuándo, Cuánto)   ¿*How much* cuesta este libro?
4. (De quién, A quién)   ¿*Whom* mira Vd.?
5. (Quién, Quiénes)   ¿*Who* hablan?
6. (Cuál, Qué)   ¿*Which one* es su hermano?
7. (Cómo, Cuántos)   ¿*How many* quiere Vd.?
8. (Cuál, Qué)   ¿*Which* periódico tiene Vd.?
9. (Cuál, Qué)   ¿*What* es el número de su teléfono?
10. (Cuándo, Cuando)   *When* estoy enfermo, no voy a la escuela.

C. Complete each sentence with **qué, cuál** or **cuáles**.

1. ¿----------------- es el nombre de este edificio?
2. ¿----------------- de sus amigos está ausente hoy?
3. ¿----------------- hace Vd. esta noche?
4. ¿----------------- son las montañas principales de Sud
   América?
5. ¿----------------- de las blusas es más bonita?
6. ¿----------------- es una enchilada?
7. ¿----------------- vestido prefiere Vd.?
8. ¿----------------- es la población de los Estados Unidos?
9. ¿----------------- libros lee Vd.?
10. ¿----------------- de los pasajeros son norteamericanos?

D. Form questions from each of the following statements.

EXAMPLE: Jorge vive en Colorado.   ¿Dónde vive Jorge?

1. Carlos necesita dos dólares.   ¿----------------- dólares necesita Carlos?
2. Pablo trabaja en una tienda.   ¿----------------- trabaja Pablo?
3. Los alumnos leen bien.   ¿----------------- leen los alumnos?
4. Madrid es la capital de España.   ¿----------------- es la capital de España?
5. Sus padres vienen mañana.   ¿----------------- vienen sus padres?
6. Jorge visita a Carmen.   ¿----------------- visita Jorge?
7. Pedro es muy simpático.   ¿----------------- es muy simpático?
8. Ana prefiere la blusa blanca.   ¿----------------- de las blusas prefiere Ana?
9. Su amigo va al cine.   ¿----------------- va su amigo?
10. Es el cuaderno de Tomás.   ¿----------------- es el cuaderno?

E. Complete the Spanish sentences.

1. What are you eating?   ¿----------- comen Vds.?
2. Whose pencil is it?   ¿----------------- es el lápiz?
3. Who are your neighbors?   ¿----------------- son sus vecinos?
4. Which suit are you wearing tonight?   ¿----------- traje lleva Vd. esta noche?
5. Which one do you like?   ¿----------- le gusta?
6. When are you leaving for Europe?   ¿----------------- salen Vds. para Europa?
7. John knows where I live.   Juan sabe ----------- vivo.
8. Whom are you inviting?   ¿----------------- invita Vd.?
9. Why do you study Spanish?   ¿----------------- estudian Vds. el español?
10. What are the principal products of Mexico? ¿----------------- son los productos principale
                                         de México?

[108]

Grammar Lesson 16—NEGATIVE WORDS

no, not

nadie, no one, nobody, not . . . anyone, not . . . anybody

nada, nothing, not . . . anything

nunca, never, not . . . ever

jamás, never, not . . . ever

ninguno, -a, no, none, not . . . any

tampoco, neither, not . . . either

ni . . . ni, neither . . . nor, not . . . either . . . or

Note

1. The common negative **no** always precedes the verb.

No es necesario.   It is not necessary.

2. Other negative words may be used either before or after the verb. If they follow the verb, **no is** required before the verb.

Nadie entra.
   Or
No entra *nadie.*
               No one (Nobody) enters.

Nada sabe.
   Or
No sabe *nada.*
               He knows nothing. (*Or* He doesn't know anything.)

Tampoco fuma.
   Or
No fuma *tampoco.*
               Neither does he smoke. (*Or* He doesn't smoke either.)

3. When **nadie** is the direct object of a verb, it is preceded by the personal **a.**

No veo *a nadie.*   I don't see anyone. (*Or* I see nobody.)

4. **Ninguno** drops its **-o** when coming immediately before a masculine singular noun.

Ningún asiento es cómodo.   No seat is comfortable.
   But
Ninguna casa en esta calle tiene patio.   No house on this street has a patio.

EXERCISES

A. Complete the Spanish sentence by underlining the correct negative word in parentheses.

1. She does not eat anything. No come (nadie, nada).

2. We never work on Sundays. (Nunca, Tampoco) trabajamos los domingos.

3. None of my friends can come to the party. (Ninguno, Ningún) de mis amigos puede venir a la fiesta.

4. Haven't you ever visited the museum? ¿No ha visitado Vd. (nada, jamás) el museo?

5. No store is open today. (No, Ninguna) tienda está abierta hoy.

6. I don't ever go out at night. No salgo (nunca, tampoco) de noche.

7. Nobody speaks. (Nada, Nadie) habla.

8. He has no talent. No tiene (ninguno, ningún) talento.

9. He doesn't help anyone. No ayuda (a nadie, nadie).

10. Albert doesn't study either. Alberto no estudia (ni, tampoco).

B. Rewrite each sentence in the other negative form.

EXAMPLE: Nunca trabaja.   No trabaja nunca.

1. Nada tiene.   _____

2. Vd. no estudia nunca.   _____

3. No bebo café tampoco.   _____

4. Nadie escucha.   _____

5. Ni lápiz ni pluma tengo.   _____

6. Jamás ayuda a sus amigos.   _____

7. Ninguna carta recibí.   _____

8. No viene nadie.   _____

9. Lola nunca llega temprano.   _____

10. Ninguno de los muchachos baila.   _____

C. Complete the answers to the following questions, using a negative word or expression.

1. ¿A quién ve Vd.? No veo _____.

2. ¿Qué dice Vd.? No digo _____.

3. ¿Va Vd. al baile o al cine? No voy _____ al baile ni al cine.

4. ¿Están abiertos los mercados? No, _____ de los mercados está abierto hoy.

5. ¿Quién vive aquí? _____ vive aquí.

6. ¿Tiene Vd. algún libro interesante? No tengo _____ libro interesante.

7. ¿Ha comido Vd. alguna vez una papaya? _____ he comido una papaya.

8. ¿Lo cree Vd. también? No lo creo _____.

9. ¿Cuándo va Vd. a escribir una carta a Pedro? _____ voy a escribir una carta a Pedro.

10. ¿A quién visita Vd. esta tarde? No visito _____ esta tarde.

D. Translate the English words into Spanish.

1. No quiero *anything*.   _____

2. Manuel *never* habla de su hermano.   _____

3. No me gusta esta camisa *either*.   _____

4. ¿No le habla Vd. *ever?*   _____

5. *None* de los vestidos es nuevo.   _____

6. *Nobody* está ausente hoy.   _____

7. *No* niño es malo.   _____

8. ¿No conoce Vd. *anyone?*   _____

9. No sabe *neither* leer *nor* escribir.   _____

10. ¿No ha visto Vd. *ever* una película

española?   _____

mí, me	**nosotros, -as,** us
ti, you (*fam.*)	**vosotros, -as,** you (*fam. pl.*)
usted, you	**ustedes,** you
él, him, it (*m.*)	**ellos,** them (*m.*)
ella, her, it (*f.*)	**ellas,** them (*f.*)

Note

1. Prepositional pronouns are the same as subject pronouns with the exception of **mí** and **ti**.

2. Prepositional pronouns are used after such prepositions as **de** (*of, from*), **en** (*in*), **con** (*with*), **sin** (*without*), **para** (*for*), **cerca de** (*near*), **lejos de** (*far from*), **delante de** (*in front of*), **detrás de** (*behind*).

con él	with him
para nosotros	for us

3. The preposition **con** combines with **mí** and **ti** to form **conmigo** and **contigo**.

conmigo	with me
contigo	with you (*fam.*)

EXERCISES

A. Change the prepositional pronouns from the singular to the plural.

1. Los libros son para Vd. Los libros son para _____.
2. ¿Va Vd. con él? ¿Va Vd. con _____?
3. Vive cerca de mí. Vive cerca de _____.
4. No recibimos cartas de ti. No recibimos cartas de _____.
5. ¿Vienen Vds. conmigo? ¿Vienen Vds. _____?
6. Pedro está detrás de ella. Pedro está detrás de _____.
7. El niño desea jugar contigo. El niño desea jugar _____.

B. Translate into Spanish.

1. for him _____.
2. in them _____
3. with me _____
4. near us _____
5. without you (*fam. plur.*) _____
6. in front of her _____
7. from you _____
8. with them (*f.*) _____
9. behind me _____
10. with you (*fam. sing.*) _____

C. Substitute a prepositional pronoun for the words in italics.

1. Vivimos lejos de *nuestros amigos*. ------------------

2. ¿Quién está sentado delante de *Pablo?* ------------------

3. Los alumnos hablan con *la profesora*. ------------------

4. Pedro va a la escuela sin *su amigo*. ------------------

5. Voy a comprar regalos para *Luisa y Ana*. ------------------

6. José vive lejos de *la escuela*. ------------------

7. La madre va al mercado sin *el niño*. ------------------

8. Antonio juega con *los muchachos*. ------------------

9. Mi casa está delante de *la iglesia*. ------------------

10. El director entra en *la clase*. ------------------

D. Replace the dash with the prepositional pronoun which best completes the meaning of each sentence.

1. ¿Son estos paquetes para mí? Sí, señorita, estos paquetes son para _____.

2. ¿Vive Luisa con Vds.? No, Luisa no vive con _____.

3. Mañana voy al parque. ¿Quiere Vd. ir _____?

4. Juan ve a Rosa todos los días porque ella vive cerca de _____.

5. Los niños quieren jugar con Carlos pero él no quiere jugar con _____.

6. ¿Quién está sentado delante de Vd.? Carlos está sentado delante de _____.

7. Nuestros abuelos viven con nosotros. ¿Viven sus abuelos con _____?

8. ¿Va Vd. al teatro con sus amigas? Sí, voy con _____.

9. ¿Recibe Vd. cartas de Elena? No recibo cartas de _____.

10. Tomás desea bailar con Teresa pero ella no desea bailar con _____.

Juan Manuel de Rosas (1793-1877) was a ruthless dictator who governed Argentina for twenty-four years. His rule was a reign of terror. He suppressed all opposition, confiscated property and murdered, imprisoned or exiled his enemies. He was overthrown in 1852 and fled to England.

Grammar Lesson 18—DIRECT OBJECT PRONOUNS

me, me	**nos,** us
te, you (*fam.*)	**os,** you (*fam. pl.*)
le, him, you (*m.*) ⎫	
lo, him, it (*m.*) ⎭	**los,** them, you (*m. pl.*)
la, her, it, you (*f.*)	**las,** them, you (*f. pl.*)

Note

1. Direct object pronouns are generally placed directly *before* the verb of which they are the object.

Roberto *me* visita.   Robert visits me.
El niño no *los* ve.   The child does not see them.

2. **Le** or **lo** may be used to translate *him.*

EXERCISES

A. Complete the English translation.

1. Te amo.   I love _____.
2. ¿Quién las necesita?   Who needs _____?
3. El hombre le mira.   The man looks at _____.
4. ¿Dónde lo venden?   Where do they sell _____?
5. Los compran.   They buy _____.
6. Carlos siempre me ayuda.   Charles always helps _____.
7. No la ve.   He does not see _____.
8. Los invitamos.   We invite _____.
9. ¿Cuándo le visita Vd.?   When do you visit _____?
10. El profesor no nos comprende.   The teacher does not understand _____.

B. Rewrite the following sentences, substituting a direct object pronoun for the words in italics.

EXAMPLE: Tomo *la pluma.* La tomo.

1. El alumno lee *el libro.* _____
2. Jorge no estudia *las lecciones.* _____
3. ¿Ve Vd. *a María?* _____
4. El profesor ayuda *al muchacho.* _____
5. Pablo invita *a sus amigos.* _____
6. Escribimos *el ejercicio* en el cuaderno. _____
7. El muchacho abre *la ventana.* _____
8. No visitan *a Pedro.* _____
9. Necesitamos *los libros.* _____
10. No comprendo *las palabras.* _____

[113]

C. Rewrite each of the following, translating the English pronoun and placing it in its correct position.

1. (*him*)   Tomás invita. _____

2. (*us*)   Su amigo no ve. _____

3. (*me*)   ¿Quiere Vd.? _____

4. (*them*)   José llama. _____

5. (*it*)   ¿Quién tiene? _____

6. (*you*)   Los muchachos admiran. _____

7. (*her*)   Nadie ayuda. _____

8. (*them*)   Compro corbatas porque necesito. _____

9. (*it*)   El profesor explica la lección pero Jorge no comprende. _____

10. (*you*)   Señora, nosotros respetamos mucho. _____

D. Answer the following questions in Spanish, using direct object pronouns for the words in italics.

EXAMPLE: ¿Tiene Vd. *el dinero?* Sí, lo tengo.

1. ¿Lee Vd. *el periódico* todos los días? _____

2. ¿Ayudan los profesores *a los alumnos?* _____

3. ¿Escucha Vd. *al profesor* cuando habla? _____

4. *¿Me* comprende Vd.? _____

5. ¿Quién *le* invita a su casa? _____

6. ¿Prepara Vd. *la lección?* _____

7. ¿Come Vd. *frutas?* _____

8. ¿Estudia Vd. *el inglés?* _____

9. ¿Usa Vd. *guantes* en el invierno? _____

10. ¿Tiene Vd. *su libro de español?* _____

E. Translate into Spanish.

1. He helps me. _____

2. They invite us. _____

3. We visit them. _____

4. Do you see him? _____

5. I admire her. _____

6. The boy is calling you. _____

7. I know it. _____

8. The teacher opens them (windows). _____

9. She sells it (house). _____

10. He doesn't love her. _____

Grammar Lesson 19—INDIRECT OBJECT PRONOUNS

me, to me

te, to you (*fam.*)

le, to him, to her, to you

nos, to us

os, to you (*fam. pl.*)

les, to them, to you (*pl.*)

Note

1. Indirect object pronouns, like direct object pronouns, are generally placed *before* the verb.

Ana *le* habla.

Me escribe muchas cartas.

Ann speaks to him.

He writes many letters to me.

2. Spanish indirect object pronouns may be identified in English by the preposition *to*, which may be expressed or understood.

Les da el dinero.

He gives the money to them.

Or

He gives them the money.

3. The meanings of **le** and **les** may be clarified by adding **a él, a ella, a Vd., a ellos (-as), a Vds.** after the verb.

El profesor *le* habla *a ella*.

The teacher speaks to her.

EXERCISES

A. Complete the English translation.

1. María desea comprar una blusa y su madre le da cinco dólares.

Mary wishes to buy a blouse and her mother gives _____ five dollars.

2. Mi amigo me presta una pluma.

My friend lends _____ a pen.

3. El profesor nos explica la lección.

The teacher explains the lesson _____.

4. Carmen encuentra a su amiga en la calle y le habla.

Carmen meets her friend on the street and speaks _____.

5. Mis primos viven en Tejas. Les escribo a menudo.

My cousins live in Texas. I write _____ often.

6. ¿Prestan Vds. atención cuando el profesor les habla?

Do you pay attention when the teacher speaks _____?

7. Le mando a Vd. un cheque mañana.

I'll send _____ a check tomorrow.

8. El señor Gómez se sienta a la mesa y la criada le sirve el desayuno.

Mr. Gomez sits down at the table and the maid serves _____ breakfast.

9. El profesor nos enseña a hablar español.

The teacher teaches _____ to speak Spanish.

10. Si prometes ser bueno, te traigo un juguete.

If you promise to be good, I'll bring _____ a toy.

B. Rewrite each of the following sentences, placing the pronoun in parentheses in its correct position.

1. (nos)   La profesora lee un cuento. _____

2. (le)   Venden la casa. _____

3. (me)   El mozo sirve una taza de café. _____

4. (les)   No da el dinero. _____

5. (te)   ¿Quién habla? _____

6. (le)   Pablo dice que no puede venir. _____

7. (os)   Trae un regalo. _____

8. (nos)   ¿Cuándo manda Vd. el dinero? _____

9. (me)   Ofrece veinte dólares por el reloj. _____

10. (le)   El señor no da una propina. _____

C. Rewrite each of the following sentences, substituting an indirect object pronoun for the words in italics.

1. El director habla *al padre*. _____

2. El profesor explica la lección *a los alumnos*. _____

_____

3. José trae dulces *a Rosa*. _____

4. Damos flores *a las muchachas*. _____

5. Prestan dinero *a Tomás y Alicia*. _____

6. ¿Escribe Vd. cartas *a sus amigos*? _____

7. El hombre pasa la sal *a la señora*. _____

8. ¿Por qué no vende Vd. el automóvil *a Pablo*? _____

_____

9. El caballero canta una canción *a las señoritas*. _____

_____

10. Rosa sirve la comida *a su esposo*. _____

D. Complete the Spanish sentences.

1. His mother reads to him every night.   Su madre _ _ _ _ _ _ _ _ _ _ _ _ _ _ _ todas las noches.

2. Do your friends write to you?   ¿_ sus amigos?

3. The teacher explains the lesson to me.   El profesor _ la lección.

4. Charles does not speak to them.   Carlos no _ .

5. He gives the magazine to her.   _ _ _ _ _ _ _ _ _ _ _ _ _ la revista.

6. I bring you many presents.   _ muchos regalos.

7. What are you saying to them?   ¿Qué _ _ _ _ _ _ _ _ _ _ _ _ _ _ _ _ _ _ _ Vd.?

8. The teacher teaches us many important things.   El profesor _ _ _ _ _ _ _ _ _ _ muchas cosas importantes.

9. He lends me his bicycle.   _ su bicicleta.

10. The man sends her a telegram.   El hombre _ _ _ _ _ _ _ _ _ _ _ _ _ _ _ _ _ _ un telegrama.

E. Answer the following questions in Spanish, using indirect object pronouns for the words in italics.

EXAMPLE: ¿Qué muestra Juan *a su padre?* Juan le muestra su reloj.

1. ¿Habla Vd. *a sus amigos* cada día? _

2. ¿Escribe Vd. *a su tío?* _

3. ¿Quién *le* presta a Vd. dinero? _

4. ¿Quién enseña *a los alumnos?* _

5. *¿Les* da el profesor mucho trabajo? _

F. Translate into Spanish.

1. He writes to me. _

2. I speak to them. _

3. She reads to us. _

4. They send the package to him. _

5. What are you bringing her? _

6. She serves them a delicious meal. _

7. No one speaks to them. _

8. Who explains the lessons to you? _

9. His friend gives him a pencil. _

10. I write to her every day. _

Miguel de Unamuno (1864-1936) was a modern Spanish philosopher, essayist, poet and novelist. His most representative work is "Del Sentimiento Trágico de la Vida" (The Tragic Sense of Life).

Grammar Lesson 20—POSITION OF DIRECT AND INDIRECT
OBJECT PRONOUNS

Direct and indirect object pronouns are generally placed *before* the verb. However, they *follow* and are attached to the verb when used with:

a. an affirmative command
b. an infinitive
c. a present participle

NORMAL POSITION:

Alberto **lo tiene.**	Albert has it.
El profesor **le habla.**	The teacher speaks to him.

EXCEPTIONS:

1. *Affirmative Command.*

Háblele Vd.	Speak to him.
But	
No le hable Vd.	Don't speak to him.

2. *Infinitive.*

Van a **invitarnos.**	They are going to invite us.

3. *Present Participle.*

Está **abriéndolos**	He is opening them.

Note

1. Direct and indirect object pronouns are attached to the affirmative command, but are placed *before* the *negative command*.
2. When a direct or indirect object pronoun is attached to the affirmative command or present participle, a written accent mark is generally required on the vowel that is stressed.

EXERCISES

A. Rearrange the Spanish words in parentheses to translate the English sentence. (Caution: Add the written accent mark where needed.)

1.	Read it to the class.	(a lo la lea Vd. clase)
2.	Do you want to speak to them?	(les Vd. hablar quiere)
3.	Do not close them.	(los Vds. no cierren)
4.	A boy brings us the newspaper.	(el un trae muchacho nos periódico)
5.	The children are not listening to him.	(no los le niños escuchando están)
6.	Do you understand me?	(me Vd. comprende)
7.	Do not give the pen to her.	(no pluma dé la Vd. le)
8.	Who is selling the house to you?	(a la está quién vendiendo casa le Vd.)
9.	Bring him a glass of milk.	(leche le vaso de traiga un Vd.)
10.	Can you help her?	(ayudar Vd. puede la)

[**118**]

B. Rewrite each of the following sentences, substituting an object pronoun for the words in italics.

EXAMPLE: Escriba Vd. *la carta*. *Escríbala* Vd.

1. Pedro desea invitar *a sus amigos*. _____

2. No diga Vd. eso *a la señorita*. _____

3. Ayude Vd. *a Carlos*. _____

4. El director habla *a los alumnos*. _____

5. El profesor está explicando *la lección*. _____

6. ¿Ve Vd. *a la niña?* _____

7. Compren Vds. *el auto*. _____

8. Nunca perdemos *nuestros libros*. _____

9. No voy a hacer *el trabajo*. _____

10. ¿Quién escribe la carta *a Luisa?* _____

C. Change the following commands to the affirmative.

1. No lo vean Vds.   _____   6. No la beba Vd.   _____

2. No les hable Vd.   _____   7. No los estudien Vds.   _____

3. No nos llame Vd.   _____   8. No me cante Vd.   _____

4. No le inviten Vds.   _____   9. No las tome Vd.   _____

5. No las coma Vd.   _____   10. No le escuchen Vds.   _____

D. Translate the English words into Spanish.

1. Mi padre *helps her*. _____

2. *Write to him* inmediatamente. _____

3. El profesor va a *to lend me* un libro. _____

4. José *visits us* los domingos. _____

5. El niño no quiere *to take it*. _____

6. No tengo las revistas. *Do you have them?* _____

7. *Do not invite them* a la fiesta. _____

8. Está *speaking to her*. _____

9. *He does you* muchos favores. _____

10. Si la casa es bonita, *buy it*. _____

REVIEW OF GRAMMAR LESSONS 15-20

A. Complete the Spanish sentences by underlining the correct words in parentheses.

1. I bought a pair of shoes for him.   Compré un par de zapatos para (él, le, lo).

2. He sees his friends and invites them to a party.   Ve a sus amigos y (las, les, los) invita a una fiesta.

3. We speak to her every day.   (Le, La, Ella) hablamos todos los días.

4. The children admire you a great deal.   Los niños (Vd., Vds., le) admiran mucho.

5. His brother lives near me.   Su hermano vive cerca de (me, mi, mí).

6. The boys enjoy themselves.   Los muchachos (se, los, les) divierten.

7. Buy the camera if you need it.   Compre Vd. la cámara si (lo, la, le) necesita.

8. John sends flowers to them frequently.   Juan (los, las, les) manda flores frecuentemente.

9. The boy washes himself.   El niño (le, lo, se) lava.

10. The teacher reads to us in class.   El profesor (nosotros, os, nos) lee en la clase.

11. Whom are they calling?   ¿(Quién, Quiénes, A quién) llaman?

12. Which stories are the most interesting?   ¿(Qué, Cuál, Quiénes) cuentos son los más interesantes?

13. Whose automobile is this?   ¿(Quién, A quién, De quién) es este automóvil?

14. When do they arrive?   ¿(Cuánto, Cuándo, Cómo) llegan?

15. Where are you going?   ¿(Dónde, Donde, A dónde) va Vd.?

16. Which one do you prefer?   ¿(Qué, Cuál, Por qué) prefiere Vd.?

17. What is the name of the school?   ¿(Qué, Cuál, Cómo) es el nombre de la escuela?

18. We can't sleep either.   No podemos dormir (ni, tampoco, jamás).

19. I do not see anyone.   No veo (nada, nadie, a nadie).

20. It hasn't any value.   No tiene (ninguno, ningún, nunca) valor.

B. Rewrite each of the following sentences, substituting a pronoun for the words in italics.

1. José habla *a su amigo.* --

2. La profesora cierra *las ventanas.* ------------------------------------

3. Tome Vd. *los paquetes.* --

4. No compre Vd. *la casa.* ---

5. Antonio quiere bailar con *Elena.* -------------------------------------

6. Voy a dar un regalo *a Rosa.* --

7. El hombre está leyendo *el periódico.* ---------------------------------

8. El mozo sirve leche *a los niños.* --------------------------------------

9. Ayuden Vds. *a Pedro.* ---

10. Recibe cartas de *sus amigos.* --

C. Translate the English words into Spanish.

1. ¿*Who* es aquel hombre?   ------------------------------

2. ¿*Which ones* son los menos caros?   ------------------------------

3. ¿*Why* no viene Vd. mañana?   ------------------------------

4. *¿What* desea Vd.? ------------------------------------

5. Ésta es la casa *where* vive. ------------------------

6. Los niños no comen *anything*. ----------------------

7. *No* persona puede ayudarle. ------------------------

8. ¿No ha jugado Vd. *ever* al tenis? ------------------

9. *Nobody* está en el patio. --------------------------

10. *None* de los alumnos está ausente. ----------------

11. ¿Desea Vd. ir al centro *with me?* ------------------

12. ¿Quiénes están sentados *behind them?* -------------

13. Van al cine *without us.* ---------------------------

14. Pancho abre el libro y *it* lee. --------------------

15. El médico *him* examina. ---------------------------

16. José compra dos camisas porque *them* necesita. ----

17. Mi tía *us* visita los domingos. --------------------

18. El profesor *to him* habla. ------------------------

19. *Write to me* todos los días. ----------------------

20. Inés quiere *to invite her* al baile. ---------------

D. Translate into Spanish.

1. What is your address? -------------------------------

2. Whose books are these? ------------------------------

3. How many persons are you inviting? ------------------

4. Which restaurant is better? -------------------------

5. I don't want anything. ------------------------------

6. He doesn't invite anyone. ---------------------------

7. They aren't going either. ---------------------------

8. He never studies. -----------------------------------

9. She eats neither fruits nor vegetables. -------------

10. None of the stores sells it. -----------------------

11. Are you coming with us? ----------------------------

12. They live far from her. ----------------------------

13. We visit them. -------------------------------------

14. She is writing a letter to him. --------------------

15. Speak to her tomorrow. -----------------------------

16. Do not take it now. --------------------------------

17. He sells newspapers to them. -----------------------

18. Do you understand me? ------------------------------

19. The teacher reads to us. ---------------------------

20. I am not able to do it. ----------------------------

MASTERY EXERCISES

A. Underline the Spanish words in parentheses that correctly translate the English.

1. Escriben *the* lecciones. (el, la, los, las)

2. Tomás no tiene *a* lápiz. (un, una)

3. Mi primo asiste a *the* universidad. (el, la)

4. Carlos va *to the* cine. (al, a la, a los, a las)

5. Mi amigo es el presidente *of the* club. (de, del, de la)

6. Las flores son *pretty*. (bonito, bonita, bonitos, bonitas)

7. Los señores son *Spanish*. (español, española, españoles, españolas)

8. Ana habla *English*. (inglés, inglesa, ingleses, inglesas)

9. José tiene *many friends*. (muchos amigos, a muchos amigos)

10. Los alumnos ven *the teacher*. (el profesor, al profesor)

11. *Your* vecino es muy simpático. (Su, Sus, Vd.)

12. Son *my* libros. (me, mi, mis)

13. *Our* nación es grande. (Nuestro, Nuestra, Nuestros, Nuestras)

14. La niña juega con *her* juguetes. (su, sus, ella)

15. *This* monumento es muy interesante. (Este, Ese, Aquel)

16. *Those* asientos están reservados. (Aquellos, Estos, Esas)

17. Pablo es más alto *than* Ricardo. (que, de)

18. Este hotel es *the largest* de la ciudad. (más grande, el más grande)

19. Viven en el *first* piso. (primero, primer, primo)

20. ¿Tiene Vd. *one* dólar? (uno, una, un)

21. Perdió *a hundred* dólares. (cien, ciento)

22. Hay *thirty-one* días en el mes de marzo. (treinta y uno, treinta y un, treinta y una)

23. Josefina *is* enferma. (es, está)

24. ¿*What* es la capital de España? (Qué, Cuál)

25. Es *five minutes to one*. (la una y cinco, la una menos cinco)

26. ¿*Whom* llama Vd.? (Quién, A quién, De quién)

27. *Nothing* me interesa. (Nada, Nadie)

28. No baila *either*. (ninguno, tampoco)

29. ¿Va Vd. con *him?* (él, lo, le)

30. Jaime *us* invitó a la fiesta. (nos, nosotros, nuestros)

31. Yo *you* admiro mucho. (Vd., le, su)

32. Mis padres *them* visitan cada semana. (ellos, los, les)

33. Manuel *to her* escribe todos los días. (le, la, ella)

34. Compra una blusa porque *it* necesita. (lo, la, le)

35. Carlos *himself* lava. (le, él, se)

36. No es una *bad* idea. (malo, mala, mal)

37. *His* mujer fué al cine. (La, Su, Ella)

38. Voy al médico *on* martes. (en, el, al)

39. Es el mejor hotel *in* la ciudad. (en, de, por)

40. No *bring it* Vd. mañana. (lo traiga, tráigalo)

41. Su cumpleaños es el *third* de marzo. (tres, tercero, tercer)

42. Son las ocho *A.M.* (de la mañana, en la mañana)

43. *None* de mis hermanos quiere ir al centro. (Nadie, Ninguno)

44. Recibimos una carta *from him.* (del, de él)

45. ¿*Where* va Vd.? (Dónde, A dónde)

46. La madre visita *the school.* (la escuela, a la escuela)

47. *Saint* Luis es una ciudad importante. (San, Santo, Santa)

48. *Their* hijos son inteligentes. (Ellos, Sus, Los)

49. ¿Ve Vd. *that* avión? (esa, este, aquel)

50. José es mi hermano *oldest.* (mayor, el mayor)

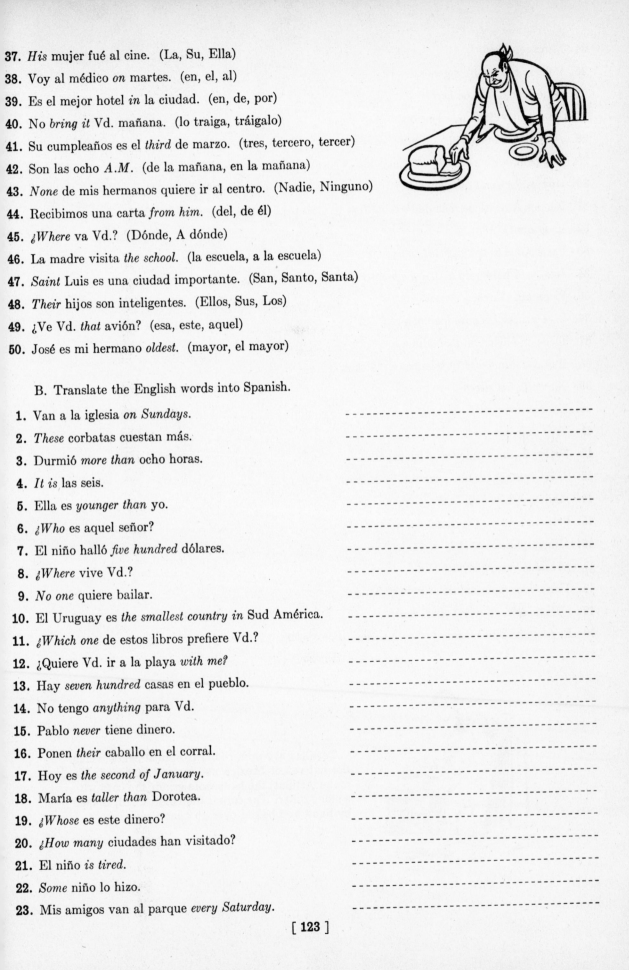

B. Translate the English words into Spanish.

1. Van a la iglesia *on Sundays.* -------------------------------

2. *These* corbatas cuestan más. -------------------------------

3. Durmió *more than* ocho horas. -------------------------------

4. *It is* las seis. -------------------------------

5. Ella es *younger than* yo. -------------------------------

6. ¿*Who* es aquel señor? -------------------------------

7. El niño halló *five hundred* dólares. -------------------------------

8. ¿*Where* vive Vd.? -------------------------------

9. *No one* quiere bailar. -------------------------------

10. El Uruguay es *the smallest country in* Sud América. -------------------------------

11. ¿*Which one* de estos libros prefiere Vd.? -------------------------------

12. ¿Quiere Vd. ir a la playa *with me?* -------------------------------

13. Hay *seven hundred* casas en el pueblo. -------------------------------

14. No tengo *anything* para Vd. -------------------------------

15. Pablo *never* tiene dinero. -------------------------------

16. Ponen *their* caballo en el corral. -------------------------------

17. Hoy es *the second of January.* -------------------------------

18. María es *taller than* Dorotea. -------------------------------

19. ¿*Whose* es este dinero? -------------------------------

20. ¿*How many* ciudades han visitado? -------------------------------

21. El niño *is tired.* -------------------------------

22. *Some* niño lo hizo. -------------------------------

23. Mis amigos van al parque *every Saturday.* -------------------------------

24. Murió en *1946*.

25. Bolívar fué un *great* general.

26. ¿Qué piensa Vd. de *her?*

27. *No* alumno estudió la lección.

28. ¿Dónde *are* los niños?

29. Llegaron *at nine o'clock*.

30. Hoy es *the worst* día del año.

31. Buenos Aires tiene más de *three million* habitantes.

32. Es la una *P.M.*

33. Los exámenes son *difficult*.

34. Julia está hablando *to Mary's brother*.

35. Es *an old church*.

36. Va a visitar *his grandparents*.

37. Tiene su oficina en *that* edificio.

38. Hay *one hundred fifty* asientos en la sala.

39. Son *half past eleven*.

40. Los hombres *are busy*.

41. Vive *near me*.

42. Carlos *to him* vende su bicicleta.

43. Si las ventanas están cerradas, *open them*.

44. ¿Quiere Vd. *to help her?*

45. Prefiero *winter* al verano.

46. Mi cumpleaños es *August 24*.

47. *¿At what time* se levanta Vd.?

48. Tiene *three thousand* dólares en el banco.

49. ¿Dónde está su reloj? Lola *has it*.

50. El profesor está *reading to them* un cuento.

Tortillas are thin, round cornmeal cakes which the natives of Mexico use instead of bread. To make tortillas, the housewife grinds the corn with a stone roller. The corn is then moistened, shaped by hand and baked over an open fire.

Part III—Idioms

Idiom Lesson 1—THE VERB *GUSTAR*

SINGULAR	PLURAL	TRANSLATION
me gusta	me gustan	I like
te gusta	te gustan	you (*fam.*) like
le gusta	le gustan	you (he, she) like(s)
nos gusta	nos gustan	we like
os gusta	os gustan	you (*fam. pl.*) like
les gusta	les gustan	you (*pl.*), they like

Note

1. The verb **gustar** (*to be pleasing*) is used to express the English verb *to like*. Sentences such as "I like the watch," "He likes the pictures," are expressed in Spanish as follows:

Me gusta el reloj.
  I like the watch.
  Literally: To me is pleasing the watch.

Le gustan los cuadros.
  He likes the pictures.
  Literally: To him are pleasing the pictures.

2. The verb **gustar** is used only in the third person singular or plural. The singular form is used when what is liked is singular. The plural form is used when what is liked is plural.

Me *gustó* el libro.   I liked the book.
Me *gustaron* los libros.   I liked the books.

3. The various meanings of **le gusta(n)** and **les gusta(n)** may be clarified by adding **a él, a ella, a Vd., a ellos (-as), a Vds.**

¿Le gusta *a Vd.* el sombrero?   Do you like the hat?
¿Les gusta *a ellos* bailar?   Do they like to dance?

EXERCISES

A. Complete each sentence with **gusta** or **gustan**.

1. Nos _____ los animales domésticos.

2. No me _____ las corbatas.

3. Les _____ jugar.

4. ¿Te _____ esta novela?

5. Le _____ las películas.

6. Me _____ el automóvil.

7. No les _____ los conciertos.

8. Nos _____ la casa.

9. ¿Le _____ a Vd. cantar?

10. ¿Te _____ las anécdotas?

B. Complete the Spanish sentences.

1. He likes to sleep.   _____ gusta dormir.

2. Do you like your classes?   ¿_____ gustan sus clases?

[125]

3. We like the Spanish class.   ------------------------------ gusta la clase de español.

4. I do not like the food of the cafeteria.   No -------------------- gusta la comida de la cafetería.

5. They like bullfights.   ------------------------------ gustan las corridas de toros.

6. She did not like the hat.   No ------------------------------------ el sombrero.

7. Do you (*fam.*) like apple pie?   ¿-------------------- gusta pastel de manzana?

8. He liked the neckties.   ------------------------------------ las corbatas.

9. They like Spanish dances.   ------------------------------ los bailes españoles.

10. Do you (*plural*) like this dress?   ¿------------------------ este vestido?

C. Translate the English words into Spanish.

1. *I like* los dulces.   ------------------------------

2. *He likes* los programas de televisión.   ------------------------------

3. *¿Do you like* este hotel?   ------------------------------

4. *We like* viajar.   ------------------------------

5. *They like* el clima.   ------------------------------

6. *They liked* las flores.   ------------------------------

7. Carlos y Roberto, *¿do you like* los deportes?   ------------------------------

8. *I do not like* el invierno.   ------------------------------

9. *She likes* nadar.   ------------------------------

10. *We do not like* estas plantas.   ------------------------------

D. Answer the following questions in complete Spanish sentences.

1. ¿Le gusta comer en un restaurante? ------------------------------

----

2. ¿Les gusta estudiar? ------------------------------

3. ¿Le gustan las legumbres? ------------------------------

4. ¿Qué mes del año le gusta más? ------------------------------

5. ¿Les gustan los exámenes? ------------------------------

E. Translate into Spanish.

1. Do you like to dance? ------------------------------

2. We like Spanish music. ------------------------------

3. They do not like romantic songs. ------------------------------

4. She liked the apartment. ------------------------------

5. Do you like the rooms? ------------------------------

6. I like to read magazines. ------------------------------

7. He likes novels. ------------------------------

8. Do you like to travel by plane? ------------------------------

9. They like the country. ------------------------------

10. We do not like the large cities. ------------------------------

Idiom Lesson 2—IDIOMS WITH *HACER*

WEATHER EXPRESSIONS

¿Qué tiempo hace?	How is the weather?
Hace buen (mal) tiempo.	It is good (bad) weather.
Hace calor (frío).	It is hot (cold).
Hace fresco.	It is cool.
Hace sol.	It is sunny.
Hacía viento.	It was windy.

Note

In weather expressions, *very* is expressed by **mucho** instead of **muy.**

Hace mucho calor.	It is very hot.
Hace mucho viento.	It is very windy.

OTHER EXPRESSIONS WITH *HACER*

hacer una pregunta, to ask a question

El muchacho *hace una pregunta.*	The boy asks a question.
Pedro *hace muchas preguntas.*	Peter asks many questions.

hacer un viaje, to take a trip

Hacen un viaje cada verano.	They take a trip each summer.

hacer una visita, to pay a visit

Hizo una visita a su abuela.	He paid a visit to his grandmother.

haga Vd. el favor de + infinitive, please

Haga Vd. el favor de abrir la ventana.	Please open the window.

EXERCISES

A. Answer true (T) or false (F).

1. Algunas personas hacen un viaje durante las vacaciones. _____

2. Hace sol a las diez de la noche. _____

3. Hace mal tiempo todos los días. _____

4. Muchas personas llevan un abrigo cuando hace mucho viento. _____

5. Hace frío en el mes de diciembre. _____

6. Generalmente hace buen tiempo en la primavera. _____

7. Hace calor en el invierno. _____

8. Hago una visita a mi amigo porque deseo verle. _____

9. Hace fresco en la zona tropical. _____

10. Una persona tímida hace muchas preguntas. _____

B. Complete the following sentences in Spanish.

1. En el verano hace _____.

2. _____ buen tiempo ayer.

3. _____ mucho viento hoy.

4. Haga Vd. _____ de cerrar la puerta.

5. Hace un _____ a Europa.

6. Hace _____ en el invierno.

7. El profesor hace una _____ y un alumno contesta.

8. Mañana vamos a _____ una visita a Elena.

9. ¿Qué _____ hace en su país?

10. Hace mal _____ hoy.

C. Answer the following questions in complete Spanish sentences.

1. ¿Qué tiempo hace hoy? _____

2. ¿En qué mes hace fresco? _____

3. ¿Cuándo hace Vd. un viaje al campo? _____
_____

4. ¿Quién hace muchas preguntas en la clase? _____
_____

5. ¿Va Vd. a hacer una visita a su amigo mañana? _____
_____

D. Translate into Spanish.

1. How is the weather today? _____

2. It is good weather. _____

3. It is sunny. _____

4. It is not very warm. _____

5. It is cool. _____

6. Is it cold today? _____

7. It was windy. _____

8. I want to take a trip to Mexico. _____

9. They asked many questions. _____

10. Please pass the sugar. _____

E. Use each of the following idioms in a complete Spanish sentence, and then translate the sentence into English.

1. hacer un viaje _____

2. hacer una visita _____
_____

3. hacer una pregunta _____

4. haga Vd. el favor de + infinitive _____
_____

5. hacer mal tiempo _____

Idiom Lesson 3—IDIOMS WITH *TENER*

IDIOMS IN WHICH *TENER* = TO BE

tener . . . años, to be . . . years old

Juan *tiene* diez *años.* — John is ten years old.
¿*Cuántos años tiene Vd.?* — How old are you?

tener calor, to be warm

¿*Tiene Vd. calor?* — Are you warm?

tener frío, to be cold

Los niños *tienen frío.* — The children are cold.

tener hambre, to be hungry

Tengo hambre. — I am hungry.

tener sed, to be thirsty

Tenemos sed. — We are thirsty.

tener razón, to be right; **no tener razón,** to be wrong

María *tiene razón.* — Mary is right.
Carlota *no tiene razón.* — Charlotte is wrong.

tener sueño, to be sleepy

¿*Tienen Vds. sueño?* — Are you sleepy?

Note

In the idioms with **tener** listed above, *very* is expressed by **mucho, -a** instead of **muy.**

Tengo *mucho* calor (frío). — I am very warm (cold).
Tenemos *mucha* hambre (sed). — We are very hungry (thirsty).

OTHER IDIOMS WITH *TENER*

tener dolor de cabeza, to have a headache

Pablo *tiene dolor de cabeza.* — Paul has a headache.

tener que + infinitive, to have to, must

Tienen que trabajar. — They have to (must) work.

tenga Vd. la bondad de + infinitive, please

Tenga Vd. la bondad de cerrar la puerta. — Please close the door.

EXERCISES

A. Select the word in parentheses that best completes the meaning of the sentence.

1. Tenga Vd. la (bondad, sed) de entrar.
2. Juan come porque tiene (mucha, muy) hambre.
3. ¿Qué bebe Vd. cuando tiene (sueño, sed)?
4. En el verano tengo (frío, calor).
5. Los niños duermen cuando tienen (sueño, años).

6. Tengo (de, que) estudiar.

7. Estoy enfermo. Tengo dolor de (cabeza, razón).

8. José tiene quince (hambre, años).

9. El muchacho confiesa que no tiene (la bondad, razón).

10. María llevaba abrigo porque tenía (frío, calor).

B. Complete the Spanish sentences.

1. My brother is twenty years old. Mi hermano _____.

2. Please sit down. _____ sentarse.

3. We must buy a new automobile. _____ un automóvil nuevo.

4. You are right. Vds. _____.

5. Arthur is very hungry. Arturo _____.

6. Who is thirsty? ¿Quién _____?

7. I am very cold. Tengo _____.

8. Jane was wrong. Juana _____.

9. How old are you? ¿_____ tiene Vd.?

10. Do you have a headache? ¿Tiene Vd. _____?

C. Answer the following questions in complete Spanish sentences.

1. ¿Tiene Vd. mucho calor hoy? _____

2. ¿Tienen Vds. que ir a la escuela mañana? _____

3. ¿Va Vd. al médico cuando tiene dolor de cabeza? _____

4. ¿Qué hace Vd. cuando tiene sueño? _____

5. ¿Cuántos años tiene su amigo(-a)? _____

6. ¿Toma Vd. una Coca-Cola cuando tiene sed? _____

7. ¿Qué come Vd. cuando tiene hambre? _____

8. ¿Qué lleva Vd. cuando tiene frío? _____

D. Translate into Spanish.

1. Are you hungry? _____

2. I am very thirsty. _____

3. We are very warm. _____

4. They were cold. _____

5. She is right. _____

6. You are wrong. _____

7. We are very sleepy. _____

8. I am fifteen years old. _____

9. He must sell the house. _____

10. Please open the window. _____

Idiom Lesson 4—MISCELLANEOUS VERBAL IDIOMS

VERBS REQUIRING A PREPOSITION BEFORE THE INFINITIVE

aprender a, to learn to

   Aprenden a nadar.   They are learning to swim.

empezar a, to begin to

   El profesor *empieza a* leer.   The teacher begins to read.

enseñar a, to teach to

   Carmen me *enseña a* bailar.   Carmen teaches me to dance.

ir a, to go to

   Voy a comprar un sombrero.   I am going to buy a hat.

venir a, to come to

   Viene a ver a su amigo.   He comes to see his friend.

volver a, to (verb) again

   Vuelven a entrar.   They enter again.

acabar de, to have just

   Luis *acaba de* salir.   Louis has just left.
   María *acababa de* entrar.   Mary had just entered.

tratar de, to try to

   Trato de estudiar.   I try to study.

VERBS REQUIRING A PREPOSITION BEFORE A NOUN

asistir a, to attend

   Los alumnos *asisten a* la escuela.   The pupils attend school.

jugar a, to play (a game)

   Ramón *juega a* la pelota.   Raymond plays ball.
   ¿*Juega Vd. al* tenis?   Do you play tennis?

querer a, to love

   Pablo *quiere a* Catalina.   Paul loves Catherine.

salir de, to leave

   Salimos de la escuela a las tres.   We leave school at three o'clock.

entrar en, to enter

   Ana *entra en* el cuarto.   Ann enters the room.

OTHER VERBAL IDIOMS

dar un paseo, to take a walk

   Dan un paseo.   They take a walk.

ir de compras, to go shopping

   La madre *va de compras.*   The mother goes shopping.

poner la mesa, to set the table

      La criada *pone la mesa.*   The maid sets the table.

prestar atención, to pay attention

      Presten Vds. atención.   Pay attention.

querer decir, to mean

      ¿Qué *quiere decir* este párrafo?   What does this paragraph mean?

saber + infinitive, to know how (to)

      El hombre no *sabe* escribir.   The man does not know how to write.

tocar el piano (el violín, etc.), to play the piano (violin, etc.)

      ¿Toca Vd. el piano?   Do you play the piano?

tomar el desayuno (el almuerzo, la comida), to have breakfast (lunch, dinner)

      Tomamos el desayuno a las ocho.   We have breakfast at eight o'clock.

EXERCISES

A. Translate into English.

1. ¿Quién sabe tocar el piano? ------------------------------------

2. ¿A qué hora toma Vd. el desayuno? ------------------------------

3. Los alumnos deben prestar atención en la clase. ----------------

4. Acabamos de dar un paseo por el parque. -------------------------

5. Asisten a la iglesia todos los domingos. -----------------------

6. Inés desea ir de compras. ------------------------------------

7. Pablo vuelve a visitar a su amigo. -----------------------------

8. La madre pone la mesa. --------------------------------------

9. El niño trató de jugar a la pelota. -----------------------------

10. ¿Qué quiere Vd. decir? --------------------------------------

B. Supply the missing preposition **a, de,** or **en.**

1. Trataré --------- llegar a tiempo.

2. El médico entró --------- el hospital.

3. Salen --------- la tienda.

4. Los soldados empiezan --------- marchar.

5. ¿Va Vd. --------- trabajar hoy?

6. Vienen --------- visitar a su tío.

7. Acabo --------- llegar.

8. Aprendemos --------- bailar.

9. Quieren _____ sus abuelos.

10. El profesor nos enseña _____ hablar español.

C. Answer the following questions in complete Spanish sentences.

1. ¿Asisten Vds. a una escuela grande? _____

_____

2. ¿Va Vd. a dar un paseo esta tarde? _____

_____

3. ¿Juega Vd. bien al béisbol? _____

4. ¿A qué hora toma Vd. el almuerzo? _____

5. ¿Toca Vd. un instrumento musical? _____

6. ¿Sabe Vd. conducir (to drive) un automóvil? _____

_____

7. ¿Quién pone la mesa en su casa? _____

8. ¿Quiere Vd. a su madre? _____

9. ¿Acaba Vd. de salir de la escuela? _____

10. ¿Tratan Vds. de prestar atención en la clase? _____

_____

D. Complete the Spanish sentences.

1. He had just returned from Mexico. _____ de México.

2. I like to take a walk in the evening. Me gusta _____ por la noche.

3. The girls are learning to sew. Las muchachas _____ coser.

4. My brother taught me to swim. Mi hermano me _____ nadar.

5. We began to eat at nine. _____ a las nueve.

6. Paul did not attend the meeting. Pablo no _____ la reunión.

7. I am going to play football. _____ fútbol.

8. He knows how to play the guitar. _____ la guitarra.

9. At what time will you leave your house? ¿A qué hora _____ su casa?

10. I do not understand what you mean. No comprendo lo que _____.

Diego Rivera was a noted Mexican mural painter. His art portrays the oppressed and downtrodden workers and peasants of his country. Rivera's murals decorate the walls of public buildings in Mexico and the United States.

Idiom Lesson 5—IDIOMS WITH *A, DE, EN* AND *POR*

IDIOMS WITH *A*

a caballo, on horseback

    Llegan *a caballo.*   They arrive on horseback.

a casa, home

    Voy *a casa.*   I am going home.

a la escuela (iglesia), to school (church)

    Los alumnos van *a la escuela.*   The pupils go to school.

a menudo, often

    Yo le veo *a menudo.*   I often see him.

a pie, on foot

    Viajan *a pie.*   They travel on foot.

a tiempo, on time

    Viene *a tiempo.*   He comes on time.

al + infinitive, on, upon

    Al entrar en el cuarto, abrió las ventanas.   On entering the room, he opened the windows.

al día siguiente, on the following day

    Partió *al día siguiente.*   He left on the following day.

al fin, finally, at last

    Al fin llegaron.   Finally they arrived.

al lado de, beside, next to

    Hay una tienda *al lado de* mi casa.   There is a store next to my house.

IDIOMS WITH *DE*

de esta manera, in this way

    Los indios viven *de esta manera.*   The Indians live in this way.

de memoria, by heart

    Aprenden la lección *de memoria.*   They learn the lesson by heart.

de nada, you're welcome, don't mention it

    Muchas gracias. *De nada.*   Thank you very much. You're welcome.

de pronto, suddenly, all of a sudden

    De pronto volvió.   Suddenly he returned.

IDIOMS WITH *EN*

en casa, at home

    Están *en casa.*   They are at home.

en medio de, in the middle of, in the midst of

    El niño jugaba *en medio de* la calle.   The child was playing in the middle of the street.

en seguida, at once, immediately

      Hágalo Vd. *en seguida.*   Do it at once.

IDIOMS WITH *POR*

por ejemplo, for example

    Por ejemplo, Pedro estudia mucho.   For example, Peter studies a great deal.

por favor, please

    Siéntese Vd., *por favor.*   Sit down, please.

por la mañana (tarde, noche), in the morning (afternoon, evening)

    Trabaja *por la mañana.*   He works in the morning.

EXERCISES

A. Complete the English sentences.

1. Venga Vd. en seguida.   Come _____.
2. De pronto empezó a llover.   _____ it began to rain.
3. Al ver a mi amigo, le hablé.   _____ my friend, I spoke to him.
4. El profesor se sentó al lado del alumno.   The teacher sat _____ the pupil.
5. Llegó al día siguiente.   He arrived _____.
6. El accidente ocurrió en medio del camino.   The accident occurred _____ the road.
7. Apréndalo Vd. de memoria.   Learn it _____.
8. Voy a prepararlo de esta manera.   I am going to prepare it _____.
9. El niño llora a menudo.   The child cries _____.
10. Al fin aceptaron el dinero.   _____ they accepted the money.

B. Underline the expression that correctly translates the English words in italics.

1. Hágalo Vd. *in this way.* (de memoria, de esta manera)
2. Llegó *on time.* (a hora, a tiempo)
3. ¿Puede Vd. venir *in the afternoon?* (por la tarde, de la tarde)
4. Es necesario ir *on foot.* (a pie, en pie)
5. Vamos *to school.* (a escuela, a la escuela)
6. Vimos a Jaime *on leaving* de la tienda. (al salir, en salir)
7. Salen *immediately.* (de pronto, en seguida)
8. Ponga Vd. las maletas *beside* la cama. (al lado de, en medio de)
9. Quieren ir *on horseback.* (a caballo, en caballo)
10. Luisa no está *at home.* (a casa, en casa)

C. Answer the following questions in complete Spanish sentences.

1. ¿Va Vd. a la escuela mañana? _____
2. ¿Juega Vd. con sus amigos al salir de la escuela? _____

_____

3. ¿A qué hora va Vd. a casa? -----------------------------------

4. ¿Estudia Vd. a menudo? -----------------------------------

5. ¿Mira Vd. la televisión por la noche? -----------------------

----

D. Translate the English words into Spanish.

1. *Upon arriving home*, José se bañó. -----------------------

2. *Finally* todos salieron. -----------------------

3. *You're welcome*, respondió el hombre. -----------------------

4. ¿Qué hace Vd. *in the morning?* -----------------------

5. Los gauchos viajan *on horseback*. -----------------------

6. Vuelvan Vds. *immediately*. -----------------------

7. Pase Vd. la sal, *please*. -----------------------

8. ¿Llega Vd. a la escuela *on time?* -----------------------

9. Celebraron la fiesta *on the following day*. -----------------------

10. *For example*, el perro es un animal doméstico. -----------------------

Idiom Lesson 6—MISCELLANEOUS IDIOMATIC EXPRESSIONS

EXPRESSIONS OF GREETING, FAREWELL AND COURTESY

buenos días	good morning
buenas tardes	good afternoon
buenas noches	good evening, good night
hasta luego	goodbye (see you later)
hasta la vista	goodbye (until I see you again)
hasta mañana	goodbye (see you tomorrow)
muchas gracias	thank you very much
no hay de qué	you're welcome, don't mention it
con mucho gusto	gladly, with great pleasure
con permiso	excuse me (in passing in front of someone)

EXPRESSIONS WITH *VEZ*

otra vez	again
una vez	once
dos veces	twice
algunas veces	sometimes
muchas veces	many times, often

OTHER IDIOMATIC EXPRESSIONS

el año (mes) pasado	last year (month)
la semana pasada	last week
el año (mes) próximo	next year (month)
la semana próxima	next week
esta noche	tonight
todos los días	every day
todo el mundo	everybody, everyone
la lección (la clase, el profesor) de español	the Spanish lesson (class, teacher)
el libro de lectura	the reader (book)
sin embargo	however, nevertheless
sobre todo	above all, especially
¡está bien!	all right!
¡Ya lo creo!	Yes, indeed! I should say so!
¿de qué color es . . . ?	what is the color of . . . ?
¿no es verdad? or ¿verdad?	isn't that so? isn't it true?

EXERCISES

A. Translate the English words into Spanish.

1. ¿Cuántos alumnos hay en *the Spanish class?* _____

2. ¿Qué hace Vd. *tonight?* _____

3. *Sometimes* es muy difícil estudiar. _____

4. Voy a comprar un automóvil nuevo *next year.* _____

5. *Good morning*, Pedro. _____

6. Elena ve a su amiga Carmen *every day.* _____

7. ¿*What is the color of* la bandera mexicana? _____

8. El hermano de Miguel es profesor, *¿isn't that true?* _____

[137]

9. Los alumnos repiten la frase *many times*. _____

10. Pablo no trabajó *last week*. _____

B. On the line before each Spanish expression in Column I, write the letter of its English meaning in Column II.

Column I	Column II
_____ **1.** no hay de qué	*a.* all right
_____ **2.** ya lo creo	*b.* again
_____ **3.** está bien	*c.* however
_____ **4.** todo el mundo	*d.* gladly
_____ **5.** otra vez	*e.* see you later
_____ **6.** con mucho gusto	*f.* you're welcome
_____ **7.** sin embargo	*g.* especially
_____ **8.** hasta luego	*h.* once
_____ **9.** una vez	*i.* everybody
_____ **10.** sobre todo	*j.* yes, indeed

C. Write the Spanish expression you would use in each of the following situations.

1. You excuse yourself as you pass in front of someone. "_____

_____"

2. Someone asks you to pass the salt. "_____

_____"

3. Someone says to you, "Muchas gracias." "_____

_____"

4. You say goodbye to your friend and tell him that you will see him tomorrow. "_____

_____"

5. You greet a friend at night. "_____

_____"

6. You wish to know the color of a new suit your friend has bought. "_____

_____"

7. You ask your friend who his Spanish teacher is. "_____

_____"

8. You wish to reply that it's O.K. "_____

_____"

9. You tell someone you'll see him later. "_____

_____"

10. You meet your neighbor Mr. Ortega in the morning and you greet him. "_____

_____"

D. Answer the following questions in complete Spanish sentences.

1. ¿Tienen Vds. un libro de lectura? _____

_____

2. ¿Va Vd. al cine esta noche? _____

3. ¿Celebra Vd. una fiesta el mes próximo? _____

_____

4. ¿Asisten Vds. a la escuela todos los días? _____

_____

5. ¿Come Vd. en una cafetería algunas veces? _____

_____

E. Use each of the following expressions in an original Spanish sentence, and then translate each sentence into English.

1. dos veces _____

_____

2. la semana próxima _____

_____

3. el año pasado _____

_____

4. todo el mundo _____

_____

5. ¿verdad? _____

_____

Large quantities of bananas are grown in Honduras. Bananas are picked green and transported in mule-drawn banana cars to the nearest port. There they are loaded on refrigerated ships for export.

[139]

MASTERY EXERCISES

A. Complete the English sentences.

1. Hace viento hoy. _____ today.

2. El niño tiene sueño.   The child _____

3. Acaban de llegar. _____ arrived.

4. Vuelven a entrar en la casa.   They enter the house _____

5. ¿Qué quiere decir eso?   What does that _____?

6. Al ver a su amigo, le saludó. _____ his friend, he greeted him.

7. De pronto desapareció. _____ he disappeared.

8. ¿Quiere Vd. verlo otra vez?   Do you wish to see it _____?

9. Venga Vd. en seguida.   Come _____.

10. Sin embargo, los cuartos son pequeños. _____ the rooms are small.

11. Hace fresco por la tarde. _____ in the afternoon.

12. Carlos asiste a esta escuela.   Charles _____ this school.

13. Es necesario verlo una vez.   It is necessary to see it _____.

14. Mi madre pone la mesa.   My mother _____.

15. Los alumnos deben prestar atención en la clase.   Students should _____ in class.

16. ¿Sabe Vd. nadar? _____ to swim?

17. ¡Ya lo creo!   Yes, _____!

18. Es importante, ¿verdad?   It's important, _____?

19. Me gusta el campo sobre todo en la primavera.   I like the country _____ in the spring.

20. Lo explicó de esta manera.   He explained it _____.

B. Write the opposite of each of the following expressions.

1. buenos días _____

2. por la mañana _____

3. Entra en la iglesia. _____ la iglesia.

4. Ramón tiene frío.   Ramón _____

5. el año pasado _____.

6. Hace buen tiempo. _____.

7. Llegan a tiempo.   Llegan _____.

8. Tiene razón. _____.

9. Hace calor. _____.

10. Nadie está contento. _____ está contento.

C. Write a synonym for each of the following expressions.

1. Viajan a Europa. _____ a Europa.

2. Haga Vd. el favor de entrar. _____ de entrar.

3. Finalmente llegaron. _____ llegaron.

4. Comienzan a comer. _____ comer.

5. ¿Quieren Vds. visitar a Pablo?   ¿Quieren Vds. _____ a Pablo?

6. Te amo mucho.   Te _____ mucho.

7. ¿Le gusta pasearse por el parque?   ¿Le gusta _____ por el parque?

8. ¿Qué significa?   ¿Qué _____?

9. Me desayuno a las ocho.   _____ a las ocho.

10. Nos visita muchas veces.   Nos visita _____.

11. Salieron inmediatamente.   Salieron _____.

12. No hay de qué.   _____.

D. Underline the word in parentheses that correctly completes the Spanish translation of the English sentence.

1. It is warm today. (Es, Está, Hace) calor hoy.

2. I like roses. Me (gusta, gustan, gusto) las rosas.

3. He is very hungry. Tiene (más, mucha, muy) hambre.

4. I must study. Tengo (que, de, a) estudiar.

5. Do you play the violin? ¿(Juega, Toca, Sabe) Vd. el violín?

6. We are going home. Vamos (a, de, en) casa.

7. He has breakfast early. (Toma, Tiene, Lleva) el desayuno temprano.

8. They take a walk. (Dan, Toman, Hacen) un paseo.

9. They arrive tonight. Llegan (anoche, de noche, esta noche).

10. Please enter. (Haga, Tenga, Ponga) Vd. la bondad de entrar.

E. Complete the Spanish sentences.

1. They like the house.   _____ la casa.

2. She asks many questions.   _____ muchas preguntas.

3. The boy is right.   El muchacho _____.

4. Do you have a headache?   ¿Tiene Vd. _____?

5. I am going to see my friend.   _____ ver a mi amigo.

6. The prisoner tried to escape.   El prisionero _____ escaparse.

7. He died on the following day.   Murió _____.

8. Thank you. You're welcome.   Muchas gracias. _____.

9. He has to buy a suit.   _____ un traje.

10. We want to take a trip to France.   Queremos _____ a Francia.

F. Complete the following sentences, and then translate them into English.

1. _____ sol hoy. _____

2. La familia está _____ casa. _____

3. Levántese Vd., _____ favor. _____

4. Tenemos _____ trabajar. _____

[141]

5. Aprenda Vd. la poesía _____ memoria. _____

6. Acabo _____ comprar un automóvil nuevo. _____

_____

7. Los indios van al mercado _____ pie. _____

8. Salen _____ la oficina. _____

9. La casa está situada _____ lado de un parque. _____

_____

10. _____ ejemplo, Vd. no necesita pasaporte para ir a México. _____

_____

G. How would you say to someone in Spanish:

1. How is the weather? _____

2. How old are you? _____

3. Are you thirsty? _____

4. Do you play tennis? _____

5. Please close the door. _____

6. All right! _____

7. Yes, indeed! _____

8. Do you like this dress? _____

9. I am going shopping. _____

10. See you later. _____

Rubber trees grow abundantly in the tropical forests of the Amazon valley. To obtain rubber, the trees are tapped and the sap collected in a cup. In recent years, the rubber industry in this region has declined in importance because of competition from countries in the Far East, and because of the development of synthetic rubber.

Part IV—*Vocabulary*

Vocabulary Lesson 1—COGNATES

Some Spanish and English words, derived from the same root, are related in spelling and meaning. Such words are called cognates: **metal,** metal; **continente,** continent; **montañoso,** mountainous.

Many Spanish words ending in **-ción** end in *-tion* in English: **la invitación,** invitation; **la sección,** section.

A. Write the English equivalent of the following Spanish words.

1. la admiración ....
2. la educación ....
3. la producción ....
4. la atención ....
5. la nación ....

6. la emoción ....
7. la imaginación ....
8. la situación ....
9. la civilización ....
10. la aviación ....

Many Spanish words ending in **-dad** end in *-ty* in English: **la sociedad,** society.

B. Write the English equivalent of the following Spanish words.

1. la universidad ....
2. la generosidad ....
3. la necesidad ....
4. la oportunidad ....
5. la capacidad ....

6. la curiosidad ....
7. la dignidad ....
8. la eternidad ....
9. la variedad ....
10. la autoridad ....

Many Spanish words ending in **-ia, -ía,** or **-io** end in *-y* in English: **la historia,** history; **la energía,** energy; **ordinario,** ordinary.

C. Write the English equivalent of the following Spanish words.

1. la gloria ....
2. la geografía ....
3. el matrimonio ....
4. la ceremonia ....
5. la familia ....

6. la industria ....
7. necesario ....
8. el remedio ....
9. la memoria ....
10. la cortesía ....

Many Spanish words ending in **-oso** end in *-ous* in English: **famoso,** famous; **precioso,** precious.

D. Write the English equivalent of the following Spanish words.

1. misterioso ....
2. nervioso ....
3. curioso ....
4. religioso ....
5. montañoso ....

6. generoso ....
7. furioso ....
8. glorioso ....
9. maravilloso ....
10. sospechoso ....

Many Spanish words ending in **-mente** end in *-ly* in English: **generalmente,** generally; **finalmente**, finally.

E. Write the English equivalent of the following Spanish words.

1. correctamente ....
2. inmediatamente ....
3. perfectamente ....
4. usualmente ....
5. exactamente ....

6. rápidamente ....
7. naturalmente ....
8. frecuentemente ....
9. silenciosamente ....
10. recientemente ....

Many Spanish words beginning with **es** plus a consonant begin with *s* plus a consonant in English: **especial,** special; **el espacio,** space.

F. Write the English equivalent of the following Spanish words.

1. la estación ....
2. la estatua ....
3. el estómago ....
4. el escándalo ....
5. el estudio ....

6. la escena ....
7. el espectáculo ....
8. el espíritu ....
9. el estilo ....
10. estúpido ....

Benito Juárez (1806-1872) was a full-blooded Indian who rose from very humble surroundings to become President of Mexico. During his administration, Napoleon III of France tried to establish an empire in Mexico. Juárez resisted stubbornly, and the French troops were forced to withdraw. Mexicans consider Juárez one of their national heroes. He has been called the "Abraham Lincoln of Mexico" because, like Lincoln, his life is an example of goodness, kindness, brotherhood and love of liberty.

[144]

Vocabulary Lesson 2—INDIRECT COGNATES

Many Spanish words are indirectly related in form and meaning to an English word. For example, *libro* means book and is related to the English word *library*.

GROUP I

SPANISH WORD	ENGLISH MEANING	ENGLISH COGNATE
alto	high	*altitude*
amable	kind	*amiable*
amor	love	*amorous, enamored*
antiguo	old	*antique*
año	year	*annual, anniversary*
aprender	to learn	*apprentice*
árbol	tree	*arbor*
avión	airplane	*aviation*
bailar	to dance	*ballet*
barba	beard, chin	*barber*
beber	to drink	*beverage*
bello	beautiful	*belle, embellish*
brazo	arm	*bracelet, embrace*
caballo	horse	*cavalry*
campo	country, field	*camp*
cantar	to sing	*chant*
cara	face	*caricature*
ciento	hundred	*century, per cent*
cine	movies	*cinema*
comprender	to understand	*comprehend*
contra	against	*contrary, contradict*
correr	to run	*courier, current*
creer	to believe	*creed, incredible*
cuánto	how much	*quantity*
cuarto	room	*quarters*
cuerpo	body	*corpse*
deber	to owe	*debt, debtor*
decir	to say, to tell	*dictate, diction*
día	day	*diary*
diente	tooth	*dentist, dental*
dios	god	*deity*
dormir	to sleep	*dormitory*
duro	hard	*durable*

EXERCISES

A. Write the Spanish word that is related to the English word; then write the English meaning of each Spanish word.

English Word	Related Spanish Word	English Meaning
1. ballet	--------	--------
2. dental	--------	--------
3. beverage	--------	--------
4. century	--------	--------
5. debt	--------	--------
6. apprentice	--------	--------

[145]

7. durable   --   --

8. aviation   --   --

9. annual   --   --

10. camp   --   --

11. quantity   --   --

12. comprehend   --   --

13. diction   --   --

14. cinema   --   --

15. altitude   --   --

16. creed   --   --

17. dormitory   --   --

18. contrary   --   --

19. diary   --   --

20. quarters   --   --

B. In the space before each Spanish word, first write the letter of the English meaning and then the letter of the English cognate.

Spanish Word	English Meaning	English Cognate
------- 1. bello	a. old	A. corpse
------- 2. correr	b. to believe	B. arbor
------- 3. antiguo	c. love	C. belle
------- 4. cuerpo	d. face	D. amiable
------- 5. amor	e. beard	E. antique
------- 6. árbol	f. arm	F. contradict
------- 7. barba	g. kind	G. chant
------- 8. creer	h. beautiful	H. cavalry
------- 9. cantar	i. god	I. amorous
------- 10. cara	j. horse	J. deity
------- 11. brazo	k. body	K. courier
------- 12. amable	l. against	L. caricature
------- 13. contra	m. to sing	M. incredible
------- 14. caballo	n. to run	N. bracelet
------- 15. dios	o. tree	O. barber

C. Underline the English word that translates the Spanish word.

1. *deber:*   to drink, to owe, to tell   6. *caballo:*   horse, hair, gentleman

2. *cantar:*   to count, to sing, to buy   7. *aprender:*   to open, to learn, to understand

3. *duro:*   tooth, dear, hard   8. *dios:*   goodbye, day, god

4. *cara:*   car, face, each   9. *correr:*   to believe, to run, to want

5. *amor:*   kind, love, old   10. *cuarto:*   room, four, picture

D. Underline the Spanish word that translates the English word.

1. *arm:*   brazo, brazalete, abrazo

2. *against:*   como, cómodo, contra

3. *kind:*   amor, amar, amable

4. *year:*   amo, año, uno

5. *airplane:*   ave, aire, avión

6. *how much:*   cuánto, cuándo, cuál

7. *tree:*   antiguo, árbol, alto

8. *to drink:*   creer, bailar, beber

9. *to sleep:*   dormir, decir, durar

10. *tooth:*   día, duro, diente

GROUP II

SPANISH WORD	ENGLISH MEANING	ENGLISH COGNATE
edificio	building	*edifice*
encontrar	to meet, to find	*encounter*
enfermo	sick	*infirmary*
entre	between, among	*international, interstate*
enviar	to send	*envoy*
escalera	stairs, staircase	*escalator*
escribir	to write	*scribble*
esposo	husband	*spouse*
fábrica	factory	*fabric*
fácil	easy	*facilitate*
flor	flower	*florist*
frío	cold	*frigid, refrigerator*
guante	glove	*gauntlet*
guerra	war	*guerrilla*
gusto	pleasure	*disgust*
iglesia	church	*ecclesiastical*
joven	young	*juvenile, rejuvenate*
lavar	to wash	*lavatory*
leer	to read	*legible*
lengua	language	*linguist*
libre	free	*liberate, liberty*
libro	book	*library*
mandar	to order	*mandatory, command*
mano	hand	*manual*
mar	sea	*mariner, maritime*
mayor	greater, larger	*major, majority*
médico	doctor	*medical*
menor	younger, smaller	*minor, minority*
menos	less	*minus*
mirar	to look at	*mirror*
morir	to die	*mortician, immortal*
mosca	fly	*mosquito*
nuevo	new	*novelty*

EXERCISES

A. Write the Spanish word that is related to the English word; then write the English meaning of each Spanish word.

English Word	Related Spanish Word	English Meaning
1. juvenile	-------------------------------------	-------------------------------------
2. escalator	-------------------------------------	-------------------------------------
3. mosquito	-------------------------------------	-------------------------------------

4. manual

5. facilitate

6. edifice

7. maritime

8. encounter

9. frigid

10. scribble

11. majority

12. minor

13. mirror

14. medical

15. lavatory

B. In the space before each Spanish word, first write the letter of the English meaning and then the letter of the English cognate.

Spanish Word	English Meaning	English Cognate
------- 1. iglesia	a. new	A. international
------- 2. enviar	b. glove	B. mandatory
------- 3. fábrica	c. husband	C. fabric
------- 4. guante	d. church	D. novelty
------- 5. leer	e. free	E. linguist
------- 6. entre	f. to die	F. infirmary
------- 7. libre	g. to read	G. envoy
------- 8. nuevo	h. war	H. guerrilla
------- 9. esposo	i. to send	I. disgust
------- 10. mandar	j. pleasure	J. gauntlet
------- 11. morir	k. among	K. spouse
------- 12. lengua	l. sick	L. mortician
------- 13. guerra	m. factory	M. ecclesiastical
------- 14. enfermo	n. language	N. liberty
------- 15. gusto	o. to order	O. legible

C. Underline the English word that translates the Spanish word.

1. *menos:* less, younger, smaller

2. *morir:* to look at, to die, to show

3. *mandar:* to order, to kill, to return

4. *escalera:* scale, escape, stairs

5. *lavar:* to wash, to arrive, to carry

6. *entre:* entrance, between, upon

7. *fácil:* easy, factory, flower

8. *edificio:* office, building, exercise

9. *mayor:* greater, better, most

10. *gusto:* wind, like, pleasure

[148]

D. Underline the Spanish word that translates the English word.

1. *younger:*   mano, menor, menos
2. *free:*   libro, libre, libra
3. *factory:*   fábrica, flor, fecha
4. *hand:*   mano, malo, marido
5. *war:*   guía, guante, guerra

6. *among:*   delante, enfrente, entre
7. *new:*   nuevo, nieve, nueve
8. *to meet:*   contar, encontrar, enseñar
9. *church:*   inglés, igual, iglesia
10. *language:*   lengua, legumbre, lejos

GROUP III

SPANISH WORD	ENGLISH MEANING	ENGLISH COGNATE
patria	(native) country	*patriotic, patriotism*
paz	peace	*pacifist, pacify*
pedir	to ask for	*petition*
periódico	newspaper	*periodical*
piedra	stone	*petrified*
pobre	poor	*poverty*
primero	first	*primary*
pronto	soon	*prompt*
pueblo	town, people	*population*
recordar	to remember	*record*
responder	to answer	*respond*
seguir	to follow, to continue	*sequence*
sentir	to feel	*sentiment*
sitio	place, spot	*site*
sol	sun	*solar*
solo	alone	*solitude, soloist*
tarde	late	*tardy*
tiempo	time	*tempo, temporary*
tierra	land, earth	*territory*
todo	all	*total*
último	last	*ultimate, ultimatum*
útil	useful	*utilize, utility*
vaca	cow	*vaccine, vaccinate*
vacío	empty	*vacant*
valer	to be worth	*valuable*
vecino	neighbor	*vicinity*
vender	to sell	*vendor*
ventana	window	*ventilation*
verdad	truth	*verify*
vida	life	*vital, vitality*
vivir	to live	*revive, vivid*
voz	voice	*vocal*

EXERCISES

A. Write the Spanish word that is related to the English word; then write the English meaning of each Spanish word.

English Word	Related Spanish Word	English Meaning
1. periodical		
2. territory		
3. poverty		
4. site		

5. primary _____ _____

6. solar _____ _____

7. total _____ _____

8. vivid _____ _____

9. prompt _____ _____

10. tempo _____ _____

B. In the space before each Spanish word, first write the letter of the English meaning and then the letter of the English cognate.

Spanish Word	English Meaning	English Cognate
_____ 1. piedra	a. peace	A. sequence
_____ 2. último	b. town	B. petition
_____ 3. paz	c. truth	C. population
_____ 4. seguir	d. useful	D. solitude
_____ 5. verdad	e. alone	E. valuable
_____ 6. pedir	f. to be worth	F. petrified
_____ 7. útil	g. stone	G. vaccinate
_____ 8. pueblo	h. voice	H. vocal
_____ 9. sentir	i. empty	I. pacify
_____ 10. solo	j. last	J. vitality
_____ 11. vaca	k. life	K. utilize
_____ 12. valer	l. to follow	L. verify
_____ 13. voz	m. to feel	M. vacant
_____ 14. vida	n. cow	N. sentiment
_____ 15. vacío	o. to ask for	O. ultimatum

C. Underline the English word that translates the Spanish word.

1. *piedra:* stone, people, town

2. *seguir:* to be sure, to continue, to hasten

3. *último:* useful, timely, last

4. *valer:* to be brave, to be worth, to fly

5. *paz:* peace, pair, nation

6. *todo:* bull, land, all

7. *vecino:* time, summer, neighbor

8. *patria:* country, father, courtyard

9. *recordar:* to remember, to receive, to answer

10. *tierra:* time, earth, terror

D. Underline the Spanish word that translates the English word.

1. *sun:* sol, sólo, solo

2. *voice:* ves, voz, vez

3. *to ask for:* pedir, perder, poder

4. *empty:* vacío, vaca, vaso

5. *first:* pronto, primero, príncipe

6. *to sell:* venir, ver, vender

7. *to feel:* sentir, sentar, saludar

8. *place:* plaza, sitio, silla

9. *late:* tiempo, tarjeta, tarde

10. *life:* vida, vivir, vivo

Vocabulary Lesson 3—SYNONYMS

SYNONYMS	MEANINGS
acabar, terminar	to finish, to end
acordarse (ue) de, recordar (ue)	to remember
alegre, feliz, contento	happy, merry, gay
algunos, unos	some
alumno, estudiante	pupil, student
amar, querer	to love
amigo, compañero	friend, companion
andar, caminar, ir a pie	to walk
aplicado, diligente, trabajador	diligent, industrious, hard-working
aún, todavía	still, yet
bastante, suficiente	enough, sufficient
bello, hermoso	beautiful
bonito, lindo	pretty
cabello, pelo	hair
comenzar (ie), empezar (ie)	to begin
comprender, entender (ie)	to understand
contestar, responder	to answer, to reply
cuarto, habitación	room
dejar, permitir	to let, to allow, to permit
desear, querer	to want, to wish
despacio, lentamente	slowly
en, sobre	on, upon
encontrar (ue), hallar	to find
enviar, mandar	to send
error, falta	mistake
esposa, mujer, señora	wife
esposo, marido	husband
grande, enorme, inmenso	large, big, huge
idioma, lengua	language
irse, marcharse	to go away
jamás, nunca	never
lugar, sitio	place
maestro, profesor	teacher
mostrar (ue), enseñar	to show
niño, chico	child, little boy
país, nación	country, nation
perdone Vd., dispense Vd.	pardon me, excuse me
partir, salir	to leave
seguir (i), continuar	to continue
sólo, solamente	only

EXERCISES

A. Underline the synonym of the word in italics.

1. *lindo:*   feliz, bonito, contento

2. *nunca:*   joven, nada, jamás

3. *lengua:*   idioma, igual, iglesia

4. *sitio:*   asiento, lugar, silla

5. *entender:*   responder, aprender, comprender

6. *esposa:*   mujer, marido, señorita

7. *lentamente:*   pronto, despacio, después

8. *país:*   pueblo, plaza, nación

9. *todavía:*   aún, allí, aquí

10. *partir:*   saber, viajar, salir

B. On the line before each word in Column I, write the letter of the synonym in Column II.

Column I	Column II
_____ **1.** terminar	_a._ en
_____ **2.** caminar	_b._ chico
_____ **3.** sobre	_c._ bello
_____ **4.** error	_d._ diligente
_____ **5.** niño	_e._ acabar
_____ **6.** feliz	_f._ suficiente
_____ **7.** aplicado	_g._ encontrar
_____ **8.** hermoso	_h._ falta
_____ **9.** hallar	_i._ alegre
_____ **10.** bastante	_j._ andar

C. Write a synonym for each italicized expression in the sentences below, using one of the following.

permite	quiere	manda
se va	contesta	muestra
se acuerda de	desea	continúe
perdone		

1. _Dispense_ Vd., señor. _____

2. _Se marcha_ hoy. _____

3. El niño no _responde_. _____

4. Su padre no le _deja_ salir de noche. _____

5. Te _ama_ mucho. _____

6. ¿_Recuerda_ la dirección? _____

7. Nos _enseña_ el camino. _____

8. ¿Qué _quiere_ Vd.? _____

9. _Siga_ Vd. leyendo. _____

10. Me _envía_ una carta. _____

D. Write a synonym of:

1. compañero _____   **6.** estudiante _____

2. unos _____   **7.** ir a pie _____

3. solamente _____   **8.** cabello _____

4. marido _____   **9.** profesor _____

5. enorme _____   **10.** habitación _____

E. Write _two_ Spanish translations for each of the following words.

1. pretty _____

2. to begin _____

3. to understand _____

4. happy _____

5. to show _____

Vocabulary Lesson 4—OPPOSITES

GROUP I

abrir, to open	cerrar (ie), to close
ahora, now	más tarde, later
alegre, gay	triste, sad
algo, something	nada, nothing
alguno, some	ninguno, none
alto, high	bajo, low
amigo, friend	enemigo, enemy
ancho, wide	estrecho, narrow
anoche, last night	esta noche, tonight
antes (de), before	después (de), after
aprisa, quickly	despacio, slowly
aquí, here	allí, there
ausente, absent	presente, present
barato, cheap	caro, dear, expensive
blanco, white	negro, black
bueno, good	malo, bad
caballero, gentleman	dama, lady
caliente, hot, warm	frío, cold
cerca de, near	lejos de, far from
comprar, to buy	vender, to sell
con, with	sin, without
contestar, to answer	preguntar, to ask
corto, short	largo, long
dar, to give	recibir, to receive
débil, weak	fuerte, strong
delante de, in front of	detrás de, in back of, behind
día, day	noche, night
difícil, difficult	fácil, easy
empezar (ie), to begin	terminar, to end
este, east	oeste, west
grande, large	pequeño, small
guerra, war	paz, peace
hallar, to find	perder (ie), to lose

EXERCISES

A. On the line before each word in Column I, write the letter of the opposite in Column II.

	Column I	*Column II*
_____	**1.** paz	*a.* alegre
_____	**2.** algo	*b.* antes
_____	**3.** triste	*c.* despacio
_____	**4.** estrecho	*d.* fuerte
_____	**5.** después	*e.* cerca
_____	**6.** lejos	*f.* largo
_____	**7.** aprisa	*g.* guerra
_____	**8.** corto	*h.* detrás
_____	**9.** débil	*i.* ancho
_____	**10.** delante	*j.* nada

B. Write the opposite of each word in italics, using one of the following.

recibe   halla   ancha
cara   baja   empieza
compra   abre   pregunta
corta

1. El profesor *cierra* la puerta. _____

2. *Vende* la casa. _____

3. *Da* muchos regalos. _____

4. ¿A qué hora *termina* la clase? _____

5. El niño *pierde* la pelota. _____

6. ¿Qué *contesta* el hombre? _____

7. La blusa es *barata*. _____

8. La calle es *estrecha*. _____

9. Es una novela *larga*. _____

10. Juana es *alta*. _____

C. Write the opposite of:

1. contestar _____
2. sin _____
3. ninguno _____
4. bajo _____
5. malo _____

6. dama _____
7. oeste _____
8. difícil _____
9. presente _____
10. barato _____

D. Translate into Spanish.

1. black, white _____
2. here, there _____
3. now, later _____
4. last night, tonight _____
5. hot, cold _____
6. friend, enemy _____
7. day, night _____
8. large, small _____
9. gay, sad _____
10. something, nothing _____

GROUP II

hermoso, beautiful   feo, ugly
hombre, man   mujer, woman
hoy, today   { mañana, tomorrow
                     { ayer, yesterday
levantarse, to get up   sentarse (ie), to sit down
limpio, clean   sucio, dirty
lleno, full   vacío, empty

llorar, to cry	**reír (i),** to laugh
madre, mother	**padre,** father
marido, husband	**esposa,** wife
más, more	**menos,** less
mayor, older	**menor,** younger
mejor, better	**peor,** worse
mismo, same	**diferente,** different
mucho, much	**poco,** little
muerte, death	**vida,** life
no, no	**sí,** yes
norte, north	**sur,** south
perezoso, lazy	**aplicado,** industrious
pobre, poor	**rico,** rich
ponerse, to put on	**quitarse,** to take off
primero, first	**último,** last
príncipe, prince	**princesa,** princess
recordar (ue), to remember	**olvidar,** to forget
rey, king	**reina,** queen
rubio, blond	**moreno,** dark, brunette
ruido, noise	**silencio,** silence
salir (de), to leave	**entrar (en),** to enter
siempre, always	**nunca,** never
tarde, late	**temprano,** early
verano, summer	**invierno,** winter
verdad, truth	**mentira,** lie
viejo, old	⎰ **joven,** young ⎱ **nuevo,** new
vivir, to live	**morir (ue),** to die

EXERCISES

A. Underline the opposite of the word in italics.

1. *menor:* mayor, más, mejor

2. *diferente:* muerte, marido, mismo

3. *nunca:* temprano, siempre, poco

4. *nuevo:* viejo, aplicado, limpio

5. *moreno:* sucio, vacío, rubio

6. *mañana:* hay, hoy, ha

7. *mucho:* poco, muy, corto

8. *último:* primo, uno, primero

9. *pobre:* ruido, rico, rubio

10. *viejo:* joven, jueves, jamás

B. On the line before each word in Column I, write the letter of the opposite in Column II.

Column I	Column II
_____ 1. feo	*a.* ayer
_____ 2. verdad	*b.* vacío
_____ 3. hoy	*c.* cerrar
_____ 4. vida	*d.* ruido
_____ 5. lleno	*e.* rico
_____ 6. peor	*f.* muerte
_____ 7. abrir	*g.* perezoso
_____ 8. silencio	*h.* hermoso
_____ 9. aplicado	*i.* mejor
_____ 10. pobre	*j.* mentira

C. Write the opposite (feminine form) for each of the following.

1. el padre; la _____   4. el rey; la _____

2. el marido; la _____   5. el hombre; la _____

3. el príncipe; la _____

D. Write the opposite of the words in italics, using one of the following.

muerte	muere	se quita
llora	recuerda	sale de
limpia	llena	tarde
se levanta		

1. Mi amigo siempre *olvida* la fecha de mi cumpleaños. _____

2. *Entra en* la tienda. _____

3. El niño *ríe*. _____

4. La mujer *se pone* los guantes. _____

5. El alumno *se sienta*. _____

6. *Vive* en paz. _____

7. La botella está *vacía*. _____

8. Juan llega *temprano*. _____

9. La servilleta no está *sucia*. _____

10. ¿Cuál es su filosofía de la *vida*? _____

E. Translate into Spanish.

1. rich, poor _____

2. north, south _____

3. yes, no _____

4. early, late _____

5. new, old _____

6. tomorrow, today _____

7. summer, winter _____

8. to live, to die _____

9. clean, dirty _____

10. more, less _____

The tapir inhabits South and Central America. It stands about three feet high and has a heavy, clumsy body. The tapir is a shy and gentle animal. It feeds principally on plants, shrubs and other vegetation.

Vocabulary Lesson 5—WORDS FREQUENTLY CONFUSED

GROUP I

There are many words in Spanish which sound alike but are different in meaning.

In the following pairs of words, an accent mark is used to distinguish one word from the other.

como, as, like	**mi,** my	**si,** if
cómo, how	**mí,** me	**sí,** yes
de, of, from		**solo,** alone
dé, give (command)	**que,** which, that	**sólo,** only
el, the	**qué,** what	**te,** you, yourself
él, he, him		**té,** tea
mas, but	**se,** himself, herself, yourself, themselves	**tu,** your
más, more	**sé,** I know	**tú,** you

The following pairs of words have distinctly different meanings depending on how they are used in a sentence.

yo amo, I love	**él nada,** he swims
el amo, master, owner, boss	**nada,** nothing
la cara, face	**yo río,** I laugh
caro, cara, expensive	**el río,** river
yo como, I eat	**sobre,** on, upon
como, as, like	**el sobre,** envelope
entre Vd., enter (command)	**tarde,** late
entre, between, among	**la tarde,** afternoon
este, this	**yo traje,** I brought
el este, east	**el traje,** suit
mañana, tomorrow	**él vino,** he came
la mañana, morning	**el vino,** wine

EXERCISES

A. Translate the italicized words into English.

1. José no *nada* bien.   ------------------------

2. Venga Vd. *mañana*.   ------------------------

3. Necesito un *sobre* para la carta.   ------------------------

4. *Río* cuando estoy alegre.   ------------------------

5. ¿Quién está sentado *entre* las dos mujeres?   ------------------------

6. El señor Molina es el *amo* de la casa.   ------------------------

7. El *vino* es de España.   ------------------------

8. Está situado al *este* del país.   ------------------------

9. Lleva un *traje* azul.   ------------------------

10. Duerme por la *tarde*.   ------------------------

[157]

B. Underline the word in parentheses that correctly completes the sentence.

1. ¿Son estas cartas para (mi, mí)?

2. ¿Tienes (tu, tú) libro?

3. ¿Quién es (el, él) profesor?

4. Tome Vd. el paquete (que, qué) está sobre la mesa.

5. José recibe un paquete (de, dé) la tienda.

6. ¿(Cómo, Como) está Vd.?

7. Yo (te, té) adoro.

8. Necesitan (solo, sólo) un dólar.

9. ¿Cómo (se, sé) llama Vd.?

10. (Sí, Si), señor, soy norteamericano.

C. Translate the English words into Spanish.

1. ¿(What) desea Vd.? _____

2. ¿No tengo (my) libro? _____

3. ¿Viene Vd. (alone)? _____

4. (I know) bailar. _____

5. ¿Quién es (he)? _____

6. No lo (give) Vd. a Enrique. _____

7. Hágalo Vd. (if) puede. _____

8. La criada sirve (tea). _____

9. Canta (like) un pájaro. _____

10. Traiga Vd. (more) café, por favor. _____

GROUP II

The following words are confusing to many students because they look and sound almost alike.

el cabello, hair
el caballo, horse

cantar, to sing
contar, to count, to relate

la ciudad, city
el cuidado, care

¿cuánto?, how much?
¿cuándo?, when?

el cuadro, picture
el cuarto, room
cuatro, four

el cuento, story
la cuenta, bill, account

el dolor, pain
el dólar, dollar

el hermano, brother
hermoso, beautiful

el hombre, man
el hombro, shoulder
el hambre, hunger

hoy, today
hay, there is, there are

llegar, to arrive
llevar, to carry, to wear

llorar, to cry
llover, to rain

la nieve, snow
nueve, nine
nuevo, new

[158]

pero, but	el queso, cheese
el perro, dog	quiso, he wanted
el primo, cousin	sentarse, to sit down
primero, first	sentirse, to feel
la puerta, door	el viaje, trip
el puerto, port	viejo, old

EXERCISES

A. Translate the italicized words into English.

1. El *cuidado* de los dientes es importante. _____

2. Es un *cuento* muy interesante. _____

3. Anoche *llovió*. _____

4. Hay siete *cuartos* en la casa. _____

5. Mi amigo no *se siente* bien. _____

6. El muchacho lleva las maletas sobre los *hombros*. _____

7. Nos *contó* una anécdota. _____

8. Teresa tiene el *cabello* rubio. _____

9. Es una muchacha *hermosa*. _____

10. ¿*Cuándo* es su cumpleaños? _____

B. Underline the word in parentheses that correctly completes the sentence.

1. ¿A qué hora (lleva, llega) el tren?

2. No (queso, quiso) aceptar el dinero.

3. Abra Vd. (la puerta, el puerto).

4. Pedro es el (hermoso, hermano) de Ana.

5. Como cuando tengo (hambre, hombro, hombre).

6. Mozo, traiga Vd. (la cuenta, el cuento), por favor.

7. Monta a (cabello, caballo).

8. ¿Tiene Vd. (dólar, dolor) de cabeza?

9. El niño está (llorando, lloviendo).

10. El señor Varga es un hombre (viaje, viejo).

C. Underline the Spanish word that translates the English word.

1. *how much?*: ¿cómo?, ¿cuándo?, ¿cuánto?

2. *trip*: viaje, viejo, vieja

3. *four*: cuarto, cuadro, cuatro

4. *there are*: ha, hoy, hay

5. *picture*: cuadro, cuarto, cuatro

6. *new*: nieve, nueve, nuevo

7. *first*: primo, primero, primavera

8. *dog*: perro, pero, para

9. *to wear*: llover, llevar, llegar

10. *to sing*: cantar, contar, caminar

11. *city*: cuida, cuidado, ciudad

12. *to sit down*: sentirse, sentarse, siéntese

[159]

MASTERY EXERCISES

A. Underline the word or expression that best completes the meaning of each sentence.

1. Es más rápido hacer un viaje (*a*) en avión (*b*) por tren (*c*) a pie (*d*) en automóvil.

2. El cuerpo humano tiene dos (*a*) barbas (*b*) caras (*c*) brazos (*d*) estómagos.

3. Felipe tiene ocho años. Josefina tiene diez años. Josefina es (*a*) menor (*b*) mejor (*c*) peo (*d*) mayor   que Felipe.

4. María es una niña hermosa. Tiene el pelo negro y los ojos pardos (brown). María es (*a*) moren (*b*) rubia (*c*) vieja (*d*) fea.

5. La señora Ortega va al médico porque está (*a*) sola (*b*) enferma (*c*) fría (*d*) sucia.

6. El traje blanco cuesta ochenta dólares. El traje azul cuesta ciento veinte dólares. El traje blanc es más (*a*) nuevo (*b*) largo (*c*) barato (*d*) caro   que el traje azul.

7. La muchacha llora porque está (*a*) alegre (*b*) triste (*c*) contenta (*d*) libre.

8. Pablo es mi vecino. Vive (*a*) cerca de (*b*) lejos de (*c*) después de (*d*) antes de   mí.

9. El hermano de Marta tiene mucho dinero. Es muy (*a*) chico (*b*) rico (*c*) pobre (*d*) estrecho.

10. José estudia poco. Es (*a*) aplicado (*b*) corto (*c*) débil (*d*) perezoso.

B. Underline the word that is most closely related in thought to the word in italics.

1. *campo:*   árbol, plata, cabello
2. *Dios:*   mañana, noche, iglesia
3. *carta:*   silla, sobre, sitio
4. *rey:*   primavera, primero, príncipe
5. *frío:*   invierno, verano, verdad
6. *guante:*   paz, mano, piedra
7. *cantar:*   nombre, cuento, voz
8. *asiento:*   sentarse, sentirse, acordarse
9. *limpio:*   llevar, lavar, llover
10. *mar:*   río, menos, pero

C. Underline the two words in each group that have similar meanings.

1. mostrar, dejar, enviar, permitir, empezar
2. bastante, más, suficiente, menos, todavía
3. pelo, bello, feo, caballo, hermoso
4. jamás, nada, alguno, nunca, nadie
5. aprender, comprender, entender, responder, preguntar
6. marido, compañero, mujer, enemigo, esposo
7. solamente, sol, despacio, sal, lentamente
8. lengua, frase, inglés, idioma, alemán
9. seguir, partir, abrir, salir, saber
10. acostarse, irse, acordarse, recordar, comenza

D. Underline the two words in each group that have opposite meanings.

1. comprar, contestar, pedir, vender, hallar
2. largo, mucho, ancho, pequeño, poco
3. delante, antes, detrás, debajo, lejos
4. sentarse, acordarse, ponerse, acostarse, quitarse
5. viejo, mismo, joven, nieve, muerte
6. lindo, barato, caro, hermoso, frío
7. verdad, oeste, invierno, mentira, norte
8. débil, fácil, Dios, fuerte, triste
9. vez, guerra, voz, paz, vida
10. corto, aprisa, algo, nadie, despacio

E. Underline the English word that translates the Spanish word.

1. *queso:* pleasure, he wanted, who, cheese
2. *viaje:* trip, old, traveler, road
3. *piedra:* town, stone, loss, wall
4. *llevar:* to rain, to wash, to arrive, to wear
5. *útil:* last, useful, another, all

6. *ruido:* noise, impolite, wind, room
7. *valer:* to know, to leave, to be worth, to see
8. *libre:* book, pound, library, free
9. *chico:* child, rich, check, too much
10. *ahora:* time, hour, now, early

F. Underline the Spanish word that translates the English word.

1. *to believe:* caer, correr, creer, comer
2. *hundred:* ciento, asiento, centavo, siento
3. *building:* fábrica, edificio, facilidad, oficina
4. *empty:* vacío, vaca, sitio, caro
5. *without:* entre, contra, sin, bajo
6. *to look at:* mandar, mirar, morir, matar
7. *to lose:* pedir, poner, pensar, perder
8. *to owe:* beber, prometer, dejar, deber

9. *place:* plaza, lugar, siglo, todo
10. *owner:* amo, amor, amable, ancho
11. *land:* temprano, torre, tiempo, tierra
12. *to walk:* enviar, andar, cerrar, partir
13. *to find:* recordar, contar, hallar, cerrar
14. *yesterday:* ayer, anoche, hoy, día
15. *same:* nunca, barato, duro, mismo

Missions were established by the Spanish friars who accompanied the conquista-
dores to the New World. Usually the mission had a church, a bell tower and a
patio surrounded by minor buildings. These contained cells for the friars, servants'
quarters, guest rooms, work shops, kitchen, etc. Missions were constructed of
stone and adobe, and had heavy arcades and red tile roofs. The missionaries
themselves were dedicated to the task of civilizing the native Indians and convert-
ing them to Christianity. Today you can see Spanish missions in Texas, New
Mexico, Arizona and California.

Part V—Hispanic Civilization

Civilization Lesson 1—SPANISH INFLUENCE IN THE UNITED STATES

A. Spanish Explorers:

1. Juan Ponce de León. Discovered Florida (1513) in his search for the Fountain of Youth; named i *la Florida* because he discovered it on Easter Sunday (el domingo de Pascua Florida).

2. Álvar Núñez Cabeza de Vaca. Shipwrecked on the Texas coast (1528), he wandered for six years exploring parts of Texas, Kansas and New Mexico; was captured by Indians and lived as a slave and medicine man; finally reached Mexico, after walking thousands of miles.

3. Francisco Vásquez de Coronado. Explored the southwestern part of the United States (1540–42) i his search for the supposedly rich and prosperous "Seven Cities of Cíbola"; discovered the Grand Canyon.

4. Hernando de Soto. Discovered the Mississippi River (1541), in which he was later buried.

5. Juan Rodríguez Cabrillo. Explored the coast of California (1542).

B. Early Spanish Settlements:

1. St. Augustine. City in Florida; oldest city in the United States; established in 1565.

2. Spanish Missions. Established by Spanish priests in the southwestern part of the United States.

  a. Fray Junípero Serra. Most famous of the Spanish missionaries; he and his followers established a chain of twenty-one missions from San Diego to San Francisco (1769–1823).
  b. El Camino Real. Road which connected the California missions; now Coast Highway 101.
  c. Famous California Missions.
  (1) San Juan Capistrano.
  (2) Santa Bárbara Mission, called "Queen of the Missions."

C. Geographic Names of Spanish Origin in the United States:

1. States. California, Colorado, Florida, Montana, Nevada.

2. Cities. El Paso, Los Angeles, Santa Fe, San Francisco, and many others.

3. Rivers and Mountains. Rio Grande, Sierra Nevada, and many others.

D. Spanish Influence in Architecture:

1. Many modern American homes and buildings show the influence of the old adobe ranch houses and mission buildings constructed by the early Spaniards.

2. Characteristics of Spanish architecture.

  a. Patio (inner courtyard). An attractive spot for family relaxation; frequently has flowers, shade trees and an ornamental fountain.
  b. Reja (iron grating on windows). Used for security or adornment; a traditional meeting place for sweethearts, with the young lady behind the reja and her suitor in the street below.
  c. Balcón (balcony). Used for displaying flags and banners during celebrations; also used by members of the family for seeing and being seen during processions and merrymaking.
  d. Tejas (tiles). Made of baked clay, red in color and used for covering roofs.
  e. Arcada (arcade). A covered passageway along the front of a building; provides protection from the weather for the stroller about town.

E. Spanish Influence on Economic Life:

1. Cattle Raising.

    a. Spaniards brought the first cows, horses, goats, pigs and sheep to the New World.
    b. From the Spanish cowboy, the American cowboy copied his dress, equipment, vocabulary and ranching techniques.

2. Mining. Spaniards developed the first gold and silver mines in the New World. Their methods influenced the mining industry in America.

F. Spanish Influence in Language:

1. Spanish explorers, missionaries and settlers in North America contributed many Spanish words to our language. Some of these words are identical in English and Spanish. Others have been slightly changed.

2. Common English words of Spanish origin.

    a. Ranch life: bronco, chaps, cinch, corral, lariat, lasso, mustang, ranch, rodeo, stampede.
    b. Foods: avocado, banana, barbecue, chili, chocolate, cocoa, potato, tomato, vanilla.
    c. Beverages: julep, sherry.
    d. Clothing: bolero, brocade, huaraches, mantilla, poncho, sombrero.
    e. Animals and insects: alligator, burro, chinchilla, cockroach, coyote, llama, mosquito.
    f. Types of people: cannibal, comrade, Creole, desperado, padre, peon, renegade, vigilante.
    g. Nature: arroyo, canyon, cordillera, hurricane, lagoon, mesa, sierra, tornado.
    h. Shipping and commerce: armada, canoe, cargo, contraband, embargo, flotilla, galleon.
    i. Buildings and streets: adobe, alameda, hacienda, patio, plaza.
    j. Miscellaneous words: bonanza, cigar, fiesta, filibuster, guerrilla, siesta, tobacco.

G. Mexican Foods Popular in the United States:

1. Tortilla (flat, thin cornmeal pancake).

2. Tamal (crushed corn mixed with seasoned chopped meat).

3. Chile con carne (red pepper, chopped meat and hot chili sauce).

4. Enchilada (rolled tortilla filled with chopped meat or chicken and cheese; served with hot chili sauce).

5. Taco (a crisp tortilla folded over and filled with seasoned chopped meat, lettuce and tomatoes).

H. Spanish American Dances Popular in the United States:

1. Tango (Argentina).

2. Rumba (Cuba).

3. Mambo (Cuba).

4. Cha-cha-chá (Cuba).

5. Merengue (Dominican Republic).

EXERCISES

A. ¿Sí o No? If the statement is true, write **sí**; if it is false, write **no**.

1. La Florida fué descubierta el domingo de Pascua Florida.

2. Fray Junípero Serra y otros misioneros españoles establecieron treinta y una misiones en California.

3. "La Reina de las Misiones" se refiere a la misión de San Juan Capistrano.

4. Coronado fué capturado por los indios y vivió entre ellos.

5. La ganadería (cattle raising) es una industria que los españoles introdujeron en América.

6. El vaquero (cowboy) americano copió mucho del vaquero español.

7. Las rejas de las casas españolas tienen flores y árboles.

8. "Rodeo" y "corral" son palabras de origen español que describen la vida del rancho.

9. Los españoles construyeron muchos edificios de adobe.

10. No hay casas de arquitectura española en los Estados Unidos.

B. Match the following items.

Column I	*Column II*
_____ 1. De Soto	*a.* Florida
_____ 2. Fray Junípero Serra	*b.* explored coast of California
_____ 3. patio	*c.* Grand Canyon
_____ 4. Ponce de León	*d.* founder of California missions
_____ 5. reja	*e.* inner courtyard
_____ 6. Cabrillo	*f.* Mississippi River
_____ 7. Coronado	*g.* road connecting California missions
_____ 8. Camino Real	*h.* iron grating
_____ 9. St. Augustine	*i.* explored parts of Texas and New Mexico
_____ 10. Cabeza de Vaca	*j.* oldest city in U.S.
_____ 11. tango	*k.* Mexican dish
_____ 12. enchilada	*l.* Argentine dance

C. Complete the following sentences in Spanish.

1. _____ es una famosa misión de California.

2. _____ fué el explorador español que buscaba (searched for) la Fuente de la Juventud (Fountain of Youth).

3. _____ fué el explorador español que buscaba las "Siete Ciudades de Cíbola."

4. _____ es un estado de los Estados Unidos que tiene un nombre de origen español.

5. _____ es una ciudad norteamericana que tiene un nombre de origen español.

6. _____ es un río de los Estados Unidos que tiene un nombre de origen español.

7. _____ es una montaña de los Estados Unidos que tiene un nombre de origen español.

8. _____ es un animal que los españoles trajeron de España al Nuevo Mundo.

9. Dos bailes cubanos muy populares en los Estados Unidos son _____ y _____.

10. Dos platos mexicanos son _____ y _____.

D. Define the following words in English. Consult the English dictionary if necessary. In each case, note the Spanish word from which the English word is derived.

1. mustang _____

2. julep _____

3. chinchilla _____

4. peon _____

5. Creole _____

6. arroyo _____

7. cordillera _____

8. sierra _____

9. alameda _____

10. guerrilla _____

11. bonanza _____

12. filibuster _____

13. flotilla _____

14. armada _____

15. galleon _____

Civilization Lesson 2—OUR SPANISH AMERICAN NEIGHBORS

A. Countries of Spanish America:

1. Mexico.
2. In Central America: Guatemala, El Salvador (smallest), Honduras, Nicaragua (largest), Cost Rica, Panama.
3. In South America: Venezuela, Colombia, Ecuador, Peru, Bolivia, Paraguay, Uruguay (smallest Chile, Argentina (largest).
4. In the West Indies: Cuba, Dominican Republic, Puerto Rico (commonwealth of the United States

B. People of Spanish America:

1. Whites. Descendants of the original Spanish settlers or of later European immigrants (Italian Germans, Slavs, English, Irish). The population of Argentina and Uruguay is predominantly white
2. Indians. Full-blooded Indians are found in great numbers in Mexico, Ecuador, Bolivia and Peru
3. Mestizos (persons of Spanish and Indian blood). They form the majority of the population i many Spanish American countries.
4. Negroes. Descendants of slaves who were brought to Spanish America for heavy agricultural an mining labor. Most numerous in the West Indies.

C. Official Languages:

1. Spanish (spoken in 18 Latin American nations).
2. Portuguese (Brazil).
3. French (Haiti).

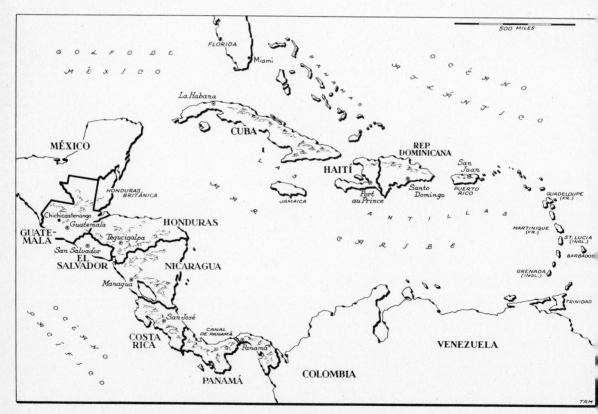

MAR CARIBE

CANAL DE PANAMÁ

La Guaira
Caracas

VENEZUELA

LLANOS

RÍO ORINOCO

GUAYANA (HOL.) (FR.)

COLOMBIA

Bogotá

RÍO MAGDALENA

LOS ANDES

OCÉANO ATLÁNTICO

ECUADOR   ECUADOR

Quito
COTOPAXI
CHIMBORAZO

Guayaquil

RÍO AMAZONAS

PERÚ

LOS ANDES

BRASIL

Natal

Callao
Lima
Cuzco

LAGO TITICACA

La Paz

BOLIVIA

Brasilia

Tacna
Arica

Sucre

LOS ANDES

GRAN CHACO

PARAGUAY

Río de Janeiro

Santos

Asunción

IGUAZÚ

Tucumán

RÍO PARANÁ

OCÉANO PACÍFICO

Córdoba

Viña del Mar
Valparaíso
Santiago

ACONCAGUA

ISLAS JUAN FERNÁNDEZ (CH.)

CHILE

PAMPAS

URUGUAY

Buenos Aires

Montevideo

RÍO DE LA PLATA

OCÉANO ATLÁNTICO

ARGENTINA

PATAGONIA

LOS ANDES

ESTRECHO DE MAGALLANES

ISLAS FALKLAND (ING.)

CABO DE HORNOS

▲ VOLCÁN Ó PICO

1000 MILES

TRM

D. Geography of Spanish America:

1. Mountain Ranges.

   a. Andes. Situated along the west coast of South America. They have peaks up to 23,000 feet.
   b. Sierra Madre. Two parallel mountain chains in Mexico. A great plateau lies between them.

2. Rivers.

   a. Río de la Plata. On its banks are two national capitals, Buenos Aires (Argentina) and Montevideo (Uruguay).
   b. Orinoco (Venezuela). Largest river in Spanish America.
   c. Magdalena (Colombia).

3. Climate.

   a. Most of Spanish America, except for northern Mexico and the southern part of South America, lies in the tropics.
   b. Although many cities and towns in Spanish America are in the tropics, they enjoy a cool climate because they are situated at high altitudes.
   c. The southern part of South America (Argentina, Chile, Uruguay, Paraguay) lies in the South Temperate Zone; seasons are the reverse of ours.

E. Animal Life:

1. Birds.

   a. Condor. Large bird of prey found in the Andes. Possibly the largest of flying birds.
   b. Quetzal. Beautiful bird found in Guatemala; it is the national emblem of Guatemala. Guatemalan dollar is called a quetzal.

2. Wild Animals. Jaguar, tapir, puma, armadillo, sloth, anteater.

3. Wool-Bearing Animals. Alpaca, guanaco, llama, vicuña.

4. Beasts of Burden.

   a. Burro. Most common beast of burden in Spanish America.
   b. Llama. Beast of burden in the Andes.

F. Important Products:

1. *Agricultural and Animal Products*	*Chief Producer*
coffee	Colombia (also Brazil)
sugar	Cuba
tobacco	Cuba
wheat	Argentina
beef	Argentina
bananas	Costa Rica, Honduras
chicle (used in the manufacture of chewing gum)	Mexico, Guatemala
cacao (bean from which chocolate is made)	Ecuador
tagua nut (used in the manufacture of buttons)	Ecuador

2. *Minerals*	*Chief Producer*
tin	Bolivia
silver	Mexico
petroleum	Venezuela
platinum	Colombia
emeralds	Colombia
copper	Chile
nitrates (used for fertilizers and explosives)	Chile

VENEZUELA

OIL

OIL

CACAO

COFFEE

IRON

COLOMBIA

SILVER

CATTLE

GOLD

HARDWOODS

GOLD

PLATINUM

COFFEE

RUBBER

OIL

HATS

CACAO

ECUADOR

SILVER

RUBBER

COTTON

ALPACA

BRASIL

RICE

COPPER

VANADIUM

PERÚ

SUGAR

RUBBER

FISH

GOLD

TIN

HARD-WOODS

BOLIVIA

TOBACCO

ANTIMONY

FISH

SHEEP

TUNGSTEN

CATTLE

LEAD

NITRATE

PARAGUAY

CINCHONA

YERBA MATÉ

COTTON

GRAPES

COPPER

QUEBRACHO

IRON

CATTLE

FISH

WHEAT

CATTLE

CATTLE

CHILE

GOLD

FLAX

CORN

SHEEP

URUGUAY

SUGAR

FISH

IODINE

SHEEP

FRUIT

FISH

WHEAT

COPPER

SHEEP

ARGENTINA

SHEEP

OIL

FISH

1000 MILES

TRM

[169]

G. Chief Cities:

1. Ciudad de México. Capital of Mexico; one of the world's most beautiful and interesting cities former capital of the Aztec Indians, who called it Tenochtitlán.

2. La Habana. Capital of Cuba; a beautiful city with a fine harbor guarded by the famous Morro Castle, a fortress built by the Spaniards in colonial times.

3. Buenos Aires. Capital of Argentina; largest Spanish-speaking city in the world; one of the world's most modern and cosmopolitan capitals.

4. Lima. Capital of Peru; contains many interesting monuments of the Spanish colonial period founded by Pizarro, who called it La Ciudad de los Reyes (City of Kings).

5. Santiago. Capital of Chile; fourth largest city of South America; one of the world's most glamorous and delightful cities.

6. Valparaíso. Seaport in Chile; most important seaport on the western coast of South America.

7. La Paz. Capital of Bolivia; situated more than two miles above sea level; highest capital city in the world.

8. Bogotá. Capital of Colombia; noted as a cultural and intellectual center.

9. Quito. Capital of Ecuador; located a few miles from the equator; famous for the beauty and lavishness of its churches.

10. Montevideo. Capital of Uruguay; one of the most progressive cities of Latin America.

EXERCISES

A. **¿Sí o No?** If the statement is true, write **sí**; if it is false, write **no**.

1. El español es la lengua oficial de diez y ocho países de la América Latina.

2. La Argentina es el país más grande de habla española.

3. Dos productos principales de Cuba son el tabaco y el café.

4. Montevideo es una de las ciudades más progresistas de la América Española.

5. Lima es la capital de la Argentina.

6. Santiago es la capital de Colombia.

7. Valparaíso es un puerto importante de Chile.

8. Quito está situada cerca del ecuador (equator).

9. Costa Rica y Honduras exportan muchas bananas a los Estados Unidos.

10. El Salvador es el país más pequeño de la América Central.

B. Underline the word or expression that correctly completes the sentence.

1. Hay (seis, nueve, veinte) países de habla española en Sud América.

2. El español no es la lengua oficial del (Perú, Brasil, Ecuador).

3. El río más grande de Venezuela es (el Orinoco, el Magdalena, el Río de la Plata).

4. Los Andes están situados en (México, Sud América, Centro América).

5. El quetzal es un pájaro que se halla principalmente en (Guatemala, Chile, Bolivia).

6. (La llama, El caballo, El burro) es una bestia de carga (beast of burden) en las alturas de los Andes.

7. En Chile, la Argentina y el Uruguay hace frío en el mes de (diciembre, julio, enero).

8. Lima fué fundada (founded) por (Cortés, Pizarro, Coronado).

9. La ciudad más grande de la América Española es (Montevideo, Lima, Buenos Aires).

10. La capital más alta del mundo es (Quito, La Paz, Bogotá).

11. Un producto importante de Guatemala es (el chicle, el cacao, la tagua).

12. La carne de vaca (beef) y el trigo (wheat) son dos productos principales de (Costa Rica, la Argentina, Nicaragua).

13. Dos minerales importantes de Colombia son las esmeraldas y (el oro, el cobre, el platino).

14. El estaño (tin) viene principalmente de (Nicaragua, Venezuela, Bolivia).

15. Los nitratos y el cobre son dos minerales importantes de (Chile, México, Venezuela).

C. Match the following items.

Column I		Column II
_____ 1. Sierra Madre		a. río en Venezuela
_____ 2. tagua		b. Tenochtitlán
_____ 3. tapir		c. chocolate
_____ 4. Ciudad de México		d. alpaca
_____ 5. La Habana		e. montañas en México
_____ 6. Orinoco		f. Ciudad de los Reyes
_____ 7. Lima		g. botones
_____ 8. cacao		h. pájaro de los Andes
_____ 9. lana		i. Castillo del Morro
_____ 10. cóndor		j. animal

D. Complete the following sentences in Spanish.

1. _____ es el país más grande de la América Central.

2. _____ es la capital del Perú.

3. El Magdalena es un _____ en Colombia.

4. El armadillo es un _____ de Sud América.

5. El _____ es una persona de sangre (blood) india y española.

6. El puerto principal de Chile es _____.

7. El Río de la Plata está situado entre (between) _____.

8. La moneda (coin) de Guatemala se llama un _____.

9. En Sud América, el país más pequeño de habla española es _____.

10. Un país de Sud América que produce mucho petróleo es _____.

A. Points of Interest in Mexico:

1. Mexico City.

   a. Cathedral of Mexico. Largest and oldest cathedral on the American continent.

   b. Piedra del Sol. Aztec calendar stone.

   c. Zócalo. Main public square.

   d. Paseo de la Reforma. Main boulevard.

   e. Chapultepec. Large, beautiful park; contains a beautiful castle which now serves as a National Museum of History.

   f. Palacio Nacional. Government building; houses the offices of the Mexican President and other government officials.

   g. Palacio de Bellas Artes. A beautiful building of white marble containing the National Theater and art galleries. The theater is noted for its magnificent glass curtain.

   h. Ciudad Universitaria of the University of Mexico. One of the largest and most beautiful university campuses in the world.

   i. Popocatépetl and Ixtaccíhuatl. Picturesque volcanoes overlooking Mexico City.

   j. Xochimilco. Town near Mexico City noted for its floating gardens.

   k. San Juan Teotihuacán. Town near Mexico City noted for its pyramids.

2. Taxco. Most picturesque town of Mexico; still preserves its Spanish colonial atmosphere.

3. Acapulco. A seaside resort on the west coast noted for its beaches, hotels and villas.

4. Guadalajara. Second largest city of Mexico; noted for its colonial architecture, colorful plazas and beautiful pottery. Important industrial city.

B. Points of Interest in South and Central America:

1. Cartagena. A seaport in Colombia surrounded by fortifications built by the Spaniards to protect the city from pirates.
2. Cuzco. Ancient city in Peru; former capital of the Incas; contains many remains of the Inca civilization.
3. Lake Titicaca. Situated in the Andes Mountains between Bolivia and Peru; highest navigable lake in the world.
4. Iguazú Falls. Spectacular waterfalls between Argentina and Brazil; higher than Niagara Falls.
5. Aconcagua. Mountain peak in the Andes of Argentina; highest peak in the Western Hemisphere; reaches a height of more than 4 miles above sea level.
6. Cristo de los Andes. Giant statue of Christ located in the Andes on the border between Chile and Argentina; erected in commemoration of a peaceful settlement of a boundary dispute between these two nations.
7. Viña del Mar. Famous summer resort in Chile; noted for its beaches and casinos.
8. Punta del Este. Famous beach resort in Uruguay. Meeting place of an important Pan-American conference.
9. Teatro Colón. Famous opera house in Buenos Aires.
10. Avenida 9 de Julio. One of the widest boulevards in the world; located in Buenos Aires.
11. Pampas. Vast stretches of prairie land in Argentina; the cowboy of the pampas is called a gaucho.
12. Panama Canal. Man-made canal built by the United States; it connects the Atlantic and Pacific Oceans.

C. Interesting Facts:

1. Panama hats are not made in Panama, but in Ecuador, where they are called sombreros de jipijapa. They were given the name Panama hats by Americans, who first purchased them in Panama.
2. The highest standard-gauge railroad in the world is located in Peru. At one point it is more than three miles high. Thousands of lives were lost in its construction.
3. Some of the products which Latin America gave the world are potatoes, corn, tomatoes, peanuts, chocolate, vanilla, pineapples, pecans and cashew nuts.
4. The National University in Mexico City and the University of San Marcos in Lima, Peru, are the oldest universities on the American continent. They were founded in 1551, more than three-quarters of a century before the establishment of Harvard University, the oldest university in the United States.
5. Colombia is the only South American nation with seacoasts and major ports on both the Atlantic and Pacific Oceans.
6. Bolivia is the only country in South America without an outlet to the sea.
7. Buenos Aires is the only city in Latin America which has a subway.
8. Uruguay is the most progressive republic of Latin America. Many social reforms such as old-age pensions, accident insurance and the eight-hour work day were introduced in Uruguay before they were adopted in the United States.
9. Costa Rica is noted for its democratic government and its progressive system of education. The country boasts of having more school teachers than soldiers.
10. One of the Juan Fernández Islands off the coast of Chile was the setting for the *Adventures of Robinson Crusoe* by Daniel Defoe.
11. Bullfighting is especially popular in Mexico, Peru, Colombia and Venezuela, but is prohibited in some Spanish American countries.

D. Interesting Customs:

1. Las Posadas. Christmas celebrations in Mexico from December 16 to December 24; during the Posadas, Mexican children break the piñata, a gaily decorated earthen jar filled with candy, fruits and nuts.

[173]

2. Jarabe tapatío. National dance of Mexico; popularly referred to as the "Mexican Hat Dance"; it is performed by a man dressed in the costume of a charro (Mexican horseman), and a woman dressed in the costume of the china poblana (female companion of the charro).

3. Musical instruments found in most native Cuban orchestras are:
   a. Maracas. Gourds which contain dried seeds or pebbles, shaken in rhythm with the music.
   b. Claves. Two small round sticks which are struck against one another.
   c. Güiro. Gourd which is scraped with a rod.
   d. Bongó. Small drums fixed together by a bar of metal; played with the thumb and fingers.

4. Yerba mate. South American tea; it is sipped from a gourd (calabaza) through a small tube (bombilla); the typical tea of the gaucho.

EXERCISES

A. ¿Sí o No? If the statement is true, write sí; if it is false, write no.

1. Hay corridas de toros en todos los países de la América Latina. _____
2. Las playas de Acapulco, Viña del Mar y Punta del Este son famosas. _____
3. El Uruguay es más grande que los Estados Unidos. _____
4. La Universidad Nacional de México fué construida después de la Universidad de Harvard. _____
5. El Uruguay es un país muy progresista. _____
6. Bolivia tiene puertos en el Océano Atlántico y el Océano Pacífico. _____
7. Buenos Aires y la Ciudad de México tienen subterráneos (subways). _____
8. El ferrocarril más alto del mundo está situado en Chile. _____
9. Costa Rica tiene más profesores que soldados. _____
10. Guadalajara es la segunda ciudad de México. _____
11. Los sudamericanos beben yerba mate. _____
12. El jarabe tapatío es un baile cubano. _____

B. Underline the word or expression that correctly completes the sentence.

1. Popocatépetl e Ixtaccíhuatl son dos (pirámides, volcanes, pueblos indios).
2. Los sombreros de jipijapa se fabrican (are manufactured) en (el Ecuador, Panamá, el Perú).
3. La catedral más grande y más antigua de las Américas está situada en (Buenos Aires, Lima, la Ciudad de México).
4. El Zócalo es (una avenida, una plaza, un parque) en la Ciudad de México.
5. Cuzco fué la capital de los (incas, aztecas, mayas).
6. La construcción del Canal de Panamá fué terminada por los (franceses, españoles, norteamericanos).
7. El Aconcagua es (una montaña, un lago, una isla) de la Argentina.
8. (El Paseo de la Reforma, Chapultepec, La Piedra del Sol) es el nombre de un calendario azteca.
9. El Palacio de Bellas Artes es (un edificio de gobierno, un teatro y museo, un hotel para actores) de la Ciudad de México.
10. Las cataratas (waterfalls) del (Iguazú, Titicaca, Taxco) son más altas que las cataratas del Niágara.
11. Durante las Posadas los niños rompen (break) una (piedra, piñata, pelota).
12. Yerba mate es (una bebida, un instrumento músico, un baile) de Sud América.

C. Match the following items.

Column I

_____ **1.** Xochimilco

_____ **2.** pampas

_____ **3.** Chapultepec

_____ **4.** Cristo de los Andes

_____ **5.** San Juan Teotihuacán

_____ **6.** Teatro Colón

_____ **7.** Cartagena

_____ **8.** Titicaca

_____ **9.** Taxco

_____ **10.** Islas Juan Fernández

_____ **11.** charro

_____ **12.** maracas

Column II

a. lago

b. Robinson Crusoe

c. jardines flotantes

d. ópera

e. gaucho

f. fortificaciones

g. ciudad colonial

h. pirámides

i. estatua

j. parque

k. instrumento músico

l. china poblana

D. Complete the following sentences in Spanish.

1. _____ es la avenida principal de la Ciudad de México.

2. La Avenida _____ en Buenos Aires es una de las avenidas más anchas del mundo.

3. El Presidente de México tiene sus oficinas en _____.

4. La Ciudad Universitaria es una universidad grande y hermosa situada en _____.

5. _____ es el baile nacional de México.

6. Las Posadas se celebran en el mes de _____.

7. _____ es un producto que la América Latina dió al mundo.

8. _____ es el único (only) país de Sud América que no tiene salida (outlet) al mar.

9. _____ es la única nación sudamericana que tiene costas en el Océano Atlántico y el Océano Pacífico.

10. La Universidad de San Marcos está situada en _____.

E. Identify the following in English.

1. Acapulco _____

2. Popocatépetl _____

3. Chapultepec _____

4. Iguazú _____

5. Paseo de la Reforma _____

6. Titicaca _____

7. Las Posadas _____

8. Piedra del Sol _____

9. Taxco _____

10. pampas _____

Civilization Lesson 4—FAMOUS NAMES IN SPANISH AMERICA

A. National Heroes:

1. Simón Bolívar (1783–1830).

   a. Venezuelan general who fought for South American independence.
   b. Liberated the northern part of South America.
   c. Known as "El Libertador" and the "George Washington of South America."
   d. Country of Bolivia named in his honor.

2. José de San Martín (1778–1850).

   a. Argentine general who fought for South American independence.
   b. Liberated the southern part of South America.

3. Bernardo O'Higgins (1778–1842). Chilean general who aided San Martín in the liberation of Chile; the first president of liberated Chile.

4. Miguel Hidalgo (1753–1811). Mexican priest and patriot who began the struggle for Mexican independence.

5. Benito Juárez (1806–1872).

   a. Famous president of Mexico.
   b. Called the "Abraham Lincoln of Mexico."

6. José Martí (1853–1895). Famous poet and patriot who died fighting for Cuban independence.

B. Writers:

1. Rubén Darío (1867–1916).

   a. Greatest poet of Spanish America.
   b. Introduced a new style in poetry called modernismo.

2. Domingo Sarmiento (1811–1888).

   a. Argentine educator, statesman and president.
   b. Known as the "Schoolmaster President."
   c. Author of *Facundo*, which deals with the life of a gaucho leader and his influence on Argentine life.

3. Andrés Bello (1781–1865).

   a. One of the outstanding intellectuals of Latin America.
   b. An authority on Spanish grammar and international law.
   c. Author of *Gramática Castellana*.

4. José Hernández (1834–1886). Author of the epic poem *Martín Fierro*, one of the best works written about the life and customs of the gaucho.

5. José Enrique Rodó (1872–1918).

   a. One of the most notable essayists of Spanish America.
   b. Author of *Ariel*, an essay in which he compares the civilization of Spanish America with that of the United States.

6. Ricardo Palma (1833–1919). Author of *Tradiciones Peruanas*, a collection of historical anecdotes portraying life in Peru during colonial times.

7. Ricardo Güiraldes (1886–1927).

   a. Argentine novelist.
   b. Author of *Bon Segundo Sombra*, a novel which idealizes the life and character of the gaucho.

8. José Eustasio Rivera (1889–1929).

   a. Famous Colombian novelist.
   b. Author of *La Vorágine*, a novel portraying the lives of cruelly exploited natives toiling on rubber plantations in the Colombian jungles.

9. Mariano Azuela (1873–1952).

   a. Mexican novelist.
   b. Author of *Los de Abajo*, one of the best novels of the Mexican Revolution of 1910–1920.

10. Rómulo Gallegos (1884–   ).

   a. Famous Venezuelan novelist.
   b. Author of *Doña Bárbara*, a tale of life on the llanos (prairies) of Venezuela.

11. Gabriela Mistral (1889–1957).

   a. Famous Chilean poetess.
   b. Winner of the Nobel Prize for Literature in 1945.

C. Artists:

1. Diego Rivera (Mexican mural painter).

2. José Orozco (Mexican mural painter).

D. Composers and Musicians:

1. Carlos Chávez (Mexican composer and conductor).

2. Ernesto Lecuona (Cuban composer).

3. Claudio Arrau (Chilean pianist).

4. Manuel Ponce (Mexican composer).

E. Scientists:

1. Carlos Finlay.

   a. Cuban physician and scientist.
   b. First person to discover that yellow fever is transmitted by the mosquito.

2. Bernardo Houssay.

   a. Argentine physiologist and physician.
   b. Winner of Nobel Prize in Physiology and Medicine.
   c. First South American scientist to receive this honor.

EXERCISES

A. Identify each of the following as a national hero, writer, artist, composer, musician or scientist.

1. Miguel Hidalgo	11. José Enrique Rodó ....
2. Andrés Bello	12. Ernesto Lecuona ....
3. Carlos Finlay	13. Mariano Azuela ....
4. José Martí	14. Simón Bolívar ....
5. Diego Rivera	15. Rómulo Gallegos ....
6. Carlos Chávez	16. Domingo Sarmiento ....
7. Rubén Darío	17. Manuel Ponce ....
8. Bernardo Houssay	18. José Hernández ....
9. José de San Martín	19. José Orozco ....
10. Gabriela Mistral	20. Bernardo O'Higgins ....

B. Underline the name that correctly completes each sentence.

1. (Benito Juárez, Miguel Hidalgo, José de San Martín) se llama el "Abrahán Lincoln de México."

2. (*Martín Fierro, Ariel, La Vorágine*) es un poema que trata de (deals with) la vida de un gaucho.

3. (Ricardo Palma, Rubén Darío, Ricardo Güiraldes) es el poeta más famoso de Hispanoamérica.

4. (Simón Bolívar, José de San Martín, José Martí) se llama "El Libertador."

5. (*Doña Bárbara, Facundo, Los de Abajo*) es una de las mejores novelas de la revolución mexicana.

6. Miguel Hidalgo fué un cura que luchó (fought) por la independencia de (Cuba, México, Chile).

7. (Claudio Arrau, José Eustasio Rivera, Ernesto Lecuona) es un famoso pianista chileno.

8. Bernardo O'Higgins fué un general chileno que ayudó a (Bolívar, San Martín, Martí) en la Guerra de la Independencia.

9. Diego Rivera fué un famoso (músico, novelista, pintor).

10. (Gabriela Mistral, Bernardo Houssay, José Enrique Rodó) ganó el Premio Nobel de Literatura.

C. Match the following items.

Column I	Column II
_____ 1. Sarmiento	*a.* patriota cubano
_____ 2. Finlay	*b.* modernismo
_____ 3. San Martín	*c.* Premio Nobel de Medicina
_____ 4. Rodó	*d.* gramática
_____ 5. Bolívar	*e.* pintor mexicano
_____ 6. Orozco	*f.* Schoolmaster President
_____ 7. Houssay	*g.* ensayista famoso
_____ 8. Martí	*h.* general argentino
_____ 9. Bello	*i.* fiebre amarilla
_____ 10. Darío	*j.* George Washington of South America

D. In each of the following, write the name of a famous Spanish-American.

1. un novelista hispanoamericano _____

2. un educador argentino _____

3. un poeta hispanoamericano _____

4. una poetisa (poetess) hispanoamericana _____

5. un pintor mexicano _____

6. un compositor mexicano _____

7. un hombre de ciencia de Hispanoamérica _____

8. el autor de *Don Segundo Sombra* _____

9. el autor de *Doña Bárbara* _____

10. el autor de *Facundo* _____

MASTERY EXERCISES ON SPANISH AMERICA

Underline the word or expression that correctly completes the sentence.

1. El baile nacional de México es (el tango, el jarabe tapatío, la rumba).

2. La ciudad más grande de habla española es (Buenos Aires, Lima, Montevideo).

3. Uno de los lagos más altos del mundo se llama (Orinoco, Iguazú, Titicaca).

4. Diego Rivera fué un (pintor, autor, músico) mexicano.

5. Los antiguos habitantes de México fueron los (mestizos, incas, aztecas).

6. La primera universidad de Sud América fué establecida en (Buenos Aires, Lima, Quito).

7. El poeta más famoso de Hispanoamérica es (José Martí, Rubén Darío, Domingo Sarmiento).

8. En Hispanoamérica muchas casas tienen un (jaguar, güiro, patio).

9. Entre Chile y la Argentina está la famosa estatua de (San Marcos, Cristo de los Andes, Viña del Mar).

10. (La Paz, Montevideo, Bogotá) es la capital de Bolivia.

11. (Bolívar, Martí, Hidalgo) se llama "el Jorge Washington de Sud América."

12. La capital de la Argentina es (Santiago, Buenos Aires, Lima).

13. Un producto importante de Chile es (el hierro, los nitratos, la plata).

14. (Coronado, Ponce de León, San Martín) buscó las "siete ciudades de Cíbola."

15. Un volcán famoso de México es (el Aconcagua, Popocatépetl, Sierra Nevada).

16. (Cartagena, Guadalajara, Acapulco), en la costa mexicana, es célebre por sus playas y hoteles hermosos.

17. Un héroe importante de la Argentina fué (San Martín, Juárez, Hidalgo).

18. (Balboa, Cabeza de Vaca, Ponce de León) descubrió la Florida.

19. Las pampas están situadas en (la Argentina, Chile, el Perú).

20. El (cobre, azúcar, oro) es un producto importante de Cuba.

21. (Carlos Finlay, José Orozco, Carlos Chávez) es un director de orquesta mexicano.

22. (Gabriela Mistral, Ricardo Güiraldes, Mariano Azuela) ganó el Premio Nebol.

23. La capital del Uruguay es (Asunción, Santiago, Montevideo).

24. Un país que produce mucho estaño (tin) es (Bolivia, Chile, Venezuela).

25. La llama vive en (los Andes, las pampas, Centro América).

26. El producto más importante de Venezuela es (el chicle, el petróleo, la plata).

27. Miguel Hidalgo comenzó la revolución para ganar la independencia de (Chile, el Perú, México).

28. Un país de Sud América que no tiene costa de mar es (el Uruguay, Bolivia, el Ecuador).

29. (Andrés Bello, Domingo Sarmiento, José Enrique Rodó) escribió una gramática de la lengua española.

30. Se usa la bombilla para tomar (yerba mate, tortillas, tacos).

31. La capital del Perú es (Bogotá, La Paz, Lima).

32. Pizarro fundó a (Bogotá, Buenos Aires, Lima).

33. El pico más elevado de Sud América es (Aconcagua, Ixtaccíhuatl, Sierra Madre).

34. José Orozco es un pintor de (México, Venezuela, Chile).

35. El Castillo de Chapultepec se halla en (Buenos Aires, la Ciudad de México, la Habana).

36. José Martí fué un gran patriota de (Cuba, México, Venezuela).

37. Valparaíso es un puerto de (Colombia, Chile, la Argentina).

38. Un presidente famoso de México fué (Benito Juárez, Andrés Bello, Domingo Sarmiento).

39. (Colombia, La Argentina, Venezuela) exporta mucho trigo y carne de vaca.

40. El Camino Real se halla en el estado de (Arizona, California, Nevada).

41. El río Magdalena está en (Colombia, México, Venezuela).

42. El descubridor del río Misisipí fué (Balboa, De Soto, Cabrillo).

43. En la ciudad de Tenochtitlán vivían los (aztecas, incas, mayas).

44. El armadillo es un (animal, instrumento, mineral) de Sud América.

45. (Balboa, Coronado, Cabeza de Vaca) descubrió el Gran Cañón de Colorado.

46. Bernardo O'Higgins fué un gran héroe de (Cuba, Chile, Venezuela).

47. El estado de los Estados Unidos que tiene muchas misiones españolas es (Texas, Nuevo México, California).

48. (Santa Fe, San Antonio, San Agustín) es la ciudad más vieja de los Estados Unidos.

49. El país de la América del Sur que tiene puertos en dos océanos es (Colombia, Venezuela, la Argentina).

50. El (quetzal, cóndor, guanaco) es un pájaro de Guatemala.

Civilization Lesson 5—SPAIN, THE LAND

A. Location:

    1. Situated in the southwestern part of Europe.

    2. Occupies four-fifths of the Iberian Peninsula (Spain and Portugal).

B. Size and Population:

    1. About 200,000 square miles (approximately four times the size of New York State).

    2. Third largest country in Europe.

    3. More than 30,000,000 inhabitants.

C. Boundaries:

    1. North: France and Bay of Biscay (Mar Cantábrico).

    2. East: Mediterranean Sea.

    3. South: Mediterranean Sea and Atlantic Ocean.

    4. West: Portugal and Atlantic Ocean.

D. Mountains:

1. Los Pirineos (northeast). Separate Spain from France.
2. Los Montes Cantábricos (northwest).
3. La Sierra de Guadarrama (center). Near Madrid.
4. La Sierra Morena (south).
5. La Sierra Nevada (near the southern coast).

E. Rivers:

1. El Ebro (north). Flows into the Mediterranean.
2. El Duero (north). Flows into the Atlantic.
3. El Tajo (center). Longest river; flows into the Atlantic.
4. El Guadiana (south). Flows into the Atlantic.
5. El Guadalquivir (south). Deepest and most navigable river; flows into the Atlantic; the cities of Sevilla and Córdoba are on its banks.

F. Outlying Possessions:

1. Las Islas Baleares. A group of islands in the Mediterranean which have become a popular resort area; Mallorca is the largest island of the group.

2. Las Islas Canarias. A group of islands in the Atlantic, off the coast of Africa.

3. Several overseas provinces and possessions in Africa.

G. Important Products:

1. Spain is essentially an agricultural country.

2. Main crops are olives, oranges, grapes, rice, almonds, cork.

   a. Spain occupies third place in Europe in the production of wine.
   b. Wines of Málaga and Jerez (sherry) are world famous.
   c. Spain is also a leading producer of olive oil.

3. Mineral resources are coal, iron, mercury, lead, copper.

H. Regions of Spain: Politically, Spain and its possessions are divided into 54 provinces. Historically, Spain is divided into 13 regions.

1. Galicia (northwest).
2. Asturias (north).
3. Las Provincias Vascongadas (north; bordering the Pyrenees).
4. Navarra (north).
5. Aragón (northeast).
6. Cataluña (northeast).
7. León (northwest).
8. Castilla la Vieja (north and center).
9. Castilla la Nueva (center).
10. Valencia (east).
11. Extremadura (west).
12. Murcia (southeast).
13. Andalucía (south).

I. Principal Cities and Points of Interest:

1. Madrid.
   a. Capital and largest city of Spain.
   b. Modern, cosmopolitan city.
   c. El Prado, famous art museum.
   d. El Escorial (near Madrid), monastery, palace, library and burial place of Spanish kings, built in 1584 by Philip II.

2. Barcelona.
   a. Second largest city.
   b. Chief industrial city.
   c. Most important seaport on the Mediterranean Sea.

3. Valencia.
   a. Third largest city.
   b. Leading export center for oranges.

4. Málaga.
   a. Important seaport and resort on the Mediterranean.
   b. Famous for its wine.

5. Sevilla.
   a. Colorful and romantic city, located on the Guadalquivir River.
   b. La Catedral de Sevilla, largest cathedral in Spain.
   c. La Giralda, Moorish bell tower of the Cathedral.
   d. El Alcázar, ancient Moorish palace.

6. Bilbao.
   a. Industrial town famous for its iron and steel industry.
   b. Known as the "Pittsburgh of Spain."

7. Cádiz.
   a. Seaport on the Atlantic Ocean.
   b. Founded by the Phoenicians over 3000 years ago, it is one of the oldest cities in Europe.

8. Córdoba.
   a. Ancient Moorish city, located on the Guadalquivir River.
   b. La Mezquita (Mosque), a famous Moorish temple now used as a cathedral.

9. Granada.
   a. Picturesque Moorish city, situated at the foot of the Sierra Nevada Mountains.
   b. The last city in Spain held by the Moors; recaptured by Christians in 1492.
   c. La Alhambra, ancient Moorish palace.

10. Toledo.
   a. Famous medieval city, located on the Tajo River.
   b. Contains many artistic and historical treasures.

11. San Sebastián and Santander.
   a. Fashionable summer resorts on the northern coast of Spain.
   b. Famous for their beaches.

EXERCISES

A. **¿Sí o No?** If the statement is true, write **sí**; if it is false, write **no**.

1. Los Pirineos separan a España de Francia. _____

2. El Mar Mediterráneo está situado al oeste de España. _____

3. El Ebro es el único río grande de España que desemboca en (flows into) el Mar Mediterráneo. _____

4. España y Portugal forman la Península Ibérica. _____

5. San Sebastián y Santander están en el sur de España. _____

6. Barcelona y Málaga son puertos importantes del Atlántico. _____

7. España es principalmente un país industrial. _____

8. La catedral más grande de España está en Sevilla. _____

9. España tiene más de treinta millones de habitantes. _____

10. Cataluña y Aragón son dos ciudades de España. _____

B. Underline the word or expression that best completes the sentence.

1. (La Alhambra, La Giralda, La Mezquita) es un palacio moro en Granada.

2. Las Islas (Baleares, Canarias, Juan Fernández) son posesiones de España en el Atlántico.

3. (El Duero, El Guadiana, El Guadalquivir) es el río más navegable de España.

4. España es (más grande que, menos grande que, tan grande como) el Estado de Nueva York.

5. España está dividida aproximadamente en (cincuenta, trece, quince) provincias.

6. (Andalucía, Asturias, Galicia) es una región del sur de España.

7. (La Sierra Morena, La Sierra Nevada, La Sierra de Guadarrama) está situada en la parte central de España.

8. Valencia es famosa por sus (minerales, naranjas, vinos).

9. (El Prado, El Escorial, El Alcázar) es un famoso museo de arte en Madrid.

10. (Cádiz, Córdoba, Toledo) es célebre (famous) por su mezquita.

C. Match the following items.

	Column I	Column II
_____	1. Cádiz	a. templo moro
_____	2. La Mezquita	b. río de España
_____	3. Bilbao	c. vino
_____	4. La Giralda	d. Islas Baleares
_____	5. Asturias	e. palacio moro
_____	6. El Tajo	f. antigua ciudad fenicia
_____	7. Mallorca	g. torre mora
_____	8. Jerez	h. ciudad medieval
_____	9. El Alcázar	i. Pittsburgh of Spain
_____	10. Toledo	j. región de España

D. Complete the following sentences in Spanish.

1. _____ es la capital de España.

2. _____ es el río más largo de España.

3. _____ son islas del Mediterráneo que pertenecen (belong) a España.

4. _____ es una región de la parte central de España.

5. La ciudad de _____ es famosa por su vino.

6. _____ es la ciudad industrial más importante de España.

7. Los reyes españoles están enterrados (buried) en _____.

8. La ciudad de _____, situada en el norte de España, es famosa por sus playas.

9. _____ es un puerto español del Atlántico.

10. Las ciudades de Sevilla y Córdoba están situadas a orillas (on the shores) del río_____

E. Identify the following in English.

1. Granada _____

2. El Ebro _____

3. Santander _____

4. El Prado _____

5. Iberian Peninsula _____

6. Toledo _____

7. El Escorial _____

8. Extremadura _____

9. La Giralda _____

10. Los Pirineos _____

Civilization Lesson 6—SPAIN, THE PEOPLE

A. Early Inhabitants:

1. Los iberos (Iberians). First inhabitants of Spain.

2. Los celtas (Celts). Mingled with Iberians to form the Celtiberian or Spanish race.

3. Los fenicios (Phoenicians).

   a. Established trading posts on southern coast of Spain.
   b. Founded the city of Cádiz about 1100 B.C.

4. Los griegos (Greeks). Founded colonies on eastern coast of Spain about the 8th century B.C.

5. Los cartagineses (Carthaginians).

   a. Defeated the Celtiberians and invaded Spain in the 3rd century B.C.
   b. Founded the city of Cartagena, a port on the Mediterranean Sea.

6. Los romanos (Romans).

   a. Defeated the Carthaginians in 201 B.C.
   b. Ruled Spain for six centuries.
   c. Built aqueducts, bridges and roads.
   d. Romans spoke Latin, from which the Spanish language is derived.

7. Los visigodos (Visigoths). Germanic tribe which defeated the Romans in 409 A.D. and invaded Spain.

8. Los moros (Moors).

   a. Defeated the Visigoths in the years 711–713 A.D.
   b. Ruled large areas of Spain for more than seven centuries.
   c. Built palaces, mosques (Moorish temples) and homes with patios.
   d. Established an irrigation system by means of waterwheels (norias).
   e. Contributed many Arabic words to the Spanish language. Most of these begin with **al** (álgebra, algodón, alcalde).
   f. Driven out by the Spaniards in 1492.

B. Modern Spaniards:

1. Los castellanos (Castilians).

   a. Inhabitants of the regions of Castilla la Vieja and Castilla la Nueva.
   b. Consider themselves the true Spaniards because their ancestors drove out the Moors and unified Spain.
   c. Their language, el castellano, is the official language of Spain.

2. Los catalanes (Catalonians).

   a. Inhabitants of the region of Cataluña.
   b. People of great commercial and industrial ability.
   c. Besides Spanish, they speak catalán, the traditional language of the region.
   d. Cataluña has tried several times to break away from Spain and set up a separate government.

3. Los vascos (Basques).

   a. Inhabitants of Las Provincias Vascongadas (Basque Provinces).
   b. Origin of the Basques is unknown. They are said to be descendants of the early Iberians.
   c. Basques are great sailors and fishermen, and are noted for feats of strength and skill.
   d. El vascuence is the regional language spoken by the Basques.
   e. Because of their reputation as hard-working people, many Basque shepherds have been brought into our western states.

4. Los andaluces (Andalusians).

   a. Inhabitants of the region of Andalucía.
   b. Most picturesque people of Spain; noted for their wit and charm, and fondness for music and dancing.
   c. Life and customs show influence of Moorish occupation.

5. Los gallegos (Galicians).

    a. Inhabitants of the region of Galicia.

    b. Descendants of the early Celts.

    c. Hard-working people, many of whom emigrated to foreign lands because of the poverty in which they lived.

    d. Besides Spanish, they speak gallego, a dialect which closely resembles Portuguese.

C. Picturesque Spanish Types:

1. Sereno (night watchman). Patrols the houses in his district; carries a lantern and a bunch of keys; opens the door for those who come home in the late hours of the evening.

2. Mendigo (beggar). Often called pordiosero because he asks for alms (limosna) in the name of God (por Dios).

3. Gitano (gypsy). Found in southern part of Spain; Spanish gypsies have a reputation for being shrewd fortune tellers and nimble dancers.

4. Aguador (water seller). Obtains water from mountain springs and sells it to the people of the towns.

5. Lavandera (washerwoman). Can be seen in small towns washing clothes at the banks of a stream.

D. Religion:

1. Most people of Spain are Roman Catholics.

E. Government:

1. Dictatorship under the rule of General Francisco Franco.

2. Spanish parliament called Las Cortes.

3. Falange, the only political party permitted in Spain.

EXERCISES

A. Underline the word or expression that correctly completes the sentence.

1. El español se deriva del (latín, portugués, catalán).

2. Los gallegos son descendientes de los (iberos, celtas, griegos).

3. Los (romanos, cartagineses, moros) construyeron casas con patios.

4. Muchas palabras españolas que comienzan con "al" son de origen (portugués, griego, árabe).

5. La mayor parte de los españoles son (católicos, protestantes, romanos).

6. El general Francisco Franco es el (rey, presidente, dictador) de España.

7. Los habitantes de Castilla la Vieja y Castilla la Nueva se llaman (vascos, castellanos, catalanes).

8. Los moros tuvieron una gran influencia en la vida y costumbres de los (gallegos, andaluces, catalanes).

9. El origen de los (españoles, romanos, vascos) es incierto (uncertain).

10. La lengua oficial de España es el (castellano, catalán, vascuence).

B. Match the following items.

Column I	Column II
_____ **1.** noria	*a.* washerwoman
_____ **2.** Las Cortes	*b.* night watchman
_____ **3.** pordiosero	*c.* Cádiz
_____ **4.** Falange	*d.* early Spaniards
_____ **5.** fenicios	*e.* gypsy
_____ **6.** sereno	*f.* Moorish waterwheel
_____ **7.** gitano	*g.* Spanish parliament
_____ **8.** lavandera	*h.* water seller
_____ **9.** celtíberos	*i.* political party
_____ **10.** aguador	*j.* mendigo

C. If the statement is true, write TRUE in the space provided. If the statement is false, make it true by changing the incorrect word in italics.

1. Los *celtas* _____ fueron los primeros habitantes de España.

2. Los cartagineses fundaron (founded) la ciudad de *Cádiz* _____.

3. Los *cartagineses* _____ construyeron acueductos, puentes y caminos en España.

4. Los *romanos* _____ vencieron (conquered) a los cartagineses.

5. Los españoles expulsaron (drove out) de España a los *visigodos* _____ en 1492.

6. Los moros gobernaron en España por *dos* _____ siglos.

7. Los catalanes son los habitantes de *Castilla* _____.

8. Los habitantes más pintorescos de España son los *andaluces* _____.

9. Los *catalanes* _____ son buenos hombres de negocios (businessmen).

10. El parlamento español se llama *Falange* _____.

D. Complete the following sentences in Spanish.

1. Muchos pastores (shepherds), que trabajan en el oeste de los Estados Unidos, han venido de
_____.

2. _____ dominaron a España por seis siglos.

3. Los visigodos vencieron a los _____.

4. Los moros vencieron a los _____.

5. Los _____ piden limosna.

6. Los gallegos viven en la región de _____.

7. Los habitantes de las Provincias Vascongadas hablan el _____, además del (besides) español.

8. Los gitanos viven en el _____ de España.

9. La ciudad más industrial de España es _____.

10. Los _____ se consideran los verdaderos españoles.

[189]

Civilization Lesson 7—FAMOUS PEOPLE OF SPAIN

A. Heroes:

1. Pelayo.

    a. Began the Reconquista (reconquest) of Spain from the Moors.
    b. Defeated the Moors at the Battle of Covadonga in 718.

2. Rodrigo Díaz de Vivar.

    a. National hero of Spain.
    b. Continued the struggle against the Moors.
    c. Nicknamed El Cid ("Lord") by the Moors.

B. Rulers:

1. Fernando e Isabel.

    a. Known as Los Reyes Católicos.
    b. Completed the reconquest of Spain by driving out the Moors in 1492.
    c. Aided Columbus in the discovery of America.

2. Carlos V.

    a. Grandson of Ferdinand and Isabella.
    b. During his reign, Spain had possessions in Germany, Austria, Italy, the Netherlands and America.

3. Felipe II.

    a. Son of Charles V.
    b. Involved Spain in long, costly wars.
    c. His "Armada Invencible" was defeated by an English fleet under Drake in 1588.

C. Conquerors:

1. Cortés.

    a. Conquered Mexico in 1519.
    b. Defeated the Aztec Indians under Montezuma.

2. Pizarro.

    a. Conquered Peru in 1532.
    b. Defeated the Inca Indians under Atahualpa.

D. Writers:

1. Cervantes (1547–1616).

    a. Spain's greatest novelist.
    b. Author of the world-famous novel, *Don Quijote de la Mancha*.

2. Lope de Vega (1562–1635).

    a. Spain's leading dramatist.
    b. Founder of the Spanish national drama.

3. Calderón (1600–1681).

    a. Famous dramatist, known for his philosophical plays.
    b. Most famous work is *La Vida es Sueño*.

4. Pérez Galdós (1845–1920).

    a. Most famous novelist of Spain in the 19th century.
    b. Greatest Spanish novelist since Cervantes.

5. Blasco Ibáñez (1867–1928).

    a. Famous novelist.
    b. Author of *Los Cuatro Jinetes del Apocalipsis* (The Four Horsemen of the Apocalypse) and *Sangre y Arena* (Blood and Sand), which were filmed in Hollywood.

6. Jacinto Benavente (1866–1954).

    a. Famous dramatist.

    b. Winner of the Nobel Prize for Literature in 1922.

7. Juan Ramón Jiménez (1881–1958).

    a. Famous contemporary poet.

    b. Received the Nobel Prize for Literature in 1956.

. Painters:

1. El Greco (1548–1625).

    a. Greek painter who settled in Toledo in the 16th century.

    b. His paintings portray intense religious emotion.

2. Velázquez (1599–1660). Spain's greatest painter of portraits.

3. Goya (1746–1828).

    a. Greatest Spanish painter of the 18th and 19th centuries.

    b. His work portrays the degraded society of 18th and 19th century Spain.

4. Picasso (1881–   ).

    a. Contemporary Spanish painter who makes southern France his home.

    b. Creator of a movement in modern painting called cubism.

. Composers and Musicians:

1. Isaac Albéniz. Composed music for piano.

2. Manuel de Falla. Spain's greatest composer and foremost representative of contemporary Spanish music.

3. José Iturbi. Pianist, composer and guest conductor with leading American symphony orchestras.

4. Andrés Segovia. Guitarist; has given many recitals in the United States.

5. Pablo Casals. Violoncellist (cellist); has achieved international fame for his musical accomplishments.

. Scientists:

1. Santiago Ramón y Cajal. Physician and leader in medical research; received the Nobel Prize for Medicine in 1906.

2. Juan de la Cierva. Engineer; inventor of the autogiro, the forerunner of the helicopter.

. Dancers:

1. Vicente Escudero. Considered Spain's greatest male dancer; greatest interpreter of flamenco dancing.

2. Carmen Amaya. Spanish gypsy dancer; prominent female dancer (died 1963).

EXERCISES

A. Underline the word or expression that correctly completes the sentence.

1. El novelista más famoso de España es (Pérez Galdós, Cervantes, Blasco Ibáñez).

2. (Cortés, Pizarro, Pelayo) conquistó a los incas.

3. El héroe nacional de España es (El Cid, Calderón, El Greco).

4. El compositor más célebre de España es (Isaac Albéniz, Pablo Casals, Manuel de Falla).

5. El pintor más importante de España en el siglo diez y ocho fué (Goya, Velázquez, Picasso).

6. El gran maestro de la guitarra es (Segovia, Escudero, Casals).

7. (Ramón y Cajal, Juan de la Cierva, Benavente) inventó el autogiro.

8. Felipe II fué el hijo de (Carlos V, los Reyes Católicos, El Cid).

9. Lope de Vega fué un famoso (novelista, dramaturgo, pintor) español.

10. Juan Ramón Jiménez fué un famoso (poeta, músico, bailarín) español.

B. Match the following.

Column I	*Column II*
------- 1. Fernando e Isabel	*a.* Don Quijote de la Mancha
------- 2. Atahualpa	*b.* Rodrigo Díaz de Vivar
------- 3. Felipe II	*c.* violoncelista
------- 4. Pablo Casals	*d.* aztecas
------- 5. Pelayo	*e.* Premio Nobel
------- 6. Cervantes	*f.* Los Reyes Católicos
------- 7. Benavente	*g.* cubismo
------- 8. El Cid	*h.* Covadonga
------- 9. Picasso	*i.* incas
------- 10. Cortés	*j.* Armada Invencible

C. Complete the following sentences in Spanish.

1. _____ fué un pintor famoso de España.

2. _____ expulsaron a los moros de España.

3. Moctezuma fué el emperador de los _____.

4. _____ fué el novelista más famoso de España en el siglo diez y nueve.

5. *Sangre y Arena* fué escrita por _____.

6. El autor de *La Vida es Sueño* fué _____.

7. Un pintor griego que vivió en España en el siglo diez y seis fué _____.

8. _____ es un famoso guitarrista español.

9. _____ fué un famoso médico español que ganó el Premio Nobel.

10. _____ es un famoso pianista, compositor y director de orquesta.

D. Underline the item that does not belong in each group.

1. Calderón, Lope de Vega, Rodrigo Díaz de Vivar, Benavente

2. Velázquez, Blasco Ibáñez, Goya, El Greco, Picasso

3. Pizarro, Perú, incas, Atahualpa, Cortés

4. Pelayo, Reconquista, moros, Felipe II, Los Reyes Católicos

5. Benavente, Juan Ramón Jiménez, Premio Nobel, Pérez Galdós, Ramón y Cajal

6. Manuel de Falla, Cervantes, Blasco Ibáñez, Pérez Galdós

Civilization Lesson 8—SPANISH LIFE AND CUSTOMS

A. Family Life:

1. Spanish family names.
    a. Spanish people have two family names, the family name of the father followed by the maiden name of the mother, often joined by **y**. Example: Pedro Ortega (y) Gómez. This is sometimes shortened to Pedro Ortega by omitting the mother's family name.
    b. When a woman marries, she retains her family name and takes on the family name of her husband, which is preceded by **de**. Example: Elena López de Ortega.
2. El día del santo.
    a. The given name of most Spanish children is the name of a saint.
    b. Spanish children generally celebrate their saint's day (el día del santo) instead of their birthday (el cumpleaños).

B. Social Customs:

1. El café. Coffee house frequented by men who gather there to meet friends, to discuss current topics, to play cards or dominoes and to partake of such light refreshments as coffee, wine and liqueur.
2. La tertulia. Informal social gathering for the purpose of entertaining and chatting with friends.
3. Pelando la pava. Courting one's sweetheart by speaking to her through the reja or window grille.
4. Siesta. Afternoon nap or rest following the noon meal.
5. La lotería. Government-controlled lottery; tickets may be purchased from street vendors or in special stores; drawings are held regularly throughout the year.

C. Religious Life:

1. Navidad (Christmas).
    a. Nochebuena. Christmas Eve.
    b. Misa del Gallo. Midnight Mass.
    c. Villancicos. Christmas carols.
    d. Nacimiento. Cardboard or clay figures representing the scene of the birth of Christ; Christmas trees are not widely used.
    e. Día de los Reyes Magos. Religious holiday celebrated on January 6; Spanish children receive their Christmas gifts on this day; the Magi kings (The Three Wise Men), called "Los Reyes Magos," play the same role in Spanish life as Santa Claus does in ours.
2. Carnaval. Spanish Mardi Gras; celebrated the last three days before Lent (Cuaresma).
3. Semana Santa. Holy Week is the week before Easter (Pascua Florida); this holiday is observed in Seville with impressive and elaborate ceremonies.
4. Verbena. An evening festival in honor of a patron saint.
5. Romería. A pilgrimage, accompanied by picnicking, to the shrine of a patron saint.
6. Día de los Difuntos (All Souls' Day). Memorial day for all the dead, observed November 2; cemeteries are visited and flowers placed on the graves of relatives and friends.

D. National Holidays:

1. Dos de Mayo. Commemorates the resistance of the Spanish people to Napoleonic rule (1808).
2. Día de la Raza. Columbus Day, October 12.

E. Sports and Spectacles:

1. Corrida de toros (bullfight).
    a. Plaza de toros. Bull ring.
    b. Torero. The general term for a bullfighter.
       (1) Picador. Bullfighter on horseback who uses a pike or lance.
       (2) Banderillero. Bullfighter who sticks darts into the bull's neck.
       (3) Matador. Bullfighter who kills the bull with a sword.

2. Jai-alai (also called pelota).

    a. Basque game somewhat similar to handball.

    b. Frontón. Three-walled court on which jai-alai is played.

    c. Cesta. Curved racket strapped to the player's wrist in which the ball is caught and thrown against the wall.

3. Fútbol (Spanish word for soccer). A very popular sport in Spain and Spanish America.

F. Dances:

1. Bolero, fandango, flamenco (Andalucía). Generally accompanied by guitar.
2. Jota (Aragón). A dance of northern Spain.
3. Sardana (Cataluña). A circle dance.

G. Musical Instruments:

1. Guitarra (guitar).
2. Castañuelas (castanets).

H. Foods (Platos):

1. Cocido (stew).
2. Paella. A dish of rice with chicken and seafood.
3. Arroz con pollo. Chicken and rice; popular in Spain and Spanish America.

I. Beverages:

1. Chocolate. Thick hot chocolate served for breakfast.
2. Horchata. Cold drink of crushed almonds, water and sugar.

J. Clothing:

1. Mantilla. Silk lace scarf worn by women as a headdress.
2. Peineta. High shell comb worn with the mantilla.

EXERCISES

A. Underline the word or expression that correctly completes the sentence.

1. La fiesta nacional de España se celebra (el dos de mayo, el doce de octubre, el dos de noviembre).

2. Los niños españoles reciben sus regalos de Navidad (el diez y seis de diciembre, el veinticuatro de diciembre, el seis de enero).

3. La ciudad de (Valencia, Sevilla, Granada) es famosa por sus ceremonias religiosas durante la Semana Santa.

4. Los españoles visitan los cementerios el (Día de los Difuntos, día del santo, Día de la Raza).

5. La lotería es controlada por (la iglesia, el gobierno, los mendigos).

6. El jai-alai se juega en (un frontón, una plaza de toros, un café).

7. Un plato popular de España se llama (sardana, paella, romería).

8. Los españoles toman (chocolate, té, horchata) para el desayuno.

9. La (tertulia, verbena, cesta) es una fiesta religiosa.

10. La jota es un (baile, instrumento músico, plato) español.

B. Match the following items.

	Column I	Column II
_____	1. siesta	a. cumpleaños
_____	2. mantilla	b. villancicos
_____	3. Navidad	c. social gathering
_____	4. día del santo	d. torero
_____	5. pelando la pava	e. soccer
_____	6. tertulia	f. afternoon nap
_____	7. romería	g. peineta
_____	8. banderillero	h. religious picnic
_____	9. fútbol	i. instrumento músico
_____	10. castañuelas	j. reja

C. Complete the following sentences in Spanish.

1. Juan López y Serrano se casa con (marries) Dolores Moreno y Ortega. El nombre completo de su esposa es _____.

2. El _____ es un sitio público donde los amigos se reúnen para charlar (chat) y tomar un refresco.

3. El torero que mata al toro se llama el _____.

4. El _____ es un deporte de origen vasco.

5. _____ es un baile andaluz.

6. Un plato típico de España se llama _____.

7. La víspera (eve) de Navidad se llama la _____.

8. Pedro Vargas y López está casado (married) con Ana Aragón y Villa y tienen un hijo Carlos. El nombre completo de Carlos es _____.

9. El _____ se celebra el doce de octubre.

10. La costumbre de hablar a una señorita por la reja se llama _____.

D. Identify the following in English.

1. Nacimiento _____

2. verbena _____

3. picador _____

4. Misa del Gallo _____

5. sardana _____

6. horchata _____

7. Carnaval _____

8. Cuaresma_____

9. flamenco _____

10. Los Reyes Magos _____

MASTERY EXERCISES ON SPAIN

Underline the word or expression that correctly completes the sentence.

1. La famosa torre mora que está en Sevilla se llama (la Giralda, la Alhambra, el Generalife).
2. (Pelayo, El Cid, El Greco) venció a los moros en la Batalla de Covadonga.
3. Las montañas entre España y Francia se llaman (la Sierra Morena, los Montes Cantábricos, los Pirineos).
4. Carmen Amaya fué una (bailarina, actriz, poetisa) famosa.
5. Un plato español es (la lavandera, el cocido, el gitano).
6. El flamenco es (un baile, una bebida, un instrumento músico).
7. El héroe nacional de España es (El Cid, Cervantes, Atahualpa).
8. Las canciones que se cantan en la Nochebuena se llaman (castañuelas, villancicos, nacimientos).
9. Toledo está situado en el río (Guadiana, Duero, Tajo).
10. Después de Cervantes, el novelista principal de España fué (Galdós, Juan Ramón Jiménez, Calderón).
11. El inventor del autogiro fué (Juan de la Cierva, Calderón, Vicente Escudero).
12. El Escorial es un famoso monasterio cerca de (Málaga, Barcelona, Madrid).
13. Un famoso médico español fué (Lope de Vega, Ramón y Cajal, Juan Ramón Jiménez).
14. El río más navegable de España es (el Ebro, el Guadiana, el Guadalquivir).
15. La fiesta religiosa que se celebra el dos de noviembre es (la Pascua Florida, el Día de la Raza, el Día de los Difuntos).
16. Otro nombre por la pelota vasca es (jai-alai, jipijapa, corrida de toros).
17. Velázquez fué un famoso (escritor, compositor, pintor) español.
18. Los (romanos, españoles, moros) construyeron la Mezquita de Córdoba.
19. El Prado es un famoso (museo, catedral, palacio) en Madrid.
20. Andalucía es una región del (norte, este, sur) de España.
21. Pérez Galdós fué un gran (actor, escritor, músico) español.
22. Las Islas Baleares están en el (Atlántico, Pacífico, Mediterráneo).
23. (Cortés, Pizarro, Rodrigo Díaz de Vivar) venció a Atahualpa.
24. (Benavente, Lope de Vega, Calderón) ganó el Premio Nobel.
25. Se terminó la Reconquista en el año (718, 1492, 1571, 1808).
26. El flamenco es (un baile, una fiesta, un plato).
27. La (paella, peineta, banderilla) es un plato español.
28. Barcelona es un puerto en el (Atlántico, Mar Cantábrico, Mediterráneo).
29. Lope de Vega escribió (dramas, ensayos, novelas).
30. El río que pasa por Sevilla es el (Ebro, Duero, Guadalquivir).
31. Un baile de Andalucía es (el fandango, la jota, la sardana).
32. Andrés Segovia es un (músico, escritor, pintor) español.
33. La española lleva en la cabeza (un poncho, una mantilla, una reja).
34. La última ciudad de los moros en España fué (Granada, Sevilla, Córdoba).
35. *Don Quijote de la Mancha* es (un drama, una poesía, una novela).

36. El Día de los Reyes Magos cae el (seis de enero, dos de mayo, veinticinco de diciembre).

37. La jota es (una bebida, un baile, un plato).

38. Un puerto de mar de España en el Mediterráneo es (Cádiz, Málaga, Santander).

39. España produce mucho (café, tabaco, corcho).

40. El gran guitarrista de España es (Casals, Escudero, Segovia).

41. Valencia se halla en el (este, norte, oeste) de España.

42. La Alhambra está en (Córdoba, Granada, Valencia).

43. El Greco fué un célebre (autor, músico, pintor) de España.

44. La fiesta nacional de España se celebra el (catorce de abril, dos de mayo, doce de octubre).

45. El único (only) río grande de España que desemboca en (flows into) el Mar Mediterráneo es el (Duero, Ebro, Tajo).

46. En los días que preceden a la Cuaresma, los españoles celebran (el Carnaval, la Semana Santa, la Pascua Florida).

47. Los primeros habitantes de España fueron los (griegos, iberos, romanos).

48. El frontón es el lugar donde se juega (el jai-alai, el fútbol, el tenis).

49. La verbena es una fiesta religiosa que se celebra por la (mañana, tarde, noche).

50. El torero que va montado a caballo se llama un (picador, banderillero, matador).

EXAMINATION

BOARD OF EDUCATION, CITY OF NEW YORK

I. Select the correct word or phrase: [5]

1. Simón Bolívar was   (a) a dancer   (b) a musician   (c) a writer   (d) a patriot.
2. A "sereno" is   (a) a serenade   (b) a night watchman   (c) a policeman   (d) a sailor.
3. La Giralda is   (a) in Seville   (b) in Córdoba   (c) in Madrid   (d) in Valencia.
4. Don Quijote was written by   (a) Lope de Vega   (b) Cervantes   (c) Sancho Panza   (d) Calderón.
5. El Greco was a famous Spanish   (a) king   (b) painter   (c) musician   (d) bullfighter.

II. Select the word or phrase which best completes the meaning: [10]

[EXAMPLE: El perro es   (1) un hombre   (2) un animal   (3) un pájaro   (4) oír.]

1. Yo uso los ojos para   (1) oler   (2) ver   (3) respirar   (4) oír.
2. Nueva York es   (1) un país   (2) una legumbre   (3) una puerta   (4) una ciudad.
3. Cuando tengo sed   (1) estudio   (2) bebo   (3) como   (4) canto.
4. Yo escribo en la pizarra con   (1) tiza blanca   (2) tinta negra   (3) lápiz amarillo   (4) una pluma.
5. La ventana es de   (1) oro   (2) plata   (3) vidrio   (4) papel.
6. Ocho y siete son   (1) catorce   (2) cinco   (3) quince   (4) cincuenta y seis.
7. Mi madre prepara la comida en   (1) la biblioteca   (2) el gabinete   (3) la alcoba   (4) la cocina.
8. Mi amigo me dice—Gracias. Yo contesto   (1) ¿Cómo está Vd.?   (2) de nada   (3) ¡hola!   (4) buenas tardes.
9. El 4 de julio es un día importante en   (1) los Estados Unidos   (2) el otoño   (3) los campos de España   (4) Inglaterra.
10. Cuando estoy muy enfermo   (1) voy al cine   (2) hago ejercicios   (3) escribo la lección   (4) voy al médico.

III. Read the following passage:

El señor Brown es un médico rico que desea pasar unos meses viajando con su familia por varios países latinoamericanos.

La familia Brown está ahora en Nuevo Laredo, el primer pueblo mexicano al otro lado del Puente Internacional (International Bridge) y del Río Grande. En el grupo hay el padre, la madre Carmen, y los dos hijos Juan y Ana. Juan es un muchacho de diez y seis años y su hermana tiene catorce años. Viajan en automóvil por la Carretera Panamericana (Pan-American Highway).

El padre habla muy bien el español y todo el grupo tiene mucho interés en la vida, las costumbres y la cultura hispanoamericana. Hacen un viaje de "Buen Vecino."

Write T for each statement that is true and F for each that is false: [10]

1. El señor Brown es un abogado famoso.
2. Desea pasar un año viajando por Centro América.
3. La familia Brown está ahora en México.
4. El grupo consiste en cuatro personas.
5. La madre se llama Ana.
6. El hijo tiene quince años.
7. Viajan por la Carretera Panamericana por ferrocarril.
8. El señor Brown habla muy bien el español.
9. El grupo tiene poco interés en las costumbres panamericanas.
10. "Buen Vecino" en inglés significa "Good Neighbor."

IV. Read the following passage:

Pedro es hijo de un campesino pobre. Es un muchacho listo y aplicado. Va a la escuela todos los días y presta atención en la clase. Pedro quiere aprender mucho para ser un hombre inteligente. No es como su hermano mayor, Luis.

Luis es muy perezoso y no quiere asistir a la escuela. Está contento de jugar en el corral.

Los dos hijos van a la misma escuela. Hoy hay examen. Pedro sabe mucho y sale muy bien en el examen. Luis no sabe nada. El profesor le pregunta a Luis.

¿Son difíciles las preguntas?

No, señor,—le contesta Luis—las preguntas son fáciles. Son las respuestas que son muy difíciles.

Select the word or phrase which best completes the statement: [5]

1. The boy's father is   (a) a carpenter   (b) a poor camper   (c) a rich man   (d) a poor farmer.
2. Peter   (a) is lazy   (b) doesn't want to go to school   (c) goes to school daily and pays attention   (d) doesn't do his work.
3. Louis is   (a) older than Peter   (b) the same age as Peter   (c) younger than Peter   (d) fifteen years old.
4. In the examination   (a) Louis knows everything   (b) Peter knows a great deal and comes out well   (c) Peter can't answer the questions   (d) Peter knows less than Louis.
5. Louis thinks   (a) the questions are not easy   (b) the answers are difficult   (c) the answers are easy   (d) both are easy.

[198]

V. Read the following story:

¿Sabe Vd. que hay ciudades norteamericanas que tienen ambiente (atmosphere) española? Una de ellas que está en el estado de California se llama Santa Barbara.

Los edificios, las tiendas, las casas con los jardines y los patios son casi todos de estilo español.

Especialmente es hermosa la ciudad cuando celebran los "Días Antiguos Españoles." Hay fiesta y muchos se visten de moda española. Una procesión pasa y todo el mundo canta y baila. La gente viene de todas partes a Santa Barbara para celebrar la vida antigua española del sudoeste.

Select the word or phrase which best completes the meaning: [5]

1. Santa Barbara is (a) an island (b) a farm (c) a mountain (d) a city.
2. The buildings in Spanish style are (a) a few (b) some (c) almost all (d) none.
3. During the "Old Spanish Days" one sees much that reminds him of (a) old life in the Southwest (b) New England (c) Argentina (d) life in the country.
4. Santa Barbara is especially beautiful (a) in winter (b) at fiesta time (c) when the sun shines (d) because it is near the seacoast.
5. Those who take part in the "Old Spanish Days" are (a) the storekeepers (b) only the young people (c) the visitors (d) everyone.

VI. Match each expression in column A with the corresponding translation in column B: [10]

A	B
1. Me gusta bailar.	a. He is thirteen years old.
2. tengo que saber	b. It is cold.
3. Quiere ir a pie.	c. Let's go.
4. a la una de la mañana	d. Where are you going?
5. hace muchos años	e. He wants to walk.
6. al fin	f. Who knows?
7. Tiene trece años.	g. I like to dance.
8. Hace frío.	h. tomorrow morning
9. ¿A dónde va usted?	i. at one A.M.
10. Tenemos frío.	j. I must know.
	k. We are cold.
	l. at last
	m. many years ago

VII. Complete the following sentences as indicated: [25]

1. Enrique escribe en (the) ----------------- pizarra.
2. Yo no tengo (a) ----------------- mapa.
3. Hablamos (to the) ----------------- muchachas.
4. Yo doy el libro (to the) ----------------- profesor.
5. Ana no es (Spanish) -----------------
6. Yo (study) ----------------- la lección.
7. El alumno (is) ----------------- en la escuela.
8. Las casas son (white) -----------------·
9. La maestra (is) ----------------- francesa.
10. El señor habló (with me) -----------------·
11. Son (two o'clock) -----------------·
12. (My) ----------------- hermana es muy inteligente.
13. (His) ----------------- familia no es grande.
14. (There are) ----------------- treinta alumnos en la clase.
15. Hoy es (Friday) -----------------·
16. ¿(What) ----------------- tiene Vd. en la mano?
17. El hombre tiene (500) ----------------- pesos.
18. Deseo comprar (those) ----------------- plumas.
19. (This) ----------------- niño es perezoso.
20. Hace frío en el mes de (December) -----------------·
21. El plural de lápiz es -----------------·
22. ¿(How) ----------------- está Vd.?
23. Tenemos los libros (of the) ----------------- señor.
24. ¿(Who) ----------------- es el presidente de los Estados Unidos?
25. (Mary's pen) ----------------- es verde.

VIII. Translate into Spanish: [30] [1½ for No. 1-10; ½ for the article]

1. the table	6. the head	11. to live	16. September	21. easy
2. the flower	7. the donkey	12. with	17. because	22. Tuesday
3. the hat	8. the water	13. nine hundred	18. pretty	23. also
4. the bread	9. the friend	14. Spain	19. to eat	24. good
5. the window	10. the chair	15. small	20. to sell	25. fourteen

EXAMINATION

Board of Education, City of New York

I. Select the correct word or phrase: [5]

1. Velázquez was a famous Spanish (a) musician (b) writer (c) painter (d) king.
2. Paricutín is a volcano in (a) Mexico (b) Peru (c) Bolivia (d) Colombia.
3. El Día de los Reyes falls on (a) October 12 (b) January 6 (c) December 25 (d) May 2.
4. Cortés conquered (a) Argentina (b) Mexico (c) Peru (d) Venezuela.
5. El Greco was a famous Spanish (a) dancer (b) author (c) painter (d) musician.

II. Select the word or phrase which best completes the meaning: [10]

[EXAMPLE: Monterrey es (1) una montaña (2) una ciudad (3) un animal (4) un torero.]

1. Nueve y cuatro son (a) catorce (b) quince (c) trece (d) doce.
2. Cuando tengo que sufrir un examen (a) juego a la pelota (b) estudio (c) voy al cine (d) visito a mi amigo.
3. California es (a) una novela (b) una mujer (c) una revista (d) un estado.
4. Las páginas de un libro son de (a) vidrio (b) papel (c) acero (d) madera.
5. La manzana es (a) una fruta (b) una legumbre (c) una campana (d) una niña.
6. Usamos la boca para (a) andar (b) hablar (c) oír (d) ver.
7. Durante el verano cuando hace calor voy para nadar (a) al cine (b) a la playa (c) al parque (d) al museo.
8. Podemos comprar café en (a) una biblioteca (b) una escuela (c) una tienda (d) una cocina.
9. La primavera es (a) una estación (b) un mes (c) una comida (d) un baile.
10. El clavel se encuentra en (a) la sala de clase (b) el jardín (c) la calle (d) el armario.

III. Read the following passage:

Los mercados de los países hispanoamericanos son muy pintorescos y la gente tiene la oportunidad de ver a sus amigos y de hablar con ellos. Todo el mundo está muy contento. Algunos traen sus guitarras y tocan música muy bonita.

Hoy es domingo y todos van al mercado para vender o comprar algo. Hay vendedores que venden tortillas y bebidas. Rosita y su hermano van al mercado que está lejos de su casa. No tienen automóvil y deben caminar por muchas horas. Los dos muchachos llevan frutas y flores para vender. Con el dinero que ganan van a comprar un regalo de Navidad para sus padres. Rosita tiene sed y compra una bebida. Su hermano tiene hambre y compra una tortilla.

Los niños vuelven a casa a las ocho. Están muy cansados y se duermen pronto. Mañana es lunes y deben ir a la escuela temprano.

Write T for each statement that is true and F for each that is false: [10]

1. El mercado está cerca de la casa de Rosita.
2. Hay música bonita de los pájaros.
3. Los muchachos van al mercado los lunes.
4. En el mercado las personas hablan con sus amigos.
5. Rosita tiene hambre y compra una tortilla.
6. Los niños van a comprar un regalo para sus padres.
7. Algunas personas traen sus maracas.
8. Todo el mundo está triste.
9. Los muchachos tienen un automóvil grande.
10. Los muchachos vuelven a casa a las ocho.

IV. Read the following passage:

Un día mi amigo Roberto y yo fuimos a visitar a mi hermano Arturo que vive con su familia en la ciudad de México. Fué necesario ir en avión porque nuestras vacaciones son de quince días.

Al llegar a México nuestros amigos nos recibieron en el aeropuerto. Eran mi hermano, su esposa Dolores, y sus hijos Manfredo, Alberto y María. Los niños, con mucha curiosidad de saber algo de mi país, nos preguntaron muchas veces:
—¿Cómo son las casas de Nueva York?
—¿Es verdad que los trenes van debajo de las calles?
—¿Cuál es más grande: México o Nueva York?
—¿Usan muchos burros allí?

Contestamos con mucha paciencia hasta llegar a la casa a las seis en punto de la tarde. Dos horas después anunciaron la comida.

Select the word or phrase which best completes the statement: [5]

1. My brother lives in (a) Guatemala (b) Mexico (c) United States (d) Argentina.
2. Our vacation was to last (a) three weeks (b) fifteen days (c) eight days (d) a month.
3. Arthur's family met us (a) in the city (b) at the airport (c) at home (d) in the station.
4. Manfredo, Alberto and María are my (a) cousins (b) brothers and sister (c) nephews and niece (d) uncles and aunt.
5. We finally ate at (a) eight o'clock (b) six o'clock (c) ten o'clock (d) seven o'clock.

V. Read the following passage:

Pancho González, un cubano recién llegado a Nueva York, entra en una barbería que está en la calle Catorce y la avenida Lexington.

El barbero es un hombre muy aplicado pero habla mucho. Habla de su familia y de sus amigos, su negocio, el tiempo, etc.

El barbero habla mucho y corta (cuts) la cabeza de nuestro amigo Pancho.

En la conversación el barbero pregunta:—¿Cuántos hermanos tiene usted?

Pancho contesta:—Nosotros somos cinco hermanos si yo salgo de aquí vivo.

Select the word or phrase which best completes each statement: [5]

1. Pancho González is from   (a) Spain   (b) Puerto Rico   (c) Cuba   (d) Mexico.
2. The barber shop is located on   (a) Fifteenth Street and Eighth Avenue   (b) The Grand Concourse   (c) Fourteenth Street and Lexington Avenue   (d) none of these.
3. The barber   (a) is a quiet man   (b) works silently and efficiently   (c) talks about the Dodgers   (d) is very talkative.
4. The barber asks Pancho   (a) how many brothers he has   (b) his impressions of New York   (c) his future plans   (d) how many sisters he has.
5. Pancho replies that   (a) he is satisfied with the service   (b) he has four brothers   (c) he has five brothers   (d) he intends to leave the country.

VI. Match each expression in column *A* with the corresponding translation in column *B*: [10]

A	B
1. Tenga Vd. cuidado.	a. You're welcome.
2. Vámonos.	b. What is the matter with you?
3. De nada.	c. He is three years old.
4. ¿Quién sabe?	d. It is 2:45.
5. ¿Qué tiene Vd.?	e. every day
6. Son las tres menos cuarto.	f. What is your name?
7. otra vez	g. Be careful.
8. todos los días	h. I have studied.
9. Tengo que estudiar.	i. Thank you.
10. ¿Cómo se llama Vd.?	j. Who knows?
	k. Let's go.
	l. I have to study.
	m. again

VII. Complete the following sentences as indicated: [25]

1. (These) _____ sombreros son bonitos.
2. Aprendemos (a) _____ lección cada semana.
3. María (is eating) _____ el pan.
4. Lima (is) _____ en el Perú.
5. ¿(What) _____ desea Vd.?
6. Las clases comienzan en (September) _____
7. (His) _____ amigos tienen frío.
8. Los alumnos salen de la escuela a (3 o'clock) _____
9. ¿(Who) _____ sabe responder?
10. Nosotros (buy) _____ muchas cosas.
11. Cada mañana voy (to the) _____ escuela.
12. Rosa y Pablo son (Mexican) _____
13. El primer día de escuela es (Monday) _____
14. Pedro (is) _____ un alumno.
15. ¿Cómo (are) _____ Vd.?
16. En mi biblioteca hay (700) _____ libros.
17. La Alhambra (is) _____ interesante.
18. (John's mother) _____ habla francés.
19. La silla es (large) _____
20. Las flores (of the) _____ jardín son para mí.
21. Vemos (the) _____ agua.
22. Escribo una carta (to the) _____ presidente.
23. (That) _____ muchacho es inteligente.
24. El plural de "lección" es _____
25. (Our) _____ pluma es verde.

VIII. Translate into Spanish: [30] [1½ for No. 1-10; ½ for the article]

1. the meat
2. the chair
3. the lamp
4. the woman
5. the grandfather
6. the language
7. the bird
8. the suit
9. the hand
10. the mouth
11. blue
12. the tailor
13. the butcher
14. always
15. Where?
16. dear
17. five hundred
18. fourteen
19. difficult
20. January
21. to fall
22. in front of
23. without
24. happy
25. to come

EXAMINATION

Board of Education, City of New York

I. Select the correct word or phrase: [5]

1. The Aztecs lived in (a) Chile (b) México (c) Perú (d) Argentina.
2. Don Quijote was written by (a) Galdós (b) Benavente (c) Blasco Ibáñez (d) Cervantes.
3. The mountains that separate Spain from France are (a) the Guadarramas (b) the Andes (c) Sierra Nevada (d) the Pyrenees.
4. Simón Bolívar was (a) a famous dancer (b) an explorer (c) the Liberator (d) a painter.
5. The Alhambra is a palace in (a) Madrid (b) Granada (c) Toledo (d) Barcelona.

II. Select the word or phrase which best completes the meaning: [10]

[EXAMPLE: Nueve y cuatro son (a) catorce (b) quince (c) _trece_ (d) doce.]

1. Cuando tengo sueño (a) me acuesto (b) me levanto (c) canto (d) corro.
2. El hijo de mi tía es mi (a) sobrino (b) abuelo (c) primo (d) hermano.
3. No hay escuela (a) los miércoles (b) los lunes (c) los domingos (d) los jueves.
4. Me gusta mirar (a) el suelo (b) la televisión (c) el papel (d) el hacha.
5. Jai-alai es (a) una comida (b) un animal (c) un deporte (d) un mercado.
6. Son las dos y cuarto = (a) 2:04 (b) 2:14 (c) 4:15 (d) 2:15.
7. En un examen deseo salir (a) bien (b) mal (c) feo (d) triste.
8. Veinte y cinco menos diez son (a) diez (b) siete (c) catorce (d) quince.
9. El pájaro vive en (a) la cocina (b) el museo (c) la tienda (d) un árbol.
10. Usamos los pies para (a) cerrar (b) decir (c) andar (d) mirar.

III. Read the following passage:

En España vive un campesino rico que se llama Sancho García. No es inteligente. Su hijo, Pablo, también es muy ignorante. No asiste a la escuela.

Un día Sancho dice a Pablo:

—Mañana tú tienes que asistir a la escuela porque la gente rica debe tener una buena educación. Aquí tienes dos cuadernos grandes, una pluma de oro y un lápiz de plata. Pablo asiste a la escuela cada día. Después de tres meses el campesino va a la escuela para hablar con el profesor. El profesor dice que Pablo no aprende nada.

—Pero, señor profesor, mi hijo tiene dos cuadernos grandes, una pluma de oro y un lápiz de plata. ¿Qué más necesita para aprender?

—Ah, señor; pero su hijo no tiene la capacidad (ability).

—Bueno, soy un hombre rico—dice Sancho. —Mañana compro una buena capacidad para mi hijo.

Write T for each statement that is true and F for each that is false: [10]

1. El campesino es muy ignorante.
2. La gente pobre debe tener una buena educación.
3. Sancho da un burro a su hijo.
4. Pablo aprende mucho en la escuela.
5. El padre va a la escuela para hablar con el maestro.
6. Pablo vive en México.
7. La capacidad es muy importante.
8. El profesor dice que Pablo es muy inteligente.
9. Sancho García no tiene dinero.
10. El campesino puede comprar la capacidad.

IV. Read the following passage:

Mamá: Levántate ahora, Luis. Ya son las ocho.

Luis: Tengo mucho sueño, mamá. Estamos todavía en vacaciones. Hoy no deseo levantarme tan temprano.

Mamá: ¡Qué perezoso! Tu hermana Teresa se levantó hace media hora. Queremos ir de compras. Esta mañana queremos comprarte un traje.

Luis: Gracias, mamá, pero—otro día. Quiero dormir.

Mamá: Tenemos que salir muy pronto. Vamos a comprar muchas cosas. Teresa también necesita un vestido, y un par de zapatos.

Luis: ¡Ay de mí! Entonces pierdo todo el día. Teresa siempre necesita tres horas para escoger (to choose) un vestido. Cada vez que ella entra en una tienda, mira veinte vestidos. En la zapatería examina doce pares de zapatos, pero no halla nada a su gusto (to her taste).

Select the word or phrase which best completes the statement: [5]

1. Louis' mother wants him to (a) wash up (b) go to bed (c) get up (d) go to school.
2. Theresa has been up since (a) eight o'clock (b) seven o'clock (c) seven-thirty (d) eight-thirty

3. The mother wants to take Louis and his sister (*a*) to the movies (*b*) to church (*c*) to the park (*d*) shopping.
4. Theresa needs (*a*) a new suit (*b*) a pair of shoes (*c*) a new coat (*d*) a pair of gloves.
5. Louis is not looking forward to this day because (*a*) he is lazy (*b*) he is on vacation (*c*) his sister wastes too much time in the stores (*d*) he doesn't need anything.

V. Read the following passage:

El Sr. Serrano es abogado. Vive en un pueblo pequeño y trabaja en la ciudad grande cerca de su pueblo. Todos los días se levanta temprano. Después del desayuno sale en su automóvil para la ciudad.

Dice adiós a sus hijos, Arturo y Luisa, y a su mujer, María. El Sr. Serrano está muy ocupado todo el día. Tiene que leer y estudiar muchos libros.

Select the word or phrase which best completes each statement: [5]

1. Mr. Serrano is a (*a*) doctor (*b*) teacher (*c*) lawyer (*d*) writer.
2. He lives (*a*) in a large city (*b*) in a small town near the city (*c*) in a small town far from the city (*d*) on the farm
3. Every day Mr. Serrano (*a*) takes a walk (*b*) gets up early (*c*) sleeps late (*d*) oversleeps.
4. Arturo is Mr. Serrano's (*a*) neighbor (*b*) friend (*c*) brother (*d*) son.
5. Mr. Serrano is (*a*) usually not busy (*b*) late for work (*c*) busy all day (*d*) reading the newspapers.

VI. Match each expression in column *A* with the corresponding translation in column *B*: [10]

A	B
1. Ella tiene dolor de cabeza.	*a.* It is 1:30.
2. Hacía mal tiempo ayer.	*b.* Do you know how to dance?
3. Es la una y media.	*c.* She has a headache.
4. Él trabaja por la noche.	*d.* We like to speak Spanish.
5. ¿Sabe Vd. bailar?	*e.* What is the meaning of this?
6. Nos gusta hablar español.	*f.* They are going to sing again.
7. Doy un paseo esta noche.	*g.* She is calling Dolores.
8. ¿Qué quiere decir esto?	*h.* It was bad weather yesterday.
9. Van a cantar de nuevo.	*i.* It is the first of the month.
10. Todo el mundo va a casa.	*j.* He works at night.
	k. I am taking a walk tonight.
	l. They can't go until 9 P.M.
	m. Everybody goes home.

VII. Complete the following sentences as indicated: [25]

1. Juan escribe en (the) _____ cuaderno.
2. Él tiene un lápiz en (the) _____ mano.
3. Ana no es (English) _____.
4. Doy la tiza (to the) _____ profesor.
5. Escribimos (to the) _____ muchachas.
6. Yo no (know) _____ la palabra.
7. El árbol (is) _____ en el jardín.
8. Las flores (are) _____ rojas.
9. La profesora (is) _____ española.
10. Son las (eleven o'clock) _____.
11. (His) _____ familia es grande.
12. (There are) _____ veinte vacas en el campo.
13. (My) _____ hermanos van a la escuela superior.
14. ¿(How many) _____ hermanas tiene Vd.?
15. No me gusta (that) _____ casa.
16. (Mary's hat) _____ es bonito.
17. ¿(Who) _____ es su profesor de español?
18. ¿(What) _____ dice el señor?
19. Hace frío en el mes de (December) _____.
20. (This) _____ alumna es perezosa.
21. Él tiene (fifteen) _____ lápices.
22. Hoy es (Thursday) _____.
23. Yo (do) _____ el trabajo.
24. ¡(Open) _____ Vd. la ventana!
25. Él (is right) tiene _____.

VIII. Translate into Spanish: [30] [1½ for No. 1-10; ½ for the article]

1. the family	6. the milk	11. green	16. tree	21. large
2. the bedroom	7. the dog	12. who?	17. to work	22. teeth
3. the man	8. the necktie	13. sick	18. doctor	23. to understand
4. the day	9. the store	14. thirteen	19. summer	24. seven hundred
5. the blouse	10. the parents	15. October	20. to buy	25. Sunday

EXAMINATION

Board of Education, City of New York

I. Select the correct word: [5]

1. Pizarro conquered the   (a) Aztecs   (b) Incas   (c) Mayas   (d) Araucanians.
2. El Prado is   (a) an art museum   (b) a river   (c) a discoverer   (d) a dancer.
3. The Guadalquivir is a river in   (a) Chile   (b) Argentina   (c) Cuba   (d) Spain.
4. Goya was a famous   (a) explorer   (b) painter   (c) dancer   (d) bullfighter.
5. San Martín is the national hero of   (a) Brazil   (b) Ecuador   (c) Argentina   (d) Venezuela.

II. Select the word or phrase which best completes the meaning: [10]

[EXAMPLE: Nueve y cuatro son   (a) catorce   (b) quince   (c) <u>trece</u>   (d) doce.]

1. Cuando tenemos hambre   (a) dormimos   (b) hablamos   (c) bebemos   (d) comemos.
2. En el invierno muchas veces tenemos   (a) calor   (b) frío   (c) agua   (d) flores.
3. El padre de mi madre es mi   (a) sobrino   (b) tío   (c) hermano   (d) abuelo.
4. El alumno escribe con tiza en   (a) el papel   (b) la carta   (c) la pizarra   (d) el libro.
5. Abrimos la puerta con   (a) los pies   (b) la mano   (c) los dientes   (d) la cabeza.
6. Tres por cinco son   (a) catorce   (b) cinco   (c) quince   (d) ocho.
7. En el mercado   (a) compramos   (b) dormimos   (c) escribimos   (d) vivimos.
8. Para recibir notas buenas tenemos que   (a) estudiar   (b) cantar   (c) hablar   (d) comer.
9. Cuando encuentro a una persona digo   (a) hasta mañana   (b) buenos días   (c) no hay de qué   (d) me gusta.
10. Son las cuatro menos diez =   (a) 4:10   (b) 3:50   (c) 10:15   (d) 9:45.

III. Read the following passage:

Alberto y Rosa son hermanos. Él tiene catorce años. Viven en la ciudad.

No asisten a la escuela porque es el mes de agosto. Su madre no está buena y el médico le dice que necesita aire puro. Su esposo, Carlos, dice,—¿Por qué no vas a pasar dos o tres semanas con tu hermana Adela?

Así es que dentro de tres días la madre, Alberto y Rosa salen por tren para la hacienda de doña Adela y su hijo Luis.

—Alberto dice, En la ciudad tenemos máquinas (machines) donde se pone dinero por un lado (side) y sale por el otro lado un paquete de chicle, cigarrillos o dulces (candy).

Luis exclama,—¡Qué extraordinario! Y aquí tenemos una máquina en que por un lado ponemos hierba y por el otro sale leche.

—Es muy interesante, dice Alberto. ¿Qué máquina es ésa?

—Se llama una vaca, responde Luis.

Write T for each statement that is true and F for each that is false: [10]

1. Rosa es la hermana de Alberto.
2. Es el tiempo de las vacaciones.
3. La madre de los niños está enferma.
4. Adela es la hermana de Carlos.
5. El padre de Alberto se llama Carlos.
6. Luis tiene catorce años.
7. Toda la familia sale de la ciudad.
8. Alberto y Rosa pasan tres días con Luis.
9. Luis no vive en una ciudad.
10. La máquina es extraordinaria, dice Luis.

IV. Read the following passage:

Paco, un indio de dieciocho años, fué a la escuela para estudiar para médico. A la puerta encontró al profesor.

—Me llamo Paco Morelos, señor, y quiero ser médico, dijo el muchacho.

El profesor le preguntó, —¿Sabe usted leer y escribir?

—Sé escribir, pero no sé leer.

—¡Eso es raro! ¡Saber escribir y no saber leer! ¡Imposible! A ver, escríbame tres o cuatro palabras en este papel.

—Con todo gusto, dijo Paco, y escribió algunas palabras en el papel.

El profesor examinó el papel pero fué imposible leer las palabras que vió.

—¿Qué significan estas palabras?

—No sé, señor profesor. Yo dije que sé escribir pero no sé leer.

Select the word or phrase which best completes each statement: [5]

1. Paco is a boy of   (a) 8   (b) 10   (c) 18   (d) 21.
2. Paco wishes to become a   (a) teacher   (b) lawyer   (c) doctor   (d) farmer.
3. The two characters in the story met   (a) at the market   (b) in the street   (c) at the school door   (d) at the corner.
4. After studying the paper, the teacher remarked   (a) "That's strange!"   (b) "What do these words mean?"   (c) "I didn't say I could read."   (d) "Can you read and write?"
5. Paco could   (a) read and write   (b) write but not read   (c) read but not write   (d) neither write nor read.

V. Read the following passage:

Dos caballeros están sentados en un tren que va de Málaga a Córdoba. Es el mes de agosto en España y hace mucho calor.

Un caballero que tiene sesenta años pregunta: —Perdone Vd. pero . . . ¿Es Vd. Carlos Alonso el hombre muy fuerte? ¿El hombre que levanta setenta y cinco libras con una mano? ¿El famoso Carlos Alonso?

El otro señor contesta: —Sí, yo soy Carlos Alonso.

El caballero responde: —Abra Vd. esta ventana para mí . . . . hace mucho calor aquí.

Select the word or phrase which best completes each statement. [5]

1. The two gentlemen are seated in a (a) boat (b) train (c) trolley car (d) plane.
2. This story takes place in (a) Mexico (b) Puerto Rico (c) Spain (d) Cuba.
3. The man who asks the questions is (a) 60 years old (b) Carlos Alonso (c) 70 years old (d) 50 years old.
4. Carlos Alonso can (a) lift 65 pounds with one hand (b) lift 75 pounds with two hands (c) lift 75 pounds with one hand (d) lift 700 pounds.
5. The gentleman asks Mr. Alonso to (a) close the window (b) look out the window (c) sign his autograph album (d) open the window.

VI. Match each expression in column *A* with the corresponding translation in column *B*: [10]

A	B
1. Acaba de cantar.	a. Every year we learn a little more.
2. No hace frío en todas partes.	b. She studies in the afternoon.
3. Todos los años aprendemos un poco más.	c. He has just sung.
4. Ella estudia por la tarde.	d. Please tell me, what time is it?
5. Le doy las gracias por la carta.	e. Do you sleep after lunch?
6. Dígame por favor, ¿qué hora es?	f. For what do you want the money?
7. Todo el mundo compra el periódico.	g. It is not cold today.
8. ¿Duerme Vd. después del almuerzo?	h. It is not cold everywhere.
9. ¿Para qué desea Vd. el dinero?	i. He is very old.
10. Vamos a ayudar al hombre.	j. I thank him for the letter.
	k. Everybody buys the newspaper.
	l. We are going to help the man.
	m. We are going to help the hungry people.

VII. Complete the following sentences as indicated: [25]

1. Tengo (a) ----------------- flor azul.
2. Hoy es (the) ----------------- día del examen.
3. Ella no ve los (pencils) -----------------·
4. El profesor habla (to the) ----------------- alumno.
5. Leo el cuento (to the) ----------------- niñas.
6. No vamos a la escuela el (Sunday) -----------------·
7. Mi amiga es (French) -----------------·
8. (John's mother) ----------------- es muy bonita.
9. Me gusta el mes de (October) -----------------·
10. Quiero presentarla a (my) ----------------- madre.
11. (Her) ----------------- hermano es bueno.
12. (This) ----------------- lección es fácil.
13. María escribe (that) ----------------- palabra.
14. Son las (nine o'clock) -----------------·
15. Yo no (know) ----------------- esa lengua.
16. Los libros (are) ----------------- interesantes.
17. El papel no (is) ----------------- sobre la mesa.
18. La casa (is) ----------------- blanca.
19. ¿(What) ----------------- hace Vd.?
20. ¿(Whose) ----------------- es este guante?
21. En este ejercicio (there is) ----------------- una falta.
22. Tenemos (fourteen) ----------------- árboles en mi jardín.
23. Yo siempre (go) ----------------- a la escuela.
24. ¡(Write) ----------------- Vd. la frase!
25. Isabel no está (at home) -----------------·

VIII. Translate into Spanish: [30] [1½ for No. 1-10; ½ for the article]

1. the breakfast	6. the park	11. red	16. poor	21. to sing
2. the door	7. the horse	12. Thursday	17. four hundred	22. to drink
3. the kitchen	8. the shoes	13. the lawyer	18. fifteen	23. studious
4. the boy	9. the map	14. spring	19. tall	24. to write
5. the uncle	10. the face	15. when?	20. December	25. to say

EXAMINATION

Board of Education, City of New York

I. Select the correct word: [10]

1. The Basques live in the (a) southern (b) northern (c) eastern (d) western part of Spain.
2. Pizarro conquered the Incas of (a) Mexico (b) Chile (c) Peru (d) Venezuela.
3. The capital of Puerto Rico is (a) San Juan (b) San José (c) Caracas (d) Buenos Aires.
4. The Emperor of the Aztecs was named (a) Atahualpa (b) Montezuma (c) Simón Bolívar (d) Fidel Castro.
5. Pablo Casals is a great Spanish (a) painter (b) writer (c) statesman (d) musician.
6. The Aqueduct of Segovia was built by the (a) Romans (b) Moors (c) Celts (d) Visigoths.
7. The national hero of Spain is (a) Cervantes (b) El Cid (c) Velázquez (d) Alfonso X.
8. Jai-alai is a popular (a) drink (b) game (c) dish (d) resort.
9. The longest river in South America is the (a) Plata (b) Orinoco (c) Amazon (d) Magdalena.
10. El Greco was (a) a famous painter (b) an author (c) a liberator (d) a well-known dancer.

II. Select the word or phrase which best completes the meaning: [10]

[EXAMPLE: El lunes es (a) un hombre (b) <u>un día</u> (c) un animal (d) una flor.]

1. España es (a) un país (b) una capital (c) una lengua (d) una ciudad.
2. Uno de los meses del verano es (a) julio (b) diciembre (c) octubre (d) mayo.
3. Son las doce menos cuarto (a) 12:15 (b) 1:45 (c) 11:45 (d) 4:12.
4. Mi hermano es el hijo de mi (a) tío (b) padre (c) primo (d) abuelo.
5. Me lavo las manos en (a) el dormitorio (b) el comedor (c) la sala (d) el cuarto de baño.
6. Para comprar algo en una tienda hay que tener (a) pan (b) leche (c) dinero (d) café.
7. Llevamos zapatos para cubrir (a) las manos (b) los pies (c) las orejas (d) las piernas.
8. El paraguas es necesario cuando (a) llueve (b) hace viento (c) hace frío (d) hace calor.
9. Uso el tenedor cuando (a) escribo (b) bebo (c) me lavo (d) como.
10. La iglesia es (a) una lengua (b) un edificio (c) una mujer (d) una fruta.

III. Read the following passage:

Alfonsín es un niño que tiene cinco años. Viaja en tren en compañía de su padre por primera vez. Alfonsín está muy contento. El padre observa que el niño saca la cabeza (puts his head out) por la ventanilla para ver mejor. Su padre le dice que no debe hacer eso porque va a perder el sombrero.

Muy pronto el niño olvida la observación del padre y repite la falta. Para corregir su desobediencia, el padre toma el sombrero del chico y lo esconde (hides) y exclama:

—¿No ves? ¿Dónde está el sombrero? Eres un niño desobediente.

Alfonsín, muy triste, busca por todas partes. Para consolar al niño, el padre dice:

—Ahora voy a llamar al sombrero y en un segundo está aquí.

Mientras el niño busca debajo del asiento, aparece (appears) otra vez el sombrero.

La alegría (joy) de Alfonsín es grande y desea probar otra vez los poderes (powers) misteriosos de su padre. Saca la cabeza por la ventanilla y deja (permits, lets) escapar el sombrero. Dice con satisfacción infantil,

—¡Papá! ¡Papá! ¡Llama (call) al sombrero ahora!

Select the word or phrase which best completes each statement: [10]

1. Alfonsín is (a) 10 years old (b) 15 years old (c) 5 years old (d) 8 years old.
2. His father tells him (a) to sit still (b) not to put his head out of the window (c) to keep his hat on (d) to take his hat off.
3. Alfonsín (a) disobeys his father (b) obeys his father (c) keeps his head in (d) gives his hat to his father.
4. The father (a) spanks Alfonsín (b) keeps the hat in his lap (c) hides the hat (d) repeats his warning.
5. Alfonsín thinks his father has mysterious powers and (a) is afraid of him (b) holds on to his hat (c) keeps his head in (d) drops the hat out of the window.

IV. Read the following passage:

Pablo y Clara son alumnos de la clase de español. Clara es muy aplicada y aprende bien porque estudia mucho. Pablo es perezoso. No aprende bien las lecciones porque no estudia.

Un día el profesor dice a los alumnos que deben preparar un discurso (speech) original, acerca de las costumbres hispano-americanas. Clara trabaja muchos días y prepara un discurso interesante y original. Pablo prepara su discurso en media hora.

Llega el día del discurso. El profesor llama a Clara. Ella se levanta y hace su discurso delante de la clase. Todos la escuchan atentamente y aplauden porque el discurso es excelente.

Pablo levanta la mano y dice,—Señor profesor, este discurso es muy interesante, pero no es original. Yo tengo en casa un libro que contiene todas esas palabras.

—¡Es imposible! Mi discurso no está en ningún libro, exclama Clara.

—Repito que todas esas palabras están en este libro. Es un libro muy famoso.

—¿Qué libro es? pregunta el profesor con curiosidad.

—¡El diccionario!

Write T for each statement that is true and F for each that is false: [10]

1. Pablo y Clara son hermanos.
2. El discurso debe ser original.
3. Clara prepara su discurso en media hora.
4. Clara está sentada cuando habla.
5. Todos los alumnos prestan atención.
6. Pablo habla de las costumbres hispanoamericanas.
7. La clase aplaude a Pablo.
8. Las palabras están en el diccionario.
9. El profesor quiere saber dónde están las palabras.
10. Es necesario estudiar para aprender bien.

V. Match each expression in column *A* with the corresponding translation in column *B*: [10]

A	B
1. Usted tiene que trabajar.	*a.* He knows how to sing well.
2. Son las tres menos cuarto.	*b.* How is the weather today?
3. ¿Qué tiempo hace hoy?	*c.* How old was she?
4. Aprenden a escribir bien.	*d.* They learn to write well.
5. Él sabe cantar bien.	*e.* Now I'm very hungry.
6. Después de comer, ellos salieron.	*f.* At three.
7. ¡Escriba la palabra otra vez!	*g.* You have to work.
8. ¿Cuántos años tenía ella?	*h.* Write me a letter soon!
9. Ahora tengo mucha hambre.	*i.* It is a quarter to three.
10. Duermo muy bien.	*j.* I sleep very well.
	k. After eating, they left.
	l. You study in the morning.
	m. Write the word again!

VI. Complete the following sentences as indicated: [25]

1. (The) _____ mapa de España es útil.
2. La bandera representa (the) _____ nación.
3. El plural de "luz" es _____.
4. Yo hablo (to the) _____ alumno.
5. Él no tiene (Carmen's book) _____.
6. Es (the boy's book) _____.
7. La alumna nueva es (Spanish) _____.
8. (This) _____ niño es muy inteligente.
9. (Those) _____ alumnas son hermanas.
10. Son (seven o'clock) _____.
11. En la clase (I put) _____ mis libros en el pupitre.
12. (We are) _____ americanos.
13. ¿(Who) _____ es el presidente?
14. Sevilla (is) _____ en España.
15. ¿(Where) _____ está mi sombrero?
16. Él quiere ir (with me) _____.
17. (We live) _____ en Nueva York.
18. (She does not speak) _____ bien en español.
19. ¿(Do you understand) _____ el inglés?
20. (Our) _____ escuela es grande.
21. Yo tengo (thirteen) _____ años.
22. (There are) _____ muchos libros aquí.
23. Yo quiero comer; (I am hungry) _____.
24. Al entrar en la clase yo digo (Good morning) _____.
25. El primer mes del año es (January) _____.

VII. Translate into Spanish: [5]

1. yellow	3. small	5. fifteen	7. easy	9. lawyer
2. when	4. spring	6. March	8. Wednesday	10. why?

a, to, at
abierto, -a, open
abogado, *m.,* lawyer
abrazo, *m.,* embrace
abrigo, *m.,* coat, overcoat
abril, *m.,* April
abrir, to open
abuelo, *m.,* grandfather; **abuela,** *f.,* grandmother; **abuelos,** *m. pl.,* grandparents
acabar, to finish, to end; **acabar de** + *inf.,* to have just . . .
aceite, *m.,* oil; **aceite de oliva,** olive oil
aceptar, to accept
acerca de, about, concerning
acercarse (a), to approach
acompañar, to accompany
acordarse (ue) (de), to remember
acostarse (ue), to go to bed, to lie down
actriz, *f.,* actress
además (de), besides, moreover
adiós, goodbye
admiración, *f.,* admiration, wonder
admirar, to admire, to wonder
adonde, where
adorar, to adore
aeroplano, *m.,* airplane
afortunado, -a, fortunate, lucky
agosto, *m.,* August
agradable, pleasant, agreeable
agua (el), *f.,* water
ahora, now; **ahora mismo,** right now
aire, *m.,* air
al, to the, at the; **al** + *inf.,* on, upon (speaking, etc.)
Alberto, Albert
alcoba, *f.,* bedroom
alegre, merry, gay, happy
alemán, alemana, German; **alemán,** *m.,* German (language)
Alemania, *f.,* Germany
alfabeto, *m.,* alphabet
algo, something
alguien, someone, somebody
alguno, -a (algún), some
Alicia, Alice
almorzar (ue), to lunch, to eat lunch
almuerzo, *m.,* lunch
alto, -a, high, tall
alumno, -a, pupil, student
allí, there
amable, kind, amiable
amar, to love
amarillo, -a, yellow
americano, -a, American
amigo, -a, friend
amo, *m.,* master, owner

amor, *m.,* love
Ana, Ann
anciano, -a, old, ancient
ancho, -a, wide
andar, to walk, to go
Andrés, Andrew
anécdota, *f.,* anecdote
ángel, *m.,* angel
animal, *m.,* animal
anoche, last night
antes (de), before; **antes (de) que,** before
antiguo, -a, old, ancient
Antonio, Anthony, Tony
anunciar, to announce
año, *m.,* year; **Año Nuevo,** New Year
aparato, *m.,* radio or television set
apartamiento, *m.,* apartment
apetito, *m.,* appetite
aplicado, -a, studious, industrious, diligent
aprender, to learn
aprisa, quickly
aproximadamente, approximately
aquel, aquella, that; **aquél, aquélla,** that one
aquellos, -as, those; **aquéllos, -as,** those
aquí, here
árabe, Arab; **árabe,** *m.,* Arabic (language)
árbol, *m.,* tree
aritmética, *f.,* arithmetic
arquitectura, *f.,* architecture
arroz, *m.,* rice
arte, *m. or f.,* art
artículo, *m.,* article
artista, *m. or f.,* artist
Arturo, Arthur
así, so, thus
asiento, *m.,* seat
asistir (a), to attend
asustarse, to be frightened
atacar, to attack
atención, *f.,* attention
atentamente, attentively
atento, -a, attentive
aún, even, still, yet
aunque, although
ausente, absent
auto, *m.,* auto, automobile
autobús, *m.,* bus
automóvil, *m.,* automobile
autor, *m.,* author
autoridad, *f.,* authority
avanzar, to advance
ave (el), *f.,* bird
avenida, *f.,* avenue
aventura, *f.,* adventure
aviación, *f.,* aviation
avión, *m.,* airplane
ayer, yesterday
ayudar, to help, to aid
azúcar, *m.,* sugar
azul, blue

bailar, to dance

bailarín, -a, dancer
baile, *m.,* dance
bajar, to go down, to descend
bajo, -a, low, short
balcón, *m.,* balcony
banana, *f.,* banana
banco, *m.,* bench, bank
bandera, *f.,* flag
bañar, to bathe; **bañarse,** to take a bath
baño, *m.,* bath
barato, -a, cheap
barba, *f.,* beard, chin
bastante, enough, quite
batalla, *f.,* battle
beber, to drink
bebida, *f.,* beverage, drink
béisbol, *m.,* baseball
bello, -a, beautiful
besar, to kiss
beso, *m.,* kiss
biblioteca, *f.,* library
bicicleta, *f.,* bicycle
bien, well; *m.,* good, welfare; **está bien,** all right
billete, *m.,* ticket, note
blanco, -a, white
blusa, *f.,* blouse
boca, *f.,* mouth
bolsa, *f.,* purse
bolsillo, *m.,* pocket
bombilla, *f.,* small tube for drinking yerba mate
bondad, *f.,* goodness, kindness; **tenga Vd. la bondad de** + *inf.,* please . . .
bonito, -a, pretty
borrador, *m.,* eraser
botella, *f.,* bottle
botón, *m.,* button
brazalete, *m.,* bracelet
brazo, *m.,* arm
bueno, -a (buen), good
buque, *m.,* boat, ship
burro, *m.,* donkey
buscar, to look for, to seek

caballero, *m.,* gentleman, knight
caballo, *m.,* horse; **a caballo,** on horseback
cabello, *m.,* hair
cabeza, *f.,* head
cacao, *m.,* chocolate bean
cada, each, every
caer, to fall; **caerse,** to fall down
café, *m.,* coffee, café
cafetería, *f.,* cafeteria
caja, *f.,* box
calcetín, *m.,* sock
calendario, *m.,* calendar
caliente, hot, warm
calor, *m.,* heat; **hace calor,** it is warm (weather); **tiene calor,** he is warm
calle, *f.,* street
cama, *f.,* bed
cámara, *f.,* camera
caminar, to walk

camino, *m.,* road
camisa, *f.,* shirt
campesino, *m.,* farmer, peasant
campo, *m.,* country, field
canción, *f.,* song
cansado, -a, tired
cantar, to sing
capacidad, *f.,* capacity
capital, *f.,* capital (city)
capitán, *m.,* captain
capítulo, *m.,* chapter
capturar, capture
cara, *f.,* face
carácter, *m.,* character
Carlota, Charlotte
carne, *f.,* meat; **carne de vaca,** beef
caro, -a, expensive, dear
carta, *f.,* letter
cartero, *m.,* letter carrier, postman
casa, *f.,* house, home; **a casa,** home; **en casa,** at home
casar, to marry; **casarse (con),** to marry
cascada, *f.,* waterfall
casi, almost, nearly
castellano, *m.,* Castilian, Spanish
Castilla, *f.,* Castile
castillo, *m.,* castle
catalán, catalana, Catalonian
Catalina, Catherine
catedral, *f.,* cathedral
católico, -a, Catholic
catorce, fourteen
causa, *f.,* cause; **a causa de,** because of
celebrar, to celebrate
célebre, famous
cementerio, *m.,* cemetery
cena, *f.,* supper
cenar, to eat supper
centavo, *m.,* cent
central, central
centro, *m.,* center; **al centro,** downtown; **Centro América,** Central America
cerca, near; **cerca de,** near
cereal, *m.,* cereal
ceremonia, *f.,* ceremony
cereza, *f.,* cherry
cero, *m.,* zero
cerrado, -a, closed
cerrar (ie), to close
cesta, *f.,* basket
cielo, *m.,* sky, heaven
ciencia, *f.,* science
ciento (cien), one hundred
cierto, -a, certain, a certain
cinco, five
cincuenta, fifty
cine, *m.,* movies
circo, *m.,* circus
cita, *f.,* date, appointment
ciudad, *f.,* city
civilización, *f.,* civilization
claro, -a, light, clear
clase, *f.,* class, kind

clavel, *m.*, carnation
clima, *m.*, climate
club, *m.*, club
cobre, *m.*, copper
cocina, *f.*, kitchen
coche, *m.*, coach, car
color, *m.*, color
combate, *m.*, fight, combat
comedia, *f.*, comedy
comedor, *m.*, dining room
comenzar (ie), to begin, to commence
comer, to eat
comerciante, *m.*, merchant
comercio, *m.*, trade, commerce
comida, *f.*, food, dinner, meal
como, as, like
¿cómo?, how?, what?
cómodo, -a, comfortable
compañero, -a, companion
completar, to complete
completo, -a, complete
compositor, *m.*, composer
compra, *f.*, purchase; ir de compras, to go shopping
comprar, to buy
comprender, to understand
común, common
con, with
concierto, *m.*, concert
conducir, to lead, to drive
confesar (ie), to confess
conmigo, with me
conocer, to know
conquista, *f.*, conquest
conquistador, *m.*, conqueror
conquistar, to conquer
consentir (ie, i), to consent
conservar, to preserve, to save, to conserve
considerar, to consider
consigo, with him (self), with her (self), etc.
consistir en, to consist of
construcción, *f.*, construction
construir, to construct, to build
contar (ue), to count, to relate
contento, -a, content
contestar, to answer
contigo, with you
continente, *m.*, continent
continuar, to continue
contra, against
contrario, -a, contrary, opposite
controlar, to control
convencer, to convince
conversación, *f.*, conversation
copiar, to copy
corazón, *m.*, heart
corbata, *f.*, necktie
corcho, *m.*, cork
corral, *m.*, yard, corral
correctamente, correctly
correo, *m.*, mail, postoffice
correr, to run
corrida (de toros), *f.*, bullfight

cortar, to cut
corte, *f.*, court
cortés, courteous, polite
cortesía, *f.*, courtesy
cortina, *f.*, curtain
corto, -a, short
cosa, *f.*, thing
coser, to sew
costa, *f.*, coast, cost
costar (ue), to cost
costumbre, *f.*, custom, habit
creer, to believe; ¡Ya lo creo!, Yes, indeed!
crema, *f.*, cream
criado, *m.*, servant; criada, *f.*, maid, servant
crimen, *m.*, crime
cristal, *m.*, glass
cristiano, -a, Christian
cruz, *f.*, cross
cruzar, to cross
cuaderno, *m.*, notebook
cuadro, *m.*, picture
¿cuál?, which?
cuando, when
¿cuándo?, when?
¿cuánto, -a?, how much?
¿cuántos, -as?, how many?; ¿a cuántos estamos?, what is the date?
cuarenta, forty
cuarto, *m.*, room, quarter, fourth; cuarto de baño, bathroom
cuatro, four
cuatrocientos, -as, four hundred
cubano, -a, Cuban
cubierto, -a, covered
cubrir, to cover
cuchara, *f.*, spoon
cuchillo, *m.*, knife
cuenta, *f.*, account, bill
cuento, *m.*, story, tale
cuerpo, *m.*, body
cuestión, *f.*, question, problem
cuidado, *m.*, care; tener cuidado, to be careful
cuidar (de), to take care of
cultivar, to cultivate
cumpleaños, *m.*, birthday
cura, *m.*, priest; *f.*, cure
curiosidad, *f.*, curiosity
curioso, -a, curious

chaqueta, *f.*, jacket
charlar, to chat
charro, *m.*, Mexican cowboy
cheque, *m.*, bank check
chico, -a, child
chileno, -a, Chilean
chocolate, *m.*, chocolate

dama, *f.*, lady
dar, to give, to strike (the hour)
de, of, from, by, than, with
debajo de, under
deber, should, ought to, to owe

débil, weak
decidir, to decide; decidirse a, to decide to
decir, to say, to tell
declarar, to declare
defender (ie), to defend
dejar, to let, to allow, to leave
del, of the, from the
delante de, in front of
delicioso, -a, delicious
demasiado, -a, too, too much
dentro, inside, within
dependiente, *m.*, clerk
deporte, *m.*, sport
derecho, -a, right, straight; a la derecha, to the right
derivar, to derive
desaparecer, to disappear
desayunarse, to eat breakfast
desayuno, *m.*, breakfast
descendiente, *m.* or *f.*, descendant
descortés, discourteous, impolite
describir, to describe
descubierto, -a, discovered
descubrir, to discover
desde, from, since
desear, to wish, to desire
despacio, slowly
despertarse (ie), to wake up
después, afterward; después de, after
destruir, to destroy
detrás (de), in back (of), behind
día, *m.*, day; buenos días, good morning; de día, by day, in the daytime
diciembre, *m.*, December
dictador, *m.*, dictator
dicho, -a, said
diente, *m.*, tooth
diez, ten
diferencia, *f.*, difference
diferente, different
difícil, difficult
dificultad, *f.*, difficulty
dignidad, *f.*, dignity
diligente, diligent
dinero, *m.*, money
Dios, God
dirección, *f.*, address, direction
director, *m.*, director, principal
disco, *m.*, phonograph record
dispensar, to excuse
distancia, *f.*, distance
divertirse (ie, i), to enjoy oneself, to have a good time
dividir, to divide
doce, twelve
docena, *f.*, dozen
doctor, *m.*, doctor
dólar, *m.*, dollar
dolor, *m.*, pain, ache, sorrow; dolor de cabeza, headache
doméstico, -a, domestic
dominar, to dominate

domingo, *m.*, Sunday
don, *m.*, doña, *f.*, (title given to a gentleman or lady, equivalent to Mr., Mrs. or Miss in English, but used only before given names)
donde, where; ¿dónde?, where?
dormir (ue, u), to sleep; dormirse, to fall asleep
Dorotea, Dorothy
dos, two
dramaturgo, *m.*, dramatist
duda, *f.*, doubt; sin duda, no doubt, without doubt
dulce, sweet; los dulces, *m. pl.*, candy
durante, during
durar, to last, to endure
duro, -a, hard

e, and (used only before a word beginning with *i* or *hi* but not before words beginning with *hie*)
echarse a, to start to
edad, *f.*, age; ¿qué edad tiene Vd.?, how old are you?
edificio, *m.*, building
educación, *f.*, education
educador, *m.*, educator
ejemplo, *m.*, example; por ejemplo, for example
ejercicio, *m.*, exercise
ejército, *m.*, army
el, the
él, he, him, it
eléctrico, -a, electric, electrical
elefante, *m.*, elephant
elegante, elegant, stylish
Elena, Helen
elevado, -a, high, lofty
elevar, to raise, to lift
ella, she, her, it
ellos, -as, they, them
embargo: sin embargo, nevertheless, however
emoción, *f.*, emotion
emperador, *m.*, emperor
empezar (ie), to begin
empleado, *m.*, employee
en, in, on
encima (de), on top (of), above
encontrar (ue), to meet, to find
enemigo, *m.*, enemy
enero, *m.*, January
enfermo, -a, sick, ill
enfrente (de), in front of
enorme, enormous
Enrique, Henry
ensalada, *f.*, salad
enseñar, to teach, to show
entender (ie), to understand
entonces, then
entrar, to enter
entre, between, among
enviar, to send
época, *f.*, epoch, time, period

equipo, *m.*, team
error, *m.*, error, mistake
escalera, *f.*, stairs, staircase
escaparse, to escape
escena, *f.*, scene
escribir, to write
escrito, -a, written
escritor, -a, writer
escritorio, *m.*, desk
escuchar, to listen (to)
escuela, *f.*, school
ese, -a, that; ése, -a, that one
esmeralda, *f.*, emerald
eso, that
esos, -as, those; ésos, -as, those
España, *f.*, Spain
español, -a, Spanish; español, *m.*, Spanish (language), Spaniard
espectáculo, *m.*, spectacle
esperar, to await, to wait for, to hope, to expect
espíritu, *m.*, spirit
esposo, *m.*, husband; esposa, *f.*, wife
establecer, to establish
estación, *f.*, station, season
estado, *m.*, state
Estados Unidos, *m. pl.*, United States
estar, to be
estatua, *f.*, statue
este, -a, this; *m.*, east; éste, -a, this one
esto, this
estómago, *m.*, stomach
estos, -as, these; éstos, -as, these
estrecho, -a, narrow
estudiante, *m. or f.*, student
estudiar, to study
estudio, *m.*, study, studio
estúpido, -a, stupid
europeo, -a, European
exactamente, exactly
examen, *m.*, examination
examinar, to examine
excelente, excellent
existir, to exist
explicar, to explain
explorador, *m.*, explorer
explosión, *f.*, explosion
exportar, to export
expresar, to express
expulsar, to expel
extranjero, -a, foreign; *m. or f.*, foreigner
extraordinario, -a, extraordinary

fábrica, *f.*, factory
fácil, easy
facilidad, *f.*, facility
fácilmente, easily
falda, *f.*, skirt
falta, *f.*, lack, mistake, error
faltar, to be lacking, to lack, to need
fama, *f.*, fame, reputation
familia, *f.*, family

famoso, -a, famous
fantasma, *m.*, ghost
favor, *m.*, favor; por favor, please; haga Vd. el favor de + *inf.*, please
favorito, -a, favorite
febrero, *m.*, February
fecha, *f.*, date
Felipe, Philip
feliz, happy
feo, -a, ugly
ferrocarril, *m.*, railroad
fiebre, *f.*, fever
fiesta, *f.*, holiday, party
fila, *f.*, row
filosofía, *f.*, philosophy
fin, *m.*, end; al fin, finally, at last; por fin, finally
finalmente, at last, finally
flor, *f.*, flower
flotante, floating
formar, to form
fotografía, *f.*, photograph, picture
francés, francesa, French; francés, *m.*, French (language), Frenchman
Francia, France
Francisca, Frances
frase, *f.*, sentence, phrase
frecuencia, *f.*, frequency; con frecuencia, frequently
frecuentemente, frequently
frente, *f.*, forehead; *m.*, front; en frente de, in front of, opposite
fresco, -a, cool, fresh
frío, -a, cold; *m.*, cold; hace frío, it is cold (weather); tiene frío, he is cold
frito, -a, fried
fruta, *f.*, fruit
fuego, *m.*, fire
fuente, *f.*, fountain
fuerte, strong
fumar, to smoke
fundar, to found, to establish
furioso, -a, furious
fútbol, *m.*, football, soccer
futuro, *m.*, future

gallego, *m.*, Galician
ganar, to win, to earn
gastar, to spend
gato, *m.*, cat
gaucho, *m.*, Gaucho, Argentine cowboy
general, general; *m.*, general (military)
generalmente, usually, generally
generoso, -a, generous
gente, *f.*, people
geografía, *f.*, geography
gitano, *m.*, gypsy
gloria, *f.*, glory
glorioso, -a, glorious
gobernador, *m.*, governor
gobernar (ie), to govern
gobierno, *m.*, government
gracias, *f. pl.*, thanks

graduarse, to graduate
gramática, *f.*, grammar
grande (gran), large, big, great
griego, -a, Greek; *m.*, Greek (language)
gris, gray
grupo, *m.*, group
guante, *m.*, glove
guapo, -a, handsome
guerra, *f.*, war
guía, *m.*, guide; *f.*, guidebook
guitarra, *f.*, guitar
gustar, to be pleasing; gustarle a uno una cosa, to like something
gusto, *m.*, pleasure; con mucho gusto, gladly

haber, to have; había, there was, there were
habitación, *f.*, room
habitante, *m.*, inhabitant
hablar, to speak, to talk
hacer, to do, to make; hace (un año), (a year) ago
hacia, toward
hallar, to find; hallarse, to be, to find oneself
hambre (el), *f.*, hunger; tener hambre, to be hungry
hasta, until, to; hasta luego, goodbye, see you later; hasta la vista, goodbye, until I see you again
hay, there is, there are; no hay de qué, you are welcome, don't mention it
hecho, -a, done, made; *m.*, deed, fact
helado, *m.*, ice cream
hermano, *m.*, brother; hermana, *f.*, sister
hermoso, -a, beautiful
héroe, *m.*, hero
hierro, *m.*, iron
hijo, *m.*, son; hija, *f.*, daughter; hijos, *m. pl.*, children
hispanoamericano, -a, Spanish American
historia, *f.*, story, history
hombre, *m.*, man
hombro, *m.*, shoulder
hora, *f.*, hour, time
hospital, *m.*, hospital
hotel, *m.*, hotel
hoy, today; hoy día, nowadays
huevo, *m.*, egg

ibero, -a, Iberian
idea, *f.*, idea
idioma, *m.*, language
iglesia, *f.*, church
igual, equal, alike
imaginación, *f.*, imagination
imitar, to imitate
imparcial, impartial
importancia, *f.*, importance
importante, important
imposible, impossible

incierto, -a, uncertain
independencia, *f.*, independence
indio, -a, Indian
industria, *f.*, industry
industrial, industrial; *m.*, industrialist
Inés, Agnes, Inez
influencia, *f.*, influence
Inglaterra, *f.*, England
inglés, inglesa, English; inglés, *m.*, English (language), Englishman
inmediatamente, immediately
inmenso, -a, immense
insecto, *m.*, insect
instrumento, *m.*, instrument
inteligente, intelligent
interesante, interesting
introducir, to introduce
inventar, to invent
invierno, *m.*, winter
invitar, to invite
ir, to go; irse, to go away
isla, *f.*, island
izquierdo, -a, left; a la izquierda, to the left

Jaime, James
jamás, never
jamón, *m.*, ham
jardín, *m.*, garden
jefe, *m.*, chief
Jorge, George
José, Joseph
joven, young
Juan, John
juego, *m.*, game
jueves, *m.*, Thursday
juez, *m.*, judge
jugar (ue), to play
juguete, *m.*, toy
julio, *m.*, July
junio, *m.*, June
justicia, *f.*, justice

la, the, her, it, you; la que, she who, the one that
lado, *m.*, side; al lado de, beside, next to
ladrón, *m.*, thief
lago, *m.*, lake
lámpara, *f.*, lamp
lana, *f.*, wool
lápiz, *m.*, pencil
largo, -a, long
lástima, *f.*, pity
latinoamericano, -a, Latin American
lavandera, *f.*, washerwoman
lavar, to wash; lavarse, to wash oneself
le, him, to him, to her, you, to you
lección, *f.*, lesson
lectura, *f.*, reading; libro de lectura, *m.*, reader
leche, *f.*, milk
leer, to read
legumbre, *f.*, vegetable

lejos, far; lejos de, far from; a lo lejos, at a distance

lengua, *f.*, language, tongue

lentamente, slowly

león, *m.*, lion

les, to them, to you

letra, *f.*, letter (of the alphabet)

levantar, to raise; levantarse, to get up, to stand up

libertad, *f.*, liberty

libertador, *m.*, liberator

libra, *f.*, pound

libre, free

librería, *f.*, bookstore

libro, *m.*, book

limón, *m.*, lemon

limpiar, to clean

limpio, -a, clean

lindo, -a, pretty

loco, -a, insane, mad, crazy

lograr + *inf.*, to succeed in

los, las, the, them, you; los (las) que, those who, the ones that

Lucía, Lucy

lucha, *f.*, fight, struggle

luchar, to fight

luego, then; hasta luego, see you later

lugar, *m.*, place; tener lugar, to take place

Luis, Louis

Luisa, Louise

luna, *f.*, moon

lunes, *m.*, Monday

luz, *f.*, light

llamar, to call; llamar a la puerta, to knock on the door; llamarse, to be called or named

llave, *f.*, key

llegar, to arrive, to reach; llegar a ser, to become

lleno, -a, full

llevar, to carry, to take, to wear

llorar, to cry

llover (ue), to rain

lluvia, *f.*, rain

madera, *f.*, wood

madre, *f.*, mother

madrileño, -a, Madrilenian (inhabitant of Madrid)

maestro, -a, teacher

magnífico, -a, magnificent

mal, badly, poorly, ill; *m.*, evil, harm

maleta, *f.*, suitcase

malo, -a (mal), bad

mamá, *f.*, mamma

mandar, to order, to send

manera, *f.*, manner; de esta manera, in this way

mano, *f.*, hand

mantel, *m.*, tablecloth

mantequilla, *f.*, butter

manzana, *f.*, apple

mañana, tomorrow; *f.*, morning; de la mañana, in the morning, A.M.; por la mañana, in the morning

mapa, *m.*, map

mar, *m.* or *f.*, sea

maravilloso, -a, marvelous

marchar, to march, to walk; marcharse, to go away

María, Mary

marido, *m.*, husband

marinero, *m.*, sailor

martes, *m.*, Tuesday

marzo, *m.*, March

más, more

matar, to kill

matrimonio, *m.*, marriage

mayo, *m.*, May

mayor, older, oldest; larger, largest; greater, greatest

me, me, to me, myself

medianoche, *f.*, midnight

medicina, *f.*, medicine

médico, *m.*, doctor

medio, -a, half; y media, half past; en medio de, in the middle of, in the midst of

mediodía, *m.*, noon

mejicano, -a, (mexicano, -a), Mexican

mejor, better, best

melón, *m.*, melon

memoria, *f.*, memory; de memoria, by heart

menor, younger, youngest; lesser, least; smaller, smallest

menos, less, minus; a menos que, unless

mentira, *f.*, lie

menú, *m.*, menu

menudo, -a, small, minute; a menudo, often

mercado, *m.*, market

mes, *m.*, month

mesa, *f.*, table

mexicano, -a, Mexican

México, Mexico

mezquita, *f.*, mosque

mi, mis, my

mí, me

mientras (que), while

miércoles, *m.*, Wednesday

Miguel, Michael

mil, one thousand

millón, *m.*, million

mineral, *m.*, mineral

minuto, *m.*, minute

mío, -a, mine, of mine

mirar, to look (at)

misión, *f.*, mission

misionero, *m.*, missionary

mismo, -a, same

misterioso, -a, mysterious

moderno, -a, modern

momento, *m.*, moment

monasterio, *m.*, monastery

moneda, *f.*, coin

montaña, *f.*, mountain

montañoso, -a, mountainous

montar, to ride

monumento, *m.*, monument

moreno, -a, dark-complexioned, brunette

morir (ue, u), to die

moro, -a, Moorish; *m.*, Moor

mosca, *f.*, fly

mostrar (ue), to show

motor, *m.*, motor

mozo, *m.*, waiter, porter, servant

muchacho, *m.*, boy; muchacha, *f.*, girl

muchísimo, very much

mucho, -a, much

muchos, -as, many

mueble, *m.*, article of furniture; *pl.*, furniture

muerte, *f.*, death

muerto, -a, dead, died

mujer, *f.*, woman

mundo, *m.*, world; todo el mundo, everybody, everyone

museo, *m.*, museum

música, *f.*, music

musical, musical

músico, -a, musical; *m.*, musician

muy, very

nacer, to be born

nacimiento, *m.*, birth, representation of the Nativity scene

nación, *f.*, nation

nacional, national

nada, nothing, not . . . anything; de nada, you are welcome, don't mention it

nadar, to swim

nadie, no one, nobody, not . . . anyone, not . . . anybody

naranja, *f.*, orange

nariz, *f.*, nose

natural, natural

navegable, navigable

Navidad, *f.*, Christmas

necesario, -a, necessary

necesidad, *f.*, necessity

necesitar, to need

negarse a, to refuse

negocio, *m.*, business transaction; *pl.*, business

negro, -a, black

nervioso, -a, nervous

nevar (ie), to snow

ni, neither, nor; ni . . . ni, neither . . . nor

nieve, *f.*, snow

ninguno, -a (ningún), no, none, no one

niño, -a, child

no, no, not

noche, *f.*, night, evening; de noche, at night; esta noche, tonight; de la noche, in the evening, P.M.; por la noche, in the evening

nombrar, to name

nombre, *m.*, name

norte, *m.*, north

norteamericano, -a, North American, American

nos, us, to us, ourselves

nosotros, -as, we, us

nota, *f.*, grade, mark

notar, to notice, to note

noticia, *f.*, news item; *pl.*, news

novecientos, -as, nine hundred

novela, *f.*, novel

noventa, ninety

noviembre, *m.*, November

nuestro, -a, our, ours, of ours

nueve, nine

nuevo, -a, new; de nuevo, again

número, *m.*, number

numeroso, -a, numerous

nunca, never

o, or

objeto, *m.*, object

océano, *m.*, ocean

octubre, *m.*, October

ocupado, -a, busy

ocurrir, to occur, to happen; se me ocurre, it occurs to me

ochenta, eighty

ocho, eight

oeste, *m.*, west

oficial, official; *m.*, officer

oficina, *f.*, office

ofrecer, to offer

oír, to hear

ojo, *m.*, eye

olvidar, to forget; olvidarse de, to forget

omitir, to omit

once, eleven

opinión, *f.*, opinion

oportunidad, *f.*, opportunity

orden, *f.*, order, command; *m.*, order, system

ordinario, -a, ordinary

oreja, *f.*, ear

origen, *m.*, origin

orilla, *f.*, shore, bank (of a river)

oro, *m.*, gold

orquesta, *f.*, orchestra

otoño, *m.*, autumn

otro, -a, other, another

Pablo, Paul

Paco, Frank

padre, *m.*, father; padres, *m. pl.*, parents

pagar, to pay

página, *f.*, page

país, *m.*, country, nation

pájaro, *m.*, bird

palabra, *f.*, word

palacio, *m.*, palace

pálido, -a, pale

pan, *m.*, bread

panamericano, -a, Pan-American

SPANISH-ENGLISH VOCABULARY

Pancho, Frank

pantalones, *m. pl.*, trousers, pants

pañuelo, *m.*, handkerchief

papá, *m.*, papa, dad

papel, *m.*, paper

paquete, *m.*, package

par, *m.*, pair

para, for, in order to

paraguas, *m.*, umbrella

pardo, -a, brown

parecer, to seem, to appear

pared, *f.*, wall

parque, *m.*, park

párrafo, *m.*, paragraph

parte, *f.*, part; **por todas partes**, everywhere; **la mayor parte de**, most of, the majority of

partir, to depart

pasado, -a, past, last

pasajero, *m.*, passenger

pasaporte, *m.*, passport

pasar, to pass, to spend (time); **que lo pase Vd. bien**, good luck to you

Pascua: **Pascua Florida**, Easter

pasear, to walk, to ride; **pasearse**, to take a walk

paseo, *m.*, walk, drive; **dar un paseo**, to take a walk

pastel, *m.*, pie, cake

pastor, *m.*, shepherd

patata, *f.*, potato

patio, *m.*, courtyard, patio

patria, *f.*, (native) country, fatherland

patriota, *m.* or *f.*, patriot

paz, *f.*, peace

pedazo, *m.*, piece

pedir (i), to ask for, to order (food)

Pedro, Peter

peinarse, to comb one's hair

peineta, *f.*, large ornamental comb

película, *f.*, film, movie

pelo, *m.*, hair

pelota, *f.*, ball

pensar (ie), to think, to intend to; **pensar en**, to think of

peor, worse, worst

Pepe, Joe

pequeño, -a, small

pera, *f.*, pear

perder (ie), to lose; **perderse**, to get lost

pérdida, *f.*, loss

perdón, *m.*, pardon

perdonar, to pardon

perezoso, -a, lazy

perfectamente, perfectly

perfecto, -a, perfect

periódico, *m.*, newspaper

permiso, *m.*, permission; **con permiso**, excuse me

permitir, to permit

pero, but

perro, *m.*, dog

persona, *f.*, person

pertenecer, to belong

peruano, -a, Peruvian

pesar, to weigh; **a pesar de**, in spite of

pescado, *m.*, fish

peseta, *f.*, peseta (monetary unit of Spain)

peso, *m.*, peso (monetary unit of several Spanish-American countries)

petróleo, *m.*, petroleum

pianista, *m.* or *f.*, pianist

piano, *m.*, piano

pico, *m.*, peak

pie, *m.*, foot; **a pie**, on foot; **de pie**, standing

piedra, *f.*, stone

pintar, to paint

pintor, *m.*, painter

pintoresco, -a, picturesque

pintura, *f.*, painting

piña, *f.*, pineapple

pirámide, *f.*, pyramid

piso, *m.*, floor, story, apartment; **piso bajo**, ground floor

pizarra, *f.*, blackboard

plan, *m.*, plan

planta, *f.*, plant

plata, *f.*, silver

plátano, *m.*, banana

platino, *m.*, platinum

plato, *m.*, plate, dish

playa, *f.*, beach

plaza, *f.*, square, plaza

pluma, *f.*, pen

población, *f.*, population, town

pobre, poor

poco, -a, little; **poco a poco**, little by little

pocos, -as, few

poder, to be able, can; *m.*, power

poesía, *f.*, poem, poetry

poeta, *m.*, poet

poetisa, *f.*, poetess

pollo, *m.*, chicken

poner, to put, to set; **ponerse**, to put on, to become

por, for, by, through

pordiosero, *m.*, beggar

porque, because; **¿por qué?**, why?

portorriqueño, -a, (puertorriqueño, -a), Puerto Rican

portugués, portuguesa, Portuguese; **portugués**, *m.*, Portuguese (language), Portuguese

posible, possible

postres, *m. pl.*, dessert

preceder, to precede

precio, *m.*, price

precioso, -a, precious

preferir (ie, i), to prefer

pregunta, *f.*, question; **hacer una pregunta**, to ask a question

preguntar, to ask

premio, *m.*, prize, reward

preparar, to prepare; **prepararse a**, to get ready to

presentar, to present, to introduce

presente, present

presidente, *m.*, president

prestar, to lend; **prestar atención**, to pay attention

primavera, *f.*, spring (season)

primero, -a (primer), first

primo, -a, cousin

princesa, *f.*, princess

principal, main, principal

principalmente, principally, mainly

príncipe, *m.*, prince

prisa, *f.*, haste; **tener prisa**, to be in a hurry

prisionero, *m.*, prisoner

problema, *m.*, problem

producir, to produce

producto, *m.*, product

profesor, -a, teacher, professor

progresivo, -a, progressive

prohibir, to prohibit, to forbid

prometer, to promise

pronto, soon; **de pronto**, suddenly; **lo más pronto posible**, as soon as possible

pronunciar, to pronounce

propietario, *m.*, proprietor

propina, *f.*, tip

protestante, Protestant

proverbio, *m.*, proverb

próximo, -a, next

proyecto, *m.*, project, plan

público, -a, public; *m.*, public

pueblo, *m.*, town, people

puente, *m.*, bridge

puerta, *f.*, door

puerto, *m.*, port

pues, then, well

puesto, placed, put; *m.*, position, post, stand

punto, *m.*, point, dot; **en punto**, exactly, on the dot

pupitre, *m.*, (pupil's) desk

que, who, whom, which, that, than

¿qué?, what?

¡qué . . . !, what a . . . !, how . . . !

quedar, to remain, to be left; **quedarse**, to remain

querer, to want, to wish, to love; **querer decir**, to mean

querido, -a, dear, beloved

queso, *m.*, cheese

quien, who, whom

¿quién?, who?, whom?, **¿de quién?**, whose?

quienquiera, whoever

quince, fifteen

quinientos, -as, five hundred

quinto, -a, fifth

quitar, to take away; **quitarse**, to take off (clothing)

radio, *m.* or *f.*, radio (generally masculine when referring to the radio set)

ramo, *m.*, bouquet

Ramón, Raymond

rancho, *m.*, ranch

rápidamente, rapidly

rápido, -a, rapid

raro, -a, rare

ratón, *m.*, mouse

raza, *f.*, race (of people)

razón, *f.*, reason; **tener razón**, to be right; **no tener razón**, to be wrong

real, real, royal

realidad, *f.*, reality

recibir, to receive

recientemente, recently

recordar (ue), to remember

recuerdo, *m.*, remembrance, souvenir; *pl.*, regards

referir (ie), to refer

refresco, *m.*, refreshment, soft drink

regalo, *m.*, gift, present

región, *f.*, region

regla, *f.*, rule, ruler

regresar, to return

regular, regular

reina, *f.*, queen

reír (i), to laugh

religioso, -a, religious

reloj, *m.*, watch, clock

remedio, *m.*, remedy, cure

repetir (i), to repeat

representar, to represent

república, *f.*, republic

reservar, to reserve

resfriado, *m.*, cold (illness)

resolver (ue), to resolve, to solve

respetar, to respect

responder, to answer, to respond

respuesta, *f.*, reply, answer

restaurante, *m.*, restaurant

retirarse a, to retire to

retrato, *m.*, picture, portrait

reunir, to gather, to bring together; **reunirse**, to meet, to assemble

revista, *f.*, magazine

revolución, *f.*, revolution

rey, *m.*, king

rico, -a, rich

río, *m.*, river

robar, to steal

rojo, -a, red

romano, -a, Roman

romántico, -a, romantic

ropa, *f.*, clothes, clothing

ropero, *m.*, closet, locker

rosa, *f.*, rose

Rosa, Rose

rubio, -a, blond

ruido, *m.*, noise

ruina, *f.*, ruin

sábado, *m.*, Saturday

saber, to know (how to)

sal, *f.*, salt

sala, *f.*, living room, parlor

salir (de), to leave, to go out (of)

salitre, *m.*, nitrate

salón, *m.*, salon; salón de actos, auditorium

salud, *f.*, health

saludar, to greet

sangre, *f.*, blood

Santo, -a (San), Saint

sarape, *m.*, Mexican blanket, serape

se, to him, to her, to you, to them, himself, herself, yourself, themselves

secretario, -a, secretary

sed, *f.*, thirst; tener sed, to be thirsty

seguida: en seguida, immediately, at once

seguir (i), to follow, to continue

según, according to

segundo, -a, second

seguro, -a, secure, sure, safe

seis, six

seiscientos, -as, six hundred

sello, *m.*, seal, stamp

semana, *f.*, week

semestre, *m.*, semester, term

sentado, -a, seated

sentarse (ie), to sit down

sentir (ie, i), to regret, to be sorry; sentirse, to feel; lo siento mucho, I'm very sorry

señor, *m.*, master, gentleman, Mr.; señora, *f.*, lady, madam, Mrs.

separar, to separate

septiembre, *m.*, September

ser, to be; *m.*, being

sereno, *m.*, night watchman

servilleta, *f.*, napkin

servir (i), to serve

sesenta, sixty

setecientos, -as, seven hundred

setenta, seventy

si, if; sí, yes, himself, herself, yourself, themselves

siempre, always

sierra, *f.*, mountain range

siesta, *f.*, siesta, afternoon nap; dormir la siesta, to take an afternoon nap

siete, seven

siglo, *m.*, century

significar, to mean

siguiente, following; al día siguiente, on the following day

silencio, *m.*, silence

silenciosamente, silently

silla, *f.*, chair

simpático, -a, nice, pleasant

sin, without; sin que, with-

out; sin embargo, nevertheless, however

sincero, -a, sincere

sitio, *m.*, place, site

situación, *f.*, situation, place

situado, -a, situated

sobre, *m.*, envelope

sobre, on, upon; sobre todo, especially, above all

sobretodo, *m.*, overcoat

sociedad, *f.*, society

sofá, *m.*, sofa, couch

sol, *m.*, sun; hace sol, it is sunny

solamente, only

soldado, *m.*, soldier

solo, -a, alone; sólo, only

sombrero, *m.*, hat

sonido, *m.*, sound

sopa, *f.*, soup

sospechoso, -a, suspicious

su, sus, his, her, your, their, its

subir, to go up, to climb

subterráneo, *m.*, subway

sucio, -a, dirty

sud, *m.*, south; sudeste, southeast; sudoeste, southwest

suelo, *m.*, floor, ground, soil

sueño, *m.*, sleep, dream; tener sueño, to be sleepy

suficiente, sufficient

sufrir, to suffer

sur, *m.*, south

tabaco, *m.*, tobacco

talento, *m.*, talent

también, also

tampoco, neither

tan, so; tan . . . como, as . . . as

tanto, -a, so much

tarde, late; *f.*, afternoon; de la tarde, in the afternoon, P.M.; por la tarde, in the afternoon

tarjeta, *f.*, card

taza, *f.*, cup

te, you, to you, yourself

té, *m.*, tea

teatro, *m.*, theatre

teléfono, *m.*, telephone

telegrama, *m.*, telegram

televisión, *f.*, television

templo, *m.*, temple

temprano, early

tenedor, *m.*, fork

tener, to have; tener que, to have to, must

tenis, *m.*, tennis

tercero, -a (tercer), third

terminar, to finish, to end

terrible, terrible

terror, *m.*, terror

tertulia, *f.*, party, social gathering

ti, you

tiempo, *m.*, time; a tiempo, on time; ¿cuánto tiempo?, how long?; hace buen tiempo, it is good weather

tienda, *f.*, store

tierra, *f.*, land, earth

tinta, *f.*, ink

tío, *m.*, uncle; tía, *f.*, aunt

típico, -a, typical

tirar de, to pull

tiza, *f.*, chalk

tocar, to touch, to play (an instrument)

todavía, still, yet

todo, -a, all; todos los días, every day; todo el mundo, everybody; *m.*, everything

tomar, to take, to have (food or drink)

Tomás, Thomas

torero, *m.*, bullfighter

toro, *m.*, bull

torre, *f.*, tower

tortilla, *f.*, tortilla

trabajador, -a, hard working

trabajar, to work

trabajo, *m.*, work

traducir, to translate

traer, to bring

traje, *m.*, suit

tranvía, *m.*, streetcar

tratar, to treat; tratar de + *inf.*, to try to

trece, thirteen

treinta, thirty

tren, *m.*, train

tres, three

trescientos, -as, three hundred

trigo, *m.*, wheat

triste, sad

tropa, *f.*, troop

tu, tus, your

tú, you

tuyo, -a, yours

u, or (used only before words beginning with *o* or *ho*)

último, -a, last

un, una, a, an, one

único, -a, only

universidad, *f.*, university

uno, -a, one

unos, -as, some, about

usar, to use

usted (abbrev. Vd or Vd.), you; *pl.* ustedes (abbrev. Vds or Vds.)

usualmente, usually

útil, useful

vaca, *f.*, cow

vacaciones, *f. pl.*, vacation

vacío, -a, empty

valer, to be worth

valiente, brave

valor, *m.*, valor, courage, value

valle, *m.*, valley

vaquero, *m.*, cowboy

variedad, *f.*, variety

varios, -as, several

vasco, -a, Basque

vascongado, -a, Basque

vascuence, *m.*, Basque language

vaso, *m.*, glass

vecino, -a, neighbor

veinte, twenty

vencer, to conquer, to defeat

vendedor, *m.*, seller, vendor

vender, to sell

venir, to come

ventana, *f.*, window

ver, to see

verano, *m.*, summer

verbo, *m.*, verb

verdad, *f.*, truth; ¿no es verdad? or ¿verdad?, isn't it so?

verdadero, -a, true, real

verde, green

vestido, *m.*, dress

vestir (i), to dress; vestirse (de), to get dressed (in)

vez, *f.*, time; otra vez, again; una vez, once; dos veces, twice; algunas veces, sometimes; muchas veces, many times, often

viajar, to travel

viaje, *m.*, trip; hacer un viaje, to take a trip

viajero, *m.*, traveler

vida, *f.*, life

vidrio, *m.*, glass

viejo, -a, old

viento, *m.*, wind; hace viento, it is windy

viernes, *m.*, Friday

vino, *m.*, wine

violeta, *f.*, violet

violín, *m.*, violin

visita, *f.*, visit; hacer una visita, to pay a visit

visitar, to visit

vivir, to live

volar (ue), to fly

volcán, *m.*, volcano

volver (ue), to return, to go back; volver a + *inf.*, to (*verb*) again

vosotros, -as, you

voz, *f.*, voice; en voz alta, aloud

vuestro, -a, your

y, and

ya, already

yo, I

zapato, *m.*, shoe

a, un, una
able: to be able, poder
about, de, acerca de
above, sobre; above all, sobre todo
absent, ausente
accept, aceptar
action, la acción
activity, la actividad
actor, el actor
actress, la actriz
address, la dirección
admire, admirar
after, después de; it is (five) after (nine), son las (nueve) y (cinco)
afternoon, la tarde; good afternoon, buenas tardes; in the afternoon, por la tarde; (at three) in the afternoon, (a las tres) de la tarde; yesterday afternoon, ayer por la tarde
again, otra vez, de nuevo; see you again, hasta la vista
against, contra
airplane, el avión, el aeroplano
Albert, Alberto
alike, igual
all, todo, -a; all right, está bien; above all, sobre todo
allow, dejar, permitir
almost, casi
alone, solo, -a
aloud, en voz alta
already, ya
also, también
always, siempre
A.M., de la mañana
American, americano, -a, norteamericano, -a
among, entre
an, un, una
ancient, antiguo, -a
and, y, e (before i or hi)
Andrew, Andrés
animal, el animal
Ann, Ana
another, otro, -a
answer, la respuesta; to answer, responder, contestar
Anthony, Antonio
any, alguno, -a (algún); not ... any, ninguno, -a (ningún)
anyone, alguien; not ... anyone, no ... nadie
anything, algo; not ... anything, no ... nada
apartment, el apartamiento
apple, la manzana
approach, acercarse (a)
April, abril
arm, el brazo
army, el ejército
Arthur, Arturo
as, como; as ... as, tan ... como

ask: ask a question, preguntar; ask for, pedir (i)
at, a
attack, atacar
attend, asistir (a)
attention, la atención; to pay attention, prestar atención
attentively, atentamente, con atención
August, agosto
aunt, la tía
author, el autor
automobile, el automóvil; to take an automobile ride, dar un paseo en automóvil
avenue, la avenida

bad, malo, -a (mal)
ball, la pelota
banana, la banana
bank, el banco
baseball, el béisbol
bath, el baño; to take a bath, bañarse
bathroom, el cuarto de baño
battle, la batalla
be, ser, estar
beach, la playa
beard, la barba
beautiful, hermoso, -a, bello, -a
because, porque
become, llegar a ser, ponerse
bed, la cama; to go to bed, acostarse (ue)
before, antes de
begin, comenzar (ie), empezar (ie)
behind, detrás (de)
believe, creer; I believe so, creo que sí
belong, pertenecer
beside, al lado de, junto a
best, el (la) mejor
better, mejor
between, entre
beverage, la bebida
bicycle, la bicicleta
big, grande, enorme
bill, la cuenta
bird, el pájaro
birth, el nacimiento
birthday, el cumpleaños
black, negro, -a
blackboard, la pizarra
blond, rubio, -a
blood, la sangre
blouse, la blusa; cotton blouse, blusa de algodón
blue, azul
boat, el barco, el buque
body, el cuerpo
book, el libro; Spanish book, el libro de español
born: to be born, nacer
both, los (las) dos
bottle, la botella
bouquet, el ramo
box, la caja
boy, el muchacho

bracelet, el brazalete
brave, valiente
bread, el pan
breakfast, el desayuno; to eat breakfast, desayunarse
bridge, el puente
bring, traer
brother, el hermano
brown, pardo, -a
brunette, moreno, -a
build, construir
building, el edificio
bull, el toro; bullfight, la corrida de toros; bullfighter, el torero
bus, el autobús
business, los negocios
busy, ocupado, -a
but, pero
butcher, el carnicero
butter, la mantequilla
buy, comprar
by, por, de

cafeteria, la cafetería
cake, el pastel
calendar, el calendario
call, llamar
camera, la cámara
can (to be able), poder; can (to know how to), saber
candy, los dulces
capital, la capital
captain, el capitán
capture, capturar, tomar
car, el coche, el automóvil
card, la tarjeta
care, el cuidado; to be careful, tener cuidado
carry, llevar
cat, el gato
cathedral, la catedral
Catherine, Catalina
Catholic, católico, -a
celebrate, celebrar
cent, el centavo
center, el centro
central, central
Central America, La América Central, Centro América
century, el siglo
certain, cierto, -a
chair, la silla
chalk, la tiza
chapter, el capítulo
Charles, Carlos
Charlotte, Carlota
chat, charlar
cheap, barato, -a
check (bank), el cheque
cheese, el queso
chicken, el pollo
child, el niño, la niña
children, los niños, los hijos
Chilean, chileno, -a
chin, la barba
chocolate, el chocolate
Christmas, la Navidad
church, la iglesia
circus, el circo

city, la ciudad
civilization, la civilización
class, la clase
clean, limpio, -a
climate, el clima
clock, el reloj
close, cerrar (ie); closed, cerrado, -a
closet, el ropero
clothes, la ropa; clothing, la ropa
club, el club
coast, la costa
coat, el abrigo
coffee, el café
cold, frío, -a; he is cold, tiene frío; it is cold (weather), hace frío
color, el color
comb one's hair, peinarse
come, venir
comedy, la comedia
comfortable, cómodo, -a
companion, el compañero, la compañera
complete, completo, -a
composer, el compositor
concert, el concierto
conquer, vencer, conquistar
consider, considerar
construct, construir; construction, la construcción
content, contento, -a
continue, continuar, seguir (i)
convince, convencer
cool, fresco, -a; it is cool (weather), hace fresco
copper, el cobre
correctly, correctamente
cost, costar (ue)
count, contar (ue)
country (nation), el país; (as contrasted with city), el campo; (native land), la patria
courteous, cortés
cousin, el primo, la prima
cover, cubrir
cow, la vaca
cowboy, el vaquero
cream, la crema
cry, llorar
cultivate, cultivar
cup, la taza
curiosity, la curiosidad
curious, curioso, -a
curtain, la cortina
custom, la costumbre

dance, el baile; to dance, bailar
dancer, el bailarín, la bailarina
date, la fecha; (appointment), la cita
daughter, la hija
day, el día; every day, todos los días, cada día
dead, muerto, -a; death, la muerte

December, diciembre

decide, decidir

deed, el hecho

defeat, vencer

defend, defender (ie)

delicious, delicioso, -a

depart, partir

descendant, el or la descendiente

describe, describir

desk, el escritorio, el pupitre

dictator, el dictador

die, morir (ue, u)

different, diferente

difficult, difícil

diligent, diligente, aplicado, -a

dining room, el comedor

dinner, la comida; to eat dinner, comer

dirty, sucio, -a

disappear, desaparecer

discover, descubrir; discovery, el descubrimiento

dish, el plato

divide, dividir

do, hacer

doctor, el doctor, el médico

dog, el perro

dollar, el dólar

domestic, doméstico, -a

donkey, el burro

door, la puerta

Dorothy, Dorotea

downtown, el centro

dozen, la docena

dramatist, el dramaturgo

dress, el vestido; to dress (oneself), to get dressed, vestirse (i)

drink, la bebida; soft drink, el refresco; to drink, beber

drive, conducir

during, durante

each (one), cada (uno, -a)

early, temprano

earn, ganar

earth, la tierra

easily, fácilmente

east, el este

Easter, la Pascua Florida

easy, fácil

eat, comer

educator, el educador

egg, el huevo

eighty, ochenta

either (after neg.), tampoco; either . . . or, o . . . o; (after neg.), ni . . . ni

elegant, elegante

emperor, el emperador

empty, vacío, -a

end, terminar

enemy, el enemigo

engineer, el ingeniero

English, inglés, inglesa; English (language), el inglés

enjoy: to enjoy oneself, divertirse (ie, i)

enormous, enorme

enough, bastante, suficiente

enter, entrar (en)

envelope, el sobre

Ernest, Ernesto

error, el error, la falta

especially, sobre todo, especialmente

Europe, Europa

even, aún, todavía; not even, ni siquiera

evening, la noche; good evening, buenas noches; in the evening, por la noche; (at ten) in the evening, (a las diez) de la noche

ever, jamás

every, todos los, todas las

everybody, todo el mundo

everything, todo

everywhere, por todas partes

exactly, exactamente, en punto

examination, el examen; examine, examinar

example, el ejemplo; for example, por ejemplo

excuse, perdonar, dispensar; excuse me, perdone Vd., dispense Vd., con permiso

exercise, el ejercicio

exit, la salida

expect, esperar

expensive, caro, -a

explain, explicar

explorer, el explorador

eye, el ojo

face, la cara

factory, la fábrica

fail, salir mal

fall, caer

family, la familia

famous, famoso, -a, célebre

far from, lejos de

father, el padre

favor, el favor; to be in favor of, estar por

favorite, favorito, -a

February, febrero

feel, sentirse (ie, i); feeling, el sentimiento

fever, la fiebre

few, pocos, -as

fight, luchar

finally, al fin, por fin, finalmente

find, hallar, encontrar (ue), dar con

finish, acabar, terminar

first, primero, -a

fish, el pescado

five, cinco

flag, la bandera

floor, el suelo, el piso

flower, la flor

fly, la mosca; to fly, volar (ue)

follow, seguir (i)

following: on the following day, al día siguiente

food, la comida

foot, el pie; on foot, a pie

football, el fútbol

for, para, por

forget, olvidarse de

fork, el tenedor

form, formar

forty, cuarenta

fountain, la fuente

four, cuatro

France, Francia

Frances, Francisca

Frank, Paco, Pancho

free, libre

French, francés, francesa; French (language), el francés

Frenchman, el francés

frequently, frecuentemente, a menudo, con frecuencia

Friday, el viernes

fried, frito, -a

friend, el amigo, la amiga

from, de, desde

front: in front of, delante de, en frente de

fruit, la fruta

full, lleno, -a

furniture, los muebles

garden, el jardín

general, el general; generally, generalmente, por lo general

gentleman, el caballero, el señor

geography, la geografía

German, alemán, alemana; German (language), el alemán

get: to get up, levantarse

gift, el regalo

girl, la muchacha

give, dar

gladly, con mucho gusto

glass, el vaso, el vidrio

glove, el guante

go, ir, andar; to go away, irse, marcharse; to go out, salir; to go up, subir

God, Dios

gold, el oro

good, bueno, -a (buen)

goodbye, adiós; to say goodbye (to), despedirse (i) (de)

govern, gobernar (ie)

government, el gobierno

grade, la nota

graduate, graduarse

grammar, la gramática

grandfather, el abuelo; grandmother, la abuela; grandparents, los abuelos

gray, gris

great, grande (gran); a great deal, mucho; greater, mayor; greatest, el (la) mayor

Greek, el griego

green, verde

greet, saludar

ground, el suelo

group, el grupo

guitar, la guitarra

gypsy, el gitano

hair, el pelo, el cabello

half, medio, -a

ham, el jamón

hand, la mano

handkerchief, el pañuelo

happen, ocurrir, suceder

happy, feliz, contento, -a, alegre

hard, duro, -a

hard-working, trabajador, trabajadora, aplicado, -a

hat, el sombrero

have (possess), tener; to have (helping verb), haber; to have to, tener que; to have just . . . , acabar de + inf.

he, él

head, la cabeza; headache, el dolor de cabeza

hear, oír

heart, el corazón; by heart, de memoria

Helen, Elena

help, ayudar

Henry, Enrique

her: her book, su libro; her books, sus libros; for her, para ella; I see her, la veo; I speak to her, le hablo

here, aquí

hero, el héroe

herself, se

high, alto, -a

him: for him, para él; I know him, le (lo) conozco; I speak to him, le hablo

himself, se

his (adj.), su, sus

holiday, la fiesta

home, la casa; at home, en casa; he goes home, va a casa

horse, el caballo; on horseback, a caballo

hospital, el hospital

hot, caliente

hotel, el hotel

hour, la hora

house, la casa

how?, ¿cómo?; how long?, ¿cuánto tiempo?; how much?, ¿cuánto, -a?; how many?, ¿cuántos, -as?

however, sin embargo

huge, enorme, inmenso, -a

hundred, ciento, cien

hungry: to be (very) hungry, tener (mucha) hambre

hurry: to be in a hurry, tener prisa

husband, el esposo, el marido

I, yo

ice cream, el helado

idea, la idea

if, si

ill, enfermo, -a

immediately, en seguida, inmediatamente

important, importante

impossible, imposible

in, en; (after superlative), de

independence, la independencia

Indian, el indio, la india

industrial, industrial

industrious, aplicado, -a, diligente

industry, la industria

influence, la influencia

inhabitant, el habitante

ink, la tinta

insect, el insecto

instead of, en vez de, en lugar de

instrument, el instrumento

intelligent, inteligente

intend, pensar (ie)

interesting, interesante

into, en

invent, inventar

invitation, la invitación; to invite, invitar, convidar

island, la isla

it: for it, para él (ella); I see it, lo (la) veo

its, su, sus

James, Jaime, Diego

Jane, Juana

January, enero

John, Juan

Josephine, Josefina

judge, el juez

July, julio

June, junio

just: to have just, acabar de + inf.

key, la llave

kill, matar

kind, bondadoso, -a, amable

king, el rey

kitchen, la cocina

knife, el cuchillo

know (a person), conocer; to know (a fact), saber; to know (how to), saber

lady, la dama, la señora

lake, el lago

land, la tierra

language, la lengua, el idioma

large, grande

last, pasado, -a, último, -a; at last, al fin, por fin

late, tarde

later: see you later, hasta luego

Latin, el latín; Latin America, la América latina, Latinoamérica; Latin American, latinoamericano, -a

laugh, reír (i)

lawyer, el abogado

lazy, perezoso, -a

learn, aprender

least, el (la) menor

leave, salir (de), dejar

lemon, el limón

lend, prestar

less, menos

lesson, la lección

let, dejar, permitir

letter, la carta; letter carrier, el cartero

liberty, la libertad

library, la biblioteca

lie, la mentira

life, la vida

light, la luz

like, como; to like (to be pleasing), gustar

listen to, escuchar

little (size), pequeño, -a; (quantity), poco, -a

live, vivir

living room, la sala

long, largo, -a; to be long (in), tardar (en)

longer: no longer, ya no

look: to look at, mirar; to look for, buscar

lose, perder (ie)

Louise, Luisa

love, el amor; to love, amar

low, bajo, -a

Lucy, Lucía

lunch, el almuerzo; to lunch or eat lunch, almorzar (ue)

magazine, la revista

magnificent, magnífico, -a

maid, la criada

main, principal

make, hacer

man, el hombre

many, muchos, -as; very many, muchísimos, -as

map, el mapa

march, marchar

March, marzo

market, el mercado

Mary, María

master, el amo

May, mayo

me: for me, para mí; with me, conmigo; he sees me, me ve; he speaks to me, me habla

meal, la comida

mean, significar, querer decir

meat, la carne

medicine, la medicina

meet, encontrar (ue); to meet (for the first time), conocer

mention: don't mention it, no hay de qué, de nada

menu, el menú, la lista de platos

Mexican, mexicano, -a

Mexico, México

Michael, Miguel

middle: in the middle of, en medio de

midnight, la medianoche

milk, la leche

million, el millón; a million

dollars, un millón de dólares

mineral, el mineral

Miss, (la) señorita

mission, la misión

missionary, el misionero

mistake, la falta, el error

modern, moderno, -a

Monday, el lunes

money, el dinero

month, el mes; last month, el mes pasado

monument, el monumento

Moorish, moro, -a

more, más

morning, la mañana; at (six) in the morning, a (las seis) de la mañana; good morning, buenos días; in the morning, por la mañana

most, más

mother, la madre

motor, el motor

mountain, la montaña

movie, la película; movies, el cine

Mr., (el) señor

Mrs., (la) señora

much, mucho, -a; so much, tanto, -a; too much, demasiado

museum, el museo

music, la música

musical, musical, músico, -a

must, deber, tener que

my, mi, mis

myself, me

name, el nombre; to name, nombrar; what is your name? ¿cómo se llama Vd.?

nap, la siesta; to take a nap, dormir (ue, u) la siesta

napkin, la servilleta

narrow, estrecho, -a

nation, la nación, el país; national, nacional

near, cerca de

necessary: it is necessary, es necesario, es preciso

necktie, la corbata

need, necesitar

neighbor, el vecino, la vecina

neither, tampoco; neither . . . nor, ni . . . ni

never, jamás, nunca

nevertheless, sin embargo

new, nuevo, -a

news, las noticias

newspaper, el periódico

New Year, el Año Nuevo

next, próximo, -a; next to, junto a, al lado de

nice, simpático, -a

night, la noche; at night, de noche; good night, buenas noches; last night, anoche

nine, nueve

no, no, ninguno, -a (ningún); no one, nadie

nobody, nadie

noise, el ruido

none, ninguno, -a (ningún)

noon, el mediodía

north, el norte

North America, La América del Norte, Norte América; North American, norteamericano, -a

not, no

notebook, el cuaderno

nothing, nada

novel, la novela

November, noviembre

now, ahora; right now, ahora mismo

number, el número

nurse, la enfermera

occur, ocurrir

ocean, el océano

o'clock: at (eight) o'clock, a las (ocho); it is (two) o'clock, son las (dos)

October, octubre

of, de

offer, ofrecer

office, la oficina

often, a menudo, muchas veces

O.K.: it's O.K., está bien

old, viejo, -a, antiguo, -a; to be . . . years old, tener . . . años; how old are you?, ¿cuántos años tiene Vd.?

older, mayor

oldest, el (la) mayor

on, en, sobre; on (speaking), al (hablar); on (Sunday), el (domingo); on (Sundays), los (domingos)

once, una vez; at once, en seguida

one, uno, -a, un; no one, nadie

only, sólo, solamente

open, abierto, -a; to open, abrir

or, o

orange, la naranja

orchestra, la orquesta

order: in order to, para; order (food), pedir (i)

other, otro, -a

ought to, deber

our, nuestro, -a, -os, -as

owe, deber

owner, el amo, el dueño

package, el paquete

page, la página

paint, pintar

painter, el pintor

pair, el par

palace, el palacio

Pan-American, panamericano, -a

paper, el papel

paragraph, el párrafo

pardon, perdonar, dispensar

pardon me, perdone Vd., dispense Vd., con permiso
parents, los padres
park, el parque
part, la parte
party, la fiesta, la tertulia; **political party**, el partido
passenger, el pasajero
passport, el pasaporte
Paul, Pablo
pay, pagar
peace, la paz
pen, la pluma
pencil, el lápiz
people, la gente
perfect, perfecto, -a
perhaps, tal vez
permit, permitir
person, la persona
Peter, Pedro
petroleum, el petróleo
Philip, Felipe
phone, el teléfono; **to phone**, llamar por teléfono
piano, el piano
picture, el cuadro, la fotografía; **(moving) picture**, la película
picturesque, pintoresco, -a
pie, el pastel; **apple pie**, pastel de manzana
place, el lugar, el sitio
plan, el plan
plant, la planta
plate, el plato
play *(a game)*, jugar (ue); **to play** *(an instrument)*, tocar
pleasant, agradable, simpático, -a
please, por favor, haga Vd. el favor de + *inf.*, tenga Vd. la bondad de + *inf.*
P.M., de la tarde, de la noche
poet, el poeta
policeman, el policía
polite, cortés
poor, pobre
popular, popular
port, el puerto
Portuguese, portugués, portuguesa; **Portuguese** *(language)*, el portugués
potato, la patata, la papa
pound, la libra
prefer, preferir (ie, i)
prepare, preparar
present, presente; *(gift)*, el regalo
president, el presidente
pretty, bonito, -a, lindo, -a
price, el precio
priest, el cura, el sacerdote
prince, el príncipe
princess, la princesa
principal, principal; *(of a school)*, el director, la directora
prisoner, el prisionero
prize, el premio
produce, producir; **product**, el producto

program, el programa
prohibit, prohibir
promise, prometer
Protestant, protestante
public, público, -a
pupil, el alumno, la alumna
put, poner; **to put on**, ponerse

quarter, el cuarto
queen, la reina
question, la pregunta; **to ask a question**, hacer una pregunta
quickly, aprisa

radio, el *or* la radio (generally masc. when referring to the radio set), el aparato de radio
railroad, el ferrocarril
rain, llover (ue)
ranch, el rancho
rapid, rápido, -a
Raymond, Ramón
read, leer
reader *(book)*, el libro de lectura
receive, recibir
record *(phonograph)*, el disco
red, rojo, -a
refreshment, el refresco
regards, recuerdos
region, la región
regret, sentir (ie, i)
relate, contar (ue)
religious, religioso, -a
remain, quedarse
remember, recordar (ue), acordarse (ue) (de)
repeat, repetir (i)
republic, la república
respect, respetar
restaurant, el restaurante
return *(come back)*, volver (ue)
revolution, la revolución
reward, el premio
rich, rico, -a
ride, el paseo; **to go for a ride**, pasearse en automóvil; **to ride a horse**, montar a caballo
right: to be right, tener razón
rise, levantarse
river, el río
road, el camino
romantic, romántico, -a
room, el cuarto, la habitación
rose, la rosa
row, la fila
ruler, la regla
run, correr

sad, triste
sailor, el marinero
Saint, Santo, -a (San)
salad, la ensalada; **chicken salad**, la ensalada de pollo
salt, la sal
same, mismo, -a

Saturday, el sábado
say, decir; **I should say so!**, ¡ya lo creo!
school, la escuela
science, la ciencia
sea, el *or* la mar
season, la estación
seat, el asiento; **seated**, sentado, -a
second, segundo, -a
see, ver; **he sees me**, me ve; **see you again**, hasta la vista; **see you later**, hasta luego; **see you tomorrow**, hasta mañana
sell, vender
send, enviar, mandar
sentence, la frase
separate, separar
September, septiembre
serve, servir (i)
set *(radio or television)*, el aparato
several, varios, -as
she, ella
shirt, la camisa
shoe, el zapato
shopping: to go shopping, ir de compras
short *(length)*, corto, -a; *(height)*, bajo, -a
should, deber
shoulder, el hombro
show, mostrar (ue), enseñar
sick, enfermo, -a
silver, la plata
sincere, sincero, -a
sing, cantar
sir, el señor
sister, la hermana
sit down, sentarse (ie)
situated, situado, -a
skirt, la falda
sleep, dormir (ue, u); **to fall asleep**, dormirse; **to be sleepy**, tener sueño
slowly, lentamente, despacio
small, pequeño, -a
smoke, fumar
snow, la nieve; **to snow**, nevar (ie)
so, tan; **so that**, para que
society, la sociedad
sofa, el sofá
soldier, el soldado
some, alguno, -a (algún)
somebody, alguien
someone, alguien
something, algo
sometimes, algunas veces
son, el hijo
song, la canción
soon, pronto
sorry: to be sorry, sentir (ie, i)
soup, la sopa; **tomato soup**, la sopa de tomates
south, el sur
South America, la América del Sur, Sud América
Spain, España

Spaniard, el español, la española
Spanish, español, española; **Spanish** *(language)*, el español; **Spanish teacher**, el profesor de español
speak, hablar; **he speaks to me**, me habla; **I speak to him (her)**, le hablo; **I speak to you**, le (les) hablo
spend *(time)*, pasar; *(money)*, gastar
sport, el deporte
spring, la primavera
staircase, la escalera
stairs, la escalera
state, el estado
station, la estación
stay, quedarse
still, todavía; **to keep still**, callarse
stone, la piedra
store, la tienda
story, el cuento, la historia
street, la calle
streetcar, el tranvía
strong, fuerte
student, el alumno, la alumna, el *or* la estudiante
studious, aplicado, -a
study, estudiar
stupid, estúpido, -a
subway, el subterráneo
suddenly, de pronto
suffer, sufrir
sugar, el azúcar
suit, el traje
suitcase, la maleta
summer, el verano
sun, el sol
Sunday, el domingo
sunny: it is sunny, hace sol, hay sol
supper, la cena; **to eat supper**, cenar
sure, seguro, -a
sweet, dulce
swim, nadar

table, la mesa
take, tomar; **to take** *(to a place)*, llevar; **to take off**, quitarse; **to take out**, sacar
talk, hablar
tall, alto, -a
tea, el té
teach, enseñar; **teacher**, el profesor, la profesora, el maestro, la maestra
team, el equipo
telegram, el telegrama
telephone, el teléfono; **to telephone**, llamar por teléfono
television, la televisión; **television set**, el aparato de televisión
tell, decir
ten, diez
tennis, el tenis
than, que, de

thank, dar las gracias a; thanks, gracias; thank you (very much), (muchas) gracias

that (*adj.*), ese, esa, aquel, aquella; that (one) (*pron.*), ése, ésa, eso, aquél, aquélla, aquello; the book that I bought, el libro que compré

the, el, la, los, las

theatre, el teatro

their, su, sus

them: for them, para ellos, -as; I know them, los (las) conozco; I speak to them, les hablo

themselves, se; with them (selves), consigo

there, allí; there is (are), hay; there was (were), había

therefore, por eso

these (*adj.*), estos, -as; (*pron.*), éstos, -as

they, ellos, -as

thing, la cosa

think, pensar (ie), creer

third, tercero, -a

thirsty: to be thirsty, tener sed

this (*adj.*), este, esta; this (one), (*pron.*), éste, ésta, esto

those (*adj.*), esos, -as, aquellos, -as; (*pron.*), ésos, -as, aquéllos, -as

thousand, mil

three, tres

through, por

Thursday, el jueves; next Thursday, el jueves que viene

ticket, el billete, el boleto

tie, la corbata

time, el tiempo; (*hour*) la hora; (*in a series*) la vez; a long time, mucho tiempo; at what time?, ¿a qué hora?; on time, a tiempo; what time is it?, ¿qué hora es?

tip, la propina

tired, cansado, -a

to, a, hasta; it is (five) to (three), son las (tres) menos (cinco)

tobacco, el tabaco

today, hoy

tomorrow, mañana; see you tomorrow, hasta mañana

tonight, esta noche

too, también

tooth, el diente

toward, hacia

tower, la torre

town, el pueblo

toy, el juguete

train, el tren

travel, viajar; traveler, el viajero

tree, el árbol

trip, el viaje; to take a trip, hacer un viaje

truth, la verdad; it is true, es verdad; true?, isn't it true?, ¿(no es) verdad?

try to, tratar de + *inf.*

Tuesday, el martes

twice, dos veces

two, dos

ugly, feo, -a

umbrella, el paraguas

uncle, el tío

under, debajo de

understand, comprender, entender (ie)

United States, los Estados Unidos

university, la universidad

until, hasta

upon, sobre; upon (reading), al (leer)

us: for us, para nosotros, -as; he knows us, nos conoce; he speaks to us, nos habla

use, usar

useful, útil

usually, generalmente

vacation, las vacaciones

value, el valor

vegetable, la legumbre

very, muy

Vincent, Vicente

violet, la violeta

violin, el violín

visit, la visita; to pay a visit, hacer una visita; to visit, visitar

voice, la voz

volcano, el volcán

wait for, esperar

waiter, el mozo

wake up, despertarse (ie)

walk: to take a walk, dar un paseo, pasearse; to walk, andar, caminar

wall, la pared

want, querer, desear

war, la guerra

warm, caliente; he is warm, tiene calor; it is warm (*weather*), hace calor

wash, lavar; to wash oneself, lavarse

watch, el reloj

water, el agua (*f.*)

way, el modo, la manera; in this (that) way, de esta (esa) manera

we, nosotros, -as

weak, débil

wear, llevar

weather, el tiempo; how is the weather?, ¿qué tiempo hace?; the weather is good (bad), hace buen (mal) tiempo

Wednesday, el miércoles

week, la semana; next week, la semana que viene

welcome: you are welcome, no hay de qué, de nada

well, bien

west, el oeste

what?, ¿qué?, ¿cuál?; what a ...!, ¡qué ...!

whatever, cualquier (a)

when, cuando; when?, ¿cuándo?

where, donde; where?, ¿dónde?; (*with verbs of motion*), ¿a dónde?

which, que; which (one)?, ¿cuál?; which (ones)?, ¿cuáles?

while, mientras (que)

white, blanco, -a

who, que; who?, ¿quién? (¿quiénes?)

whom, que; whom?, ¿a quién? (¿quiénes?)

whose?, ¿de quién?

why?, ¿por qué?

wide, ancho, -a

wife, la esposa

win, ganar

window, la ventana

windy: it is windy, hace viento

wine, el vino

winter, el invierno

wish, desear, querer

with, con

without, sin, sin que

woman, la mujer

wood, la madera

word, la palabra

work, el trabajo, la obra; to work, trabajar; worker, el obrero

world, el mundo

worse, peor; worst, el (la) peor

worth: to be worth, valer

write, escribir; written, escrito, -a

wrong: to be wrong, no tener razón

year, el año; last year, el año pasado; to be ... years old, tener ... años

yellow, amarillo, -a

yes, sí

yesterday, ayer

yet, todavía; not yet, todavía no

you, usted, ustedes; (*fam.*) tú, vosotros, -as; for you (*fam.*), para ti; with you (*fam.*), contigo; I know you, le (la, los, las) conozco; I speak to you, le (les) hablo

young, joven; younger, menor; youngest, el (la) menor

your, tu, tus, su, sus

yourself, se; (*fam.*), te

yourselves, se; (*fam.*), os

zero, cero